# THE ADVISOR'S GUIDE TO LONG-TERM CARE

EDITED BY
R. DAVID WATROS
ERIK T. REYNOLDS

Cover by Bobbie Sanchez/ABA Publishing.

Printed in the United States of America

17  16  15  14  13      5  4  3  2  1

**Library of Congress Cataloging-in-Publication Data**

R. David Watros.
    The advisor's guide to long-term care / Edited by R. David Watros and Erik T. Reynolds.— First edition.
        pages cm
Includes bibliographical references and index.
    ISBN 978-1-61438-900-2 (print : alk. paper)
    1. Nursing homes—Law and legislation—United States. 2. Long-term care facilities—Law and legislation—United States. 3. Older people—Long-term care—Law and legislation—United States. I. Title.

    KF3826.N8B67 2013
    344.7303'216—dc23

                                                                    2013001415

# Contents

## CHAPTER 4
## Long-Term Care Insurance                                           67

## CHAPTER 5
## Legislation Affecting Long-Term Care Insurance                     99

## CHAPTER 6
## Taxation Issues Affecting Long-Term Care Insurance    **111**

## CHAPTER 7
## Selecting a Long-Term Care Insurance Company    **131**

## CHAPTER 8
## Long-Term Care Insurance Applications for Individuals—
## Estate Planning and Wealth Preservation    **149**

## CHAPTER 9
## Long-Term Care and the Employer

# Acknowledgments

M Financial Group maintains a strong legacy of client advocacy that touches many areas of the financial services profession. Core to this legacy is education: sharing our knowledge and perspective to facilitate informed decisions and sustainable planning.

In addition to M Financial's primary focus—life insurance—we are actively involved in other complementary businesses, including Long-term care (LTC) insurance. Just as we have with life insurance through *The Advisor's Guide to Life Insurance*, it is M Financial's objective to expand awareness and understanding of the opportunities and benefits of LTC with *The Advisor's Guide to Long-Term Care*.

A resource of this magnitude requires the expertise and insight of many, and I truly valued the opportunity to oversee the development of *The Advisor's Guide to Long-Term Care*. I would like to thank three members of our Member Firm Community—Allan Kaplan of New Century Planners, LLC (Chicago, IL), Bill Walker of Kibble & Prentice Holding Company (Seattle, WA), and Scott Wirtz of Eslick Financial Group, Inc. (Waterloo, IA)—for reviewing the manuscript. Their feedback and perspective, as professionals who have dedicated their careers to helping individuals and families plan for the future, was invaluable.

I would also like to acknowledge the important contributions of Erik Reynolds, Mike Skiens, and Marylee Lewis, whose copy development and editing acumen made this Guide possible.

These key contributors offered timely insight and sound critique, both of which greatly enhanced the overall quality of the final product.

On behalf of the entire M Community, I want to express my hope that all readers of this *Guide*, regardless of their experience, are able to enhance their ability to advise those who rely on them for guidance and elevate the value of what they deliver to clients.

R. David Watros
January 2013

# *About the Contributors*

The creation of this *Guide* was truly a team effort that involved the expertise and insight of many from the M Community.

With more than 140 Member Firms, M Financial Group is one of the nation's leading financial services design and distribution companies. Since 1978, M Financial's network of independent insurance, investment, and executive benefit firms has served the needs of ultra-affluent individuals, corporate executives, successful entrepreneurs, and *Fortune 1000* companies. Our core values—innovation, excellence, leadership, advocacy, and collaboration—drive everything we do, including our passion to share our insight in ways that facilitate informed decisions.

M Financial Group's Member Firms are recognized in the wealth transfer, executive benefits, and wealth management markets. Our focus is differentiation, continually working to help Member Firms enhance their ability to deliver customized insurance, benefits, and investment solutions to meet the complex needs of their clients. It is our intent that this *Guide* will enhance our efforts—and our differentiation—to advocate for clients, and create and implement sustainable solutions designed to meet their objectives.

# *What Is Long-Term Care?* 1

**M**OST PEOPLE ENVISION THEMSELVES living a long life, investing and planning throughout their working years to create a financially secure future so they can spend time doing the things they enjoy the most.

But what if that plan gets derailed? While every statistic points to the high probability of needing extended health care at some point in life, most people are in denial and think it will never happen to them. It is important to help clients accept that they will likely need care and understand how getting the right care will impact their family and their finances. It is not always a pleasant conversation, but there are important questions to consider: What if their health changes? What if the unthinkable happens? What if they need long-term health care? What is long-term care?[1]

## Long-Term Care Services Defined

Long-term care (LTC) encompasses a wide range of supportive and health services for people who have lost the capacity for self-care due to illness or injury. The need for LTC services is generally defined by one's need for assistance when incapacitation renders one unable, physically or cognitively, to perform one or more of the activities of daily living for an extended period of time (typically 90 days or longer). The risk of chronic illness increases with age whereas the risk of injury is predominating throughout one's entire life. The insurance

---

1. This chapter draws in part from HARLEY GORDON, CERTIFICATION IN LONG-TERM CARE COURSE HANDBOOK, Sections A, B, C (Releases 5.0, 8.0, 9.0, Corporation for Long-Term Care Certification, 2003, 2009, 2011), and from HARLEY GORDON, IN SICKNESS & IN HEALTH: YOUR SICKNESS—YOUR FAMILY'S HEALTH, Chapter 1 (Financial Strategies Press 2007).

industry defines chronically ill people as those who are unable to perform, without substantial assistance of another individual, at least two of the activities of daily living (ADLs). The generally accepted ADLs, as defined by the industry, are as follows:

- Eating
- Bathing
- Dressing
- Toileting
- Continence
- Transferring (mobility)

Note: California requires non-tax qualified insurance policies to include ambulation[2] or substantial supervision to protect them from threat to health and safety due to severe cognitive impairment.

According to the Center for Technology and Aging, approximately 23 percent of adults age 45 to 64 have some form of disability; for those 65 to 69 years old, the likelihood of being affected by a disability nearly doubles to 45 percent. Approximately 74 percent of adults age 80 and over have a disability. Nearly 14 million adults age 65 and older (42 percent) report having one or more disabilities. A physical disability is most common (29 percent), followed by difficulty leaving the home (20 percent), disability of the senses (14 percent), and mental disabilities (11 percent). The Center for Technology and Aging defines disability as the inability to perform daily tasks, whether physical, sensory, or cognitive, and experiencing a loss of self-management and independence.

**TABLE 1-1**
**Prevalence and Types of Disabilities Experienced by Adults Aged 65 and Older**

|  | Number (millions) | Percent |
| --- | --- | --- |
| Total Older Adults | 33.3 | 100% |
| With any disability | 14.0 | 42% |
| Disability of the senses | 4.7 | 14% |
| Physical | 9.5 | 29% |
| Mental | 3.6 | 11% |
| Self-care | 3.2 | 10% |
| Leaving the home | 8.8 | 20% |

Source: Center for Technology and Aging, Assistive Technologies for Functional Improvement Technology Review, August 2010 Discussion Draft.

---

2. California Department of Insurance, GUIDE TO LONG-TERM CARE INSURANCE (2008), http://www .insurance.ca.gov/0100-consumers/0060-information-guides/0050-health/ltc-rate-history-guide /long-term-care-insurance.cfm.

According to a recent study, approximately one in four community-resident Medicare beneficiaries over age 65 had difficulty performing one or more ADLs. An additional 15 percent reported difficulties with ADLs. Older adults' ability to maintain their independence is connected to their ability to perform ADLs without requiring a great deal of assistance.[3]

Traditionally, long-term care deals with chronic as opposed to acute conditions, while typical health care services are designed to treat and improve one's overall health. Acute impairments do not always lead to extended care, but they can. Long-term care is care-oriented rather than cure-oriented and tends to be multi-dimensional, not just focused on a specific problem. The term "long-term care" generally refers to the assistance a chronically ill or frail person needs to get through the day. Long-term care can include help with very basic housekeeping chores, such as cooking meals, paying bills, and using the telephone. The assistance it provides can range from help with these day-to-day activities in the home to more advanced assistance with activities such as bathing and dressing, and, ultimately, more complex services such as skilled nursing care.

Long-term care can be provided in a variety of settings including one's own home, community care centers, adult day care centers, continuum of care communities, assisted living facilities, or nursing homes. Additionally, long-term care can include a wide variety of services such as rehabilitative care (as a result of an accident or fall), therapeutic care (post stroke or surgery), nursing care (wound care, bandage changing, and monitoring medicines), and personal and custodial care (bathing, meal preparation, transportation, and administering medications).

This spectrum of services can be segmented into three levels of care:

1. Skilled Care
   - Continuous care provided by licensed medical professionals
   - Care provided under the direction of a physician
   - Restorative care, as defined by Medicare, where the patient must be getting better
2. Intermediate Care
   - Skilled care provided occasionally or intermittently
3. Custodial Care
   - Supervisory or hands-on services
   - Chronic: non-medical personnel (nurses' aides) help with ADL (bathing, dressing, toileting, continence, eating, mobility)
   - Cognitive impairment supervision provided

The long-term care insurance industry frequently cites a statistic from the *New England Journal of Medicine's* 1991 report on nursing home care: 43 percent

---

3. Administration on Aging, *Disability and Activity Limitations,* A Profile of Older Americans: 2009 (last modified Jan. 11, 2010), http://www.aoa.gov/AoARoot/Aging_Statistics/Profile/2009/16.aspx.

of those over the age of 65 will end up in a nursing home. To clarify this point, the study predicted that of the 2.2 million people turning 65 in 1990, 946,000 (43 percent) will spend at least some time in a nursing home at some point before they die—including stays as short as one day and stays following hospitalization.

To provide some perspective, the following are data points reflecting actual experience:

- There are 42 million Americans age 65 or older.
- Of the 42 million, 12.6 million (37 percent) reported being limited by moderate to severe chronic conditions.
- Only 1.6 million (4.1 percent) of the 12.6 million are permanently confined to nursing homes:
    - 0.9 percent are between the ages of 65 and 74;
    - 3.5 percent are between the ages of 75 and 84; and
    - 14.3 percent are 85 or older.[4]
- The percentage of people over age 65 who live in nursing homes has been declining since the mid-1980s, with sharper declines among older demographics.[5]

These numbers contradict somewhat the predictions published in the *New England Journal of Medicine* in 1991 but reflect a trend that an increasing number of individuals over the age of 65 are being cared for at home. In fact, family members and friends are the sole caregivers for 70 percent of elderly people.[6]

However, despite a large growth in home care services, nursing homes continue to dominate the service system. Federal and state government programs account for this datum yet continue to struggle to manage costs of services they provide and wrangle over their financial responsibilities.

Table 1-2 shows how services and costs generally compare with each other.

## Probabilities of Long-Term Care Events

While statistics have proven to be a less than effective means of conveying to individuals and families the likelihood of an event and the subsequent need to protect against long-term care costs, it remains important to understand the probabilities of needing long-term care and the impact of the extended care period.

Seventy percent of Americans over age 65 will need long-term care at home, through adult day care, or in an assisted living facility, a nursing home, or other

---

4. Administration on Aging, A PROFILE OF OLDER AMERICANS: 2010, http://www.aoa.gov/aoaroot/aging_statistics/Profile/2010/docs/2010profile.pdf.

5. U.S. Centers for Disease Control and Prevention, *National Nursing Home Survey*, http://www.cdc.gov/nchs/nnhs.htm (last updated Oct. 19, 2011).

6. America's Health Insurance Plans, GUIDE TO LONG-TERM CARE INSURANCE (2004), http://www.ahip.org/Issues/Long-Term-Care-Insurance.aspx.

**TABLE 1-2**

|  | Help with activities of daily living | Help with additional services | Help with care needs | Range of costs |
|---|---|---|---|---|
| Community-Based Services | Yes | Yes | No | Low to medium |
| Home Health Care | Yes | Yes | Yes | Low to high |
| In-Law Apartments | Yes | Yes | Yes | Low to high |
| Housing for Aging and Disabled Individuals | Yes | Yes | No | Low to high |
| Board and Care Homes | Yes | Yes | Yes | Low to high |
| Assisted Living | Yes | Yes | Yes | Medium to high |
| Continuing Care Retirement Communities | Yes | Yes | Yes | High |
| Nursing Homes | Yes | Yes | Yes | High |

Source: Medicare, March 25, 2009, http://www.medicare.gov/longtermcare/static/home.asp.

facility. According to the *New England Journal of Medicine*, for a man over age 65, the odds are one in three (33 percent) that he will need long-term care in his life. For a woman over age 65, the odds are one in two (50 percent) that she will need long-term care in her life. In aggregate, 42 percent of all individuals over age 65 will enter a nursing home in their lifetime. And while most people think of long-term care as impacting only those in their senior years, 40 percent of people currently receiving long-term care services are ages 18 to 64.[7]

It is common to hear clients refute statistics by stating that they are in excellent health and their parents never needed long-term care. However, this is not a medical or health decision, but rather a family financial planning decision that should be discussed with a professional advisor (e.g., an attorney, accountant, or estate planning or financial advisor), not their personal physician. The facts suggest that a healthy individual will face higher lifetime health care costs than someone who deceases earlier in life due to fair or poor health conditions.

According to a report from the Center for Retirement Research at Boston College, over a lifetime, healthy individuals may pay as much as $105,000 more than those in poor health. At age 65, a typical married couple free of chronic disease can expect to spend $197,000 on remaining lifetime health care costs, excluding nursing home care, while facing a 5 percent probability that these costs will

---

7. U.S. Department of Health and Human Services, National Clearinghouse for Long Term Care Information (Oct. 22, 2008), http://www.longtermcare.gov.

exceed $311,000. Including nursing home care, the mean cost is $260,000, with a 5 percent probability of costs exceeding $570,000. Less than 15 percent of households approaching retirement have accumulated that much in total financial assets.[8]

Those in good health can expect to live significantly longer. According to the Center for Retirement Research at Boston College, at age 80, people in healthy households have a remaining life expectancy that is 29 percent longer than people in unhealthy households, hence the risk of incurring health care costs over more years. Additionally, many of those currently free of any chronic disease at age 80, based on a statistical simulation, can expect to spend one-third of their remaining life suffering from one or more diseases. People in healthy households face a higher lifetime risk of requiring nursing home care than those who are unhealthy; their greater risk is surviving to advanced old age when the need for such care is highest.[9] This evidence, and the possibility that their health will help them qualify for long-term care coverage at more favorable rates, should motivate clients who are in excellent health currently to consider long-term care insurance.

To give an example of one prevalent chronic disease affecting our nation, a recently released report from the Alzheimer's Association[10] predicts that ten million U.S. baby boomers, one of eight, will develop Alzheimer's disease. The disease is already the seventh deadliest in the nation and poses a greater risk for women. Three quarters of the individuals diagnosed will spend their remaining life in a nursing home or an assisted living facility. In 2000, there were an estimated 411,000 new cases of Alzheimer's disease. For 2010, that number was estimated to be 454,000 (a 10-percent increase); by 2030, it is projected to be 615,000 (a 50-percent increase from 2000); and by 2050, it is projected to be 959,000 (a 130-percent increase from 2000). With these expectations, caregivers and the long-term care system will quickly be overwhelmed by this one disease.

It is important to realize that most nursing home and care facility statistics do not take into account the progression of long-term care needs and the high prevalence of spouses and family members providing the care until such caregivers are no longer able. Long-term care expenses can deplete a family's income, and unfortunately conversations about care preferences, expectations, and how to fund costs and protect one's income rarely occur before the need arises.

8. Anthony Webb & Natalia Zhivan, *What Is the Distribution of Lifetime Health Care Costs from Age 65?*, Center for Retirement Research at Boston College, No. 10-4, Mar. 2010.

9. Wei Sun et al., *Does Staying Healthy Reduce Your Lifetime Health Care Costs?*, Center for Retirement Research at Boston College, No. 10-8, May 2010.

10. Alzheimer's Association, *2011 Alzheimer's Disease Facts and Figures*, 7 ALZHEIMER'S DISEASE & DEMENTIA 2, *available at* http://www.alz.org/downloads/Facts_Figures_2011.pdf.

**FIGURE 1-1**

**Caregiving Stress Dominates a Caregiver's Life**

Most Stressful Issue in Caregiver's Life

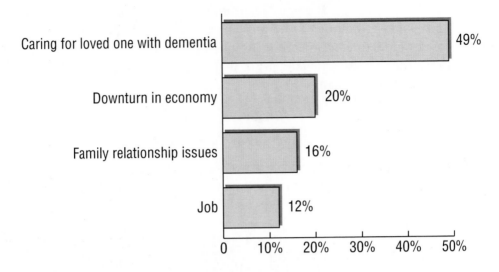

Related: 62% of Alzheimer's caregivers state they feel isolated and lonely.

Source: Caring.com Research—Alzheimer's Caregivers (August 2010). Copyright 2010 Caring, Inc.

## Increased National Awareness

Paradoxically, the recession's unforeseen benefit is that retirement portfolios have decreased in value, money for legacy has dwindled, and hard times are finally pushing long-term care planning, in particular long-term care insurance, into the forefront of people's minds and into a central role of retirement plans.

The recession not only caused significant damage to many Americans' retirement assets, it also made them more aware of the challenges facing the Social Security system, which is expected to be insolvent by 2037,[11] the uncertain future of Medicare, and the various economic stimulus plans depleting federal funds. People are increasingly concerned about the government's ability to take care of them as they age. With national debts and deficits increasing and government support of critical programs decreasing, people are realizing that they need to plan to protect themselves—the government is most likely not going to be able to provide the resources and support on which they may have counted. As a result, alternatives such as long-term care insurance are becoming increasingly attractive to those who want choice and quality care.

---

11. THE 2009 ANNUAL REPORT OF THE BOARD OF TRUSTEES OF THE FEDERAL OLD-AGE AND SURVIVORS INSURANCE AND FEDERAL DISABILITY INSURANCE TRUST FUNDS, H.R. DOC. No. 49-654 (2009), *available at* http://www.ssa.gov /OACT/TR/2009/tr09.pdf.

As publicity and legislation have been raising awareness of the subject, advisors are seeing many changes in the marketplace. With the "graying of America," the number of people who need long-term care is growing exponentially and is predicted to double over the next two decades with the aging of the baby boomer generation. New trends in the sale of products, claims data, plan designs, and product provisions continue to emerge, but the most important is the evolving attitude of potential long-term care insurance buyers who are starting to see the need for coverage and the advantages of planning ahead, yet there is still fundamental apprehension to plan:

### FIGURE 1-2

### Family Fear Factor

When asked to identify the biggest barrier to discussing long-term care, the majority of Americans cite upsetting their family more than upsetting themselves as a concern.

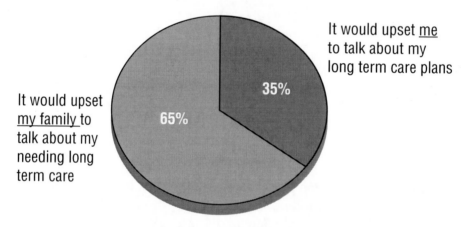

It would upset <u>me</u> to talk about my long term care plans

It would upset <u>my family</u> to talk about my needing long term care

35%

65%

Source: America Talks: Protecting Our Families' Financial Futures Survey, 2010.

In addition to significantly more favorable media coverage of long-term care insurance, as seen in the sheer volume of articles, resources, and consumer advocates, significant laws and programs enacted by federal and state governments have also greatly increased exposure to and awareness of the probabilities and consequences of long-term care. Some of the more significant legislation and programs are listed below with short descriptions. A more detailed discussion on legislative activity will follow in later chapters.

- ◆ Long-Term Care Security Act of 2000—This Act of Congress created the Federal Long Term Care Insurance Program (FLTCIP), which is a long-term care insurance program offered to federal employees, U.S. Postal Service employees and annuitants, and active and retired members of the Uniformed Services and their qualified relatives. After the Act's passage, the U.S. Office of Personnel Management (OPM) held a competitive bidding process, selecting a consortium of insurance carriers and administrators to offer the insurance under the FLTCIP for the first seven-year contract term. In May 2009, OPM selected John Hancock as the sole insurer for the FLTCIP's second seven-year contract term along with John Hancock's wholly owned subsidiary Long Term Care Partners, LLC as sole administrator of the program. The FLTCIP is the largest group long-term care insurance program in the country, as well as the largest employer-sponsored long-term care insurance program in the country, with more than 224,000 enrollees.[12]

♦ Federal Long-Term Care Awareness Campaign—The "Own Your Future" Long Term Care Insurance campaign is a joint awareness program between the federal government and individual states that was developed in January 2005. It was specifically designed to raise awareness about the need for planning for long-term care. As of the most recent report, 25 states have participated in the Own Your Future Campaign. State efforts include letters to constituents between the ages of 45 and 70, promotion of the campaign through an initial press conference, and development and dissemination of state-based information and resources, such as long-term care websites.[13]

♦ National Long-Term Care Partnership Plan—The Partnership program was designed to attract consumers who might not otherwise purchase long-term care insurance. States offer the guarantee that if benefits under a Partnership policy do not sufficiently cover the cost of care, the consumer may qualify for Medicaid under special eligibility rules while retaining a pre-specified amount of assets (though income and functional eligibility rules still apply). Consumers are thus protected from having to become impoverished to qualify for Medicaid, and states avoid the entire burden of long-term care costs. Under the Deficit Reduction Act (DRA) of 2005 all states are able to implement Long-Term Care Partnership programs through an approved State Plan Amendment, if specific requirements are met. The DRA requires programs to include certain consumer protections, most notably provisions of the National Association of Insurance Commissioners Model LTC regulations.

♦ Community Living Assistance Services and Supports Act (CLASS Act)— Under the Patient Protection and Affordable Care Act (PPACA), President Barack Obama signed into law in 2010 comprehensive health care reform legislation that contains a program known as the Community Living Assistance Services and Supports Act (CLASS Act). The CLASS Act would have created a new voluntary government program under which individuals would pay a monthly premium and be eligible for very modest benefits for their long-term care needs after five years of paying into the program.

---

12. The Federal Long Term Care Insurance Program (2011), http://www.ltcfeds.com/.

13. U.S. Department of Health and Human Services, National Clearinghouse for Long Term Care Information (2010), http://www.longtermcare.gov/LTC/Main_Site/index.aspx.

While the CLASS Act was often characterized as a long-term care program, it was primarily designed as a program to provide future assistance to the working disabled. It was not an insurance program. Traditional long-term care insurance requires that applicants meet certain insurability requirements. The CLASS Act did not have such health qualification requirements. The plan was to be offered on a guaranteed-issue basis. However, the program was plagued by financial flaws that led to its demise before it was ever implemented. In light of current federal budget challenges and the CLASS Act's failure, it is unlikely any government-sponsored long-term care program will reemerge anytime soon.

Despite years of publicly and privately funded efforts to raise consumer awareness about the importance of long-term care planning, Americans seem to understand almost all other forms of insurance better than they do long-term care insurance. Greater education is still needed about the actual need for, and costs associated with, long-term care and the realistic funding options.

Long-term care insurance continues to be one the most complicated products to understand and to market as an advisor. However, with depressed portfolios, Americans are more ready than ever to protect themselves and their families against the future consequences of needing care. Before the economic downturn, some people may have believed they could self-insure for long-term care expenses; now, with assets depleted, they realize this may not be feasible. Additionally, advisors are realizing that their clients' financial plans may be derailed if they fail to take the consequences of long-term care into consideration.

## Impact on Families and Employed Caregivers

Possibly no other expense has a more emotionally and financially overwhelming impact on a family's income and independence than long-term care. Failure to discuss extended health care with young to middle-age clients will often have severe consequences on their families. The first consequence is the emotional and physical well-being of the caregivers, who, because of the nature of long-term care, tend to be family members. The need for care is created by a chronic medical condition that compromises the individual's ability to get through the most basic of daily routines or a cognitive impairment that compromises his or her ability to safely interact with his or her environment. By its basic definition, this extended-care event is all-consuming and frequently leads to a decline in the caregiver's own health. Extended care is not a health condition—it is a life-changing event.

Extended care rarely requires skilled medical care, which is defined as services that are so inherently complex that they can only be provided under a plan of care created by a physician and executed by a skilled nursing staff and/or other trained professionals. Extended care typically requires custodial or non-skilled services, defined as supervisory or hands-on services provided to persons who suffer from chronic illnesses caused by a physical or cognitive impairment. Such care can be provided either formally, by professionals, or informally, by family or friends with no particular training in health care. Custodial care also consists of homemaking services, such as cooking and cleaning the house, and personal care assistance to help the patients get through their daily routine.

**FIGURE 1-3**

**Percent of Elderly Home Care Recipients Needing Help with Selected Activities of Daily Living**

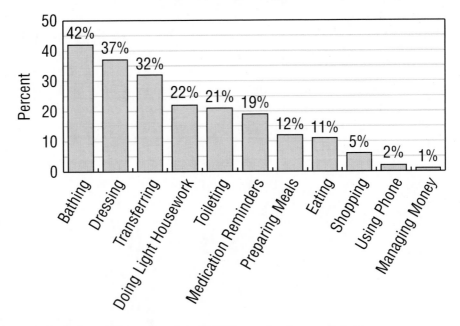

Source: Putting Home Care in Perspective, June 25, 2009, www.longtermcarelink.net.

Mitigating the impact of a long-term care event and the associated emotional and economic impact on a family can be accomplished through the creation of a plan. The plan's goal is to allow your client to remain in the community while preserving the emotional, physical, and financial well-being of his or her loved ones. In addition, the plan should attempt to get the family back to where they were emotionally, physically, and financially prior to the unexpected need for care. Unfortunately, many do not have a plan in place and find themselves struggling through these situations with little or no guidance or support. Research shows that family members who provide care to individuals with chronic or disabling conditions are themselves at risk.[14] Emotional, mental, and physical health

---

14. Family Caregiver Alliance, National Center on Caregiving, *Caregiver Health* (2006), http://www.caregiver.org/caregiver/jsp/content_node.jsp?nodeid=1822.

problems can be caused by complex caregiving situations and the strains of caring for frail or disabled relatives. These burdens and health risks can hinder the caregiver's ability to provide care, lead to higher health care costs, and adversely affect the quality of life of both the caregiver and care receivers.

- Studies have shown that an influential factor in a family caregiver's decision to place an impaired relative in a long-term care facility is the family caregiver's own physical health.[15]
- Eleven percent of caregivers report that caregiving has caused their physical health to get worse.[16]
- Family caregivers experiencing extreme stress have been shown to age prematurely. This level of stress can take as much as ten years off a family caregiver's life.[17]
- An elderly informal caregiver has a significant risk of death as a result of his or her sick spouse's hospitalization. The risk to spouses was highest when the hospitalization was for a chronic, disabling illness like dementia. "What this shows is that people are interconnected, and their health is interconnected, and seeing a person that you love suffer, seeing them ill, harms you," said study coauthor Dr. Nicholas Christakis of the Harvard Medical School.[18]

**FIGURE 1-4**

**By the Numbers**

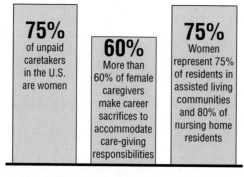

Source: Shawn Britt, Why women should be concerned with long-term care issues, Life Insurance Selling; November 2, 2010.

In addition to these numbers, women live longer than men, and as a result are more likely to reach an age where they will be without their spouse and/or require

15. G.T. Buhr et al., *Caregivers' Reasons for Nursing Home Placement: Cues for Improving Discussions with Families Prior to the Transition*, 46 THE GERONTOLOGIST 1, at 52–61 (2006).

16. CENTER ON AGING SOCIETY, HOW DO FAMILY CAREGIVERS FARE? A CLOSER LOOK AT THEIR EXPERIENCES, Profile No. 3 (Georgetown University 2005).

17. Elissa S. Epel et al., *Accelerated Telomere Shortening in Response to Life Stress*, 101 PROCEEDINGS OF THE NATIONAL ACADEMY OF SCIENCES 49 (2004).

18. N. Christakis & P. Allison, *Mortality After the Hospitalization of a Spouse*, 354 NEW ENG. J. MED. 7 (2006).

long-term care. Over two-thirds (67.5 percent) of long-term care insurance claim dollars are paid to women.[19]

Although the statistics vary depending on the research studied, the trend of more men getting involved in caregiving is increasing. It is estimated that anywhere from 34 to 51 percent of men are now considered primary caregivers.[20]

The National Alliance for Caregiving (NAC) and American Association of Retired Persons (AARP) survey found that one out of four U.S. households are involved in caregiving and that two out of three caregivers are employed full-time. As a result, employees are physically, emotionally, and financially burdened, with the following adverse effects at the worksite:

- One out of three caregivers loses up to 16 hours of work per month due to caregiver responsibilities.[21]
- Thirty percent of employees with a parent age 65 or over miss work to care for the parent.
- Thirty-one percent quit work due to providing care for a loved one.
- Sixty-seven percent adjust work schedules to care for a parent.
- Retirement and educational savings are impacted, which can cause career limits during "key wage earning" years.[22]
  - The total estimated aggregate lost wages, pension, and Social Security benefits of caregivers of parents are nearly $3 trillion.
  - For women:
    - The estimated total individual amount of lost wages due to leaving the labor force early and/or reduced hours of work because of caregiving responsibilities is $142,693.
    - The estimated impact of caregiving on lost Social Security benefits is $131,351.
    - A very conservative estimated impact on pensions is approximately $50,000.
    - In total, the estimated cost impact of caregiving on the individual female caregiver in terms of lost wages and Social Security benefits is $324,044.
  - For men:
    - The estimated total individual amount of lost wages due to leaving the labor force early and/or reduced hours of work because of caregiving responsibilities is $89,107.
    - The estimated impact of caregiving on lost Social Security benefits is $144,609.

19. AMERICAN ASSOCIATION FOR LONG-TERM CARE INSURANCE, THE 2010 SOURCEBOOK FOR LONG-TERM CARE INSURANCE INFORMATION (2010).

20. MetLife Mature Market Institute (2008, 2009, 2011).

21. NATIONAL ALLIANCE FOR CAREGIVING AND AARP, CAREGIVING IN THE U.S. (May 2005).

22. CENTERS FOR DISEASE CONTROL AND PREVENTION, THE STATE OF AGING AND HEALTH IN AMERICA 2004.

○ Adding in the conservative estimate of the impact on pensions at $50,000, the total impact is $283,716 for men or,

○ The estimated average loss for males and females age 50 and over who care for a parent is $303,880.[23]

Even when workers are able to be at work, they may not be fully present. They may be at work physically, yet mentally and emotionally they are absent. *Presenteeism* is a new term that has entered the workplace.

As a result of caregiving, U.S. businesses lose up to $33 billion annually from absenteeism, decline in productivity, interruptions (i.e., situations requiring immediate attention), decreased morale and motivation, unwillingness to travel, and inability to relocate.

**FIGURE 1-5**

**Types of Adjustments to Work Schedule Due to Caregiving**

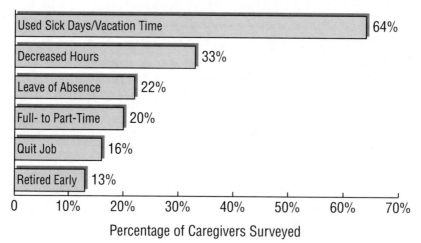

Source: Discover Financial Freedom Now, 2011.

## The Consequences of Not Having a Plan

The client who contacts the advisor for assistance with long-term care funding is often not the person needing or receiving care. It is the spouse, the children, and other family members who are already actively providing some level of care. While these families come from diverse backgrounds, they share the same story. The person needing care

♦ rarely expected to live a long life;

♦ never thought he or she would need long-term care if he or she did live a long life; and

23. THE METLIFE MATURE MARKET INSTITUTE, METLIFE INSURANCE COMPANY, THE METLIFE STUDY OF CAREGIVING COSTS TO WORKING CAREGIVERS: DOUBLE JEOPARDY FOR BABY BOOMERS CARING FOR THEIR PARENTS (June 2011).

◆ had no idea what providing care to would do to his or her family until it was too late.

Then there are the financial consequences. Clients are accustomed to living an independent life. Paying for care, however, has forced them to reallocate their retirement portfolio and adjust their spending habits due to reduced net income. The lifestyle of most has been diminished or destroyed, and many have had to turn to their children for financial help.

The consequences of being unprepared and not having a plan were never put more simply than in a statement made by a caregiver in the Public Broadcasting Service (PBS) documentary *And Thou Shalt Honor*. Asked to reflect on what taking care of her husband, who suffered from Alzheimer's disease, was doing to her, the caregiver stated:

*"When I got married, I never understood what 'in sickness and in health' meant. Now I do:*

*His sickness, my health.*

*For it to be easy for me, it would have to be over for him, and that's unacceptable.*

*I often wonder: Will there be anything left for me, will there be anything left for me?"*

This man has Alzheimer's disease; his family suffers from it.[24]

If a long-term care plan is not addressed as part of their overall financial plan, the risks associated with this oversight are numerous:

◆ Longevity risk
◆ Early death of a partner
◆ Rising health care costs
◆ Increased need for health care
◆ Expense of long-term care
◆ Impact of market volatility
◆ Sequencing of returns risk
◆ Liquidity risk
◆ Inflation risk

## Conclusions

As compelling as all the statistics stated in this chapter and the following chapters are, they are not going to help an advisor motivate a client to implement a long-term care plan. Risk does not motivate one to plan; consequences motivate

---

24. AND THOU SHALT HONOR (Public Broadcasting Service 2002).

one to plan. There are two distinct sets of consequences of the long-term care event:

1.  The damaged emotional and physical well-being of those who provide care
2.  The depletion of the family's retirement portfolio

Integrating the statement "*Tell me what's important to you*" into the initial conversation is essential; people will insure things that are important to them.

Merely suggesting clients should plan for long-term care does not mean they will take action. Whether or not someone chooses to plan for a long-term care event may seem like a personal choice, but the ramifications of not planning have an impact on the family, the community, the economy, and the nation.

The government's position is clear. Americans are to plan for long-term care on their own.

Clients who waits to address long-term care needs until the point when they actually need care are too late, as it significantly impacts their financial situation, the quality of life of their loved ones, and their ability to maintain their independence. Incorporating long-term care insurance into the financial plan can ultimately help protect assets, although income pays for care, reduce the burden of care that would otherwise fall on family members, and enable the clients to receive care in the setting they most prefer, including their home.

Long-term care is a critically important issue that affects wealth accumulation, wealth protection, wealth transfer, and wealth distribution. Long-term care insurance as part of an overall plan is a prudent risk-management choice that benefits all.

# *The Need for Long-Term Care Services* **2**

THE EFFECT OF THE BABY BOOMER generation will be felt over the next several decades and promises to have a significant impact on the frequency, nature, and overall caregiving process and marketplace. The segment of the population age 65 and older is increasing at a faster rate than the total population.[1] Tomorrow's elderly population is expected to be better educated, healthier, more culturally literate, and more discerning as consumers than those populations in the past. They are expected to differ from previous generations in that they will enjoy longer lives, better health, and more active lifestyles. Still, the overwhelming majority will also face a growing and continuous challenge to maintain their precious independence. Fifty million aging baby boomers are sparking demand for products and environments that accommodate their changing physical and sensory capabilities.[2] Recognizing the potential longevity crisis, state and federal governments are doing everything they can to encourage the purchase of private long-term care insurance.

The goal is to establish a plan for extended care, based not just on the financial risk of long-term care, but also on the severe consequences that providing care will have on the emotional, physical, and

---

1. U.S. DEPARTMENT OF HEALTH AND HUMAN SERVICES, HEALTH, UNITED STATES, 2007: WITH CHARTBOOK ON TRENDS IN THE HEALTH OF AMERICANS (National Center for Health Statistics 2007).

2. Transgenerational Design Matters, *The Demographics of Aging*, http://transgenerational.org/aging/demographics.htm#ixzz1Vb9uer8J (last visited October 28, 2012).

**17**

financial well-being of loved ones. The plan should be designed to mitigate both the risks and the consequences. Once the plan is in place, long-term care insurance can be positioned, not as a product that protects the client, but as a funding source for the plan.[3]

## Changing Demographics

Baby boomers, those born between 1946 and 1964, started turning age 65 in 2011, and the number of people age 65 and over is expected to increase significantly through 2030.

Currently, some 39 million people age 65 and older live in the United States, representing 13 percent of the total population.[4] The population over age 65 in 2030 is projected to be twice as large as the total in 2000, growing from 35 million to 72 million, nearly 20 percent of the United States population. Those age 85 and over grew from just over 100,000 in the year 1900 to 5.7 million in 2006.[5] The U.S. Census Bureau projects that the population age 85 and over could grow from 5.7 million to 19 million by 2050.

The last of the baby boomer generation will reach age 65 in the year 2029. With demand for long-term care services surging in coming decades as the early boomers reach their 80s, the aging population boom will put tremendous stress on the resources and services that communities provide for older adults. As this trend peaks in 2030, the number of people over age 65 will soar to 72 million, representing one in every five Americans. Worldwide, the percentage of adults over age 65 is expected to double, from 7 percent to 14 percent of the total population by the year 2040.[6]

The aging of the population will be accompanied by changing social, demographic, and family dynamics that will create challenges to society and caregiving. Much caregiving is provided informally by the family, and the availability of family caregivers will most likely see a decline over time. Children no longer necessarily reside near their parents, often relocating across the country or in other parts of the world. Declining family sizes, increasing childlessness, and rising divorce rates threaten the number of family caregivers.

---

3. This chapter draws in part from HARLEY GORDON, CERTIFICATION IN LONG-TERM CARE COURSE HANDBOOK, Sections A, B, C (Releases 5.0, 8.0, 9.0, Corporation for Long-Term Care Certification 2003, 2009, 2011), and from HARLEY GORDON, IN SICKNESS & IN HEALTH: YOUR SICKNESS—YOUR FAMILY'S HEALTH, Chapters 1, 2 (Financial Strategies Press 2007).

4. FEDERAL INTERAGENCY FORUM ON AGING-RELATED STATISTICS, OLDER AMERICANS 2010: KEY INDICATORS OF WELL-BEING (2010).

5. AMERICAN ASSOCIATION FOR LONG-TERM CARE INSURANCE, THE 2011 SOURCEBOOK FOR LONG-TERM CARE INSURANCE INFORMATION (2011).

6. HealthDay News, *Elder Boom Will Be Felt Worldwide*, U.S. NEWS & WORLD REPORT (July 20, 2009), http://health.usnews.com/health-news/family-health/boomer-health/articles/2009/07/20/elder-boom-will-be-felt-worldwide.

## FIGURE 2-1

### Number of people age 65 and over, by age group, selected years 1900–2000 and projected 2010–2050

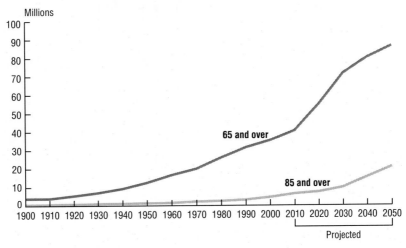

Note: Data for 2010–2050 are projections of the population.

Reference population: These data refer to the resident population.

Source: U.S. Census Bureau, Decennial Census and Projections.

Increasing participation of women in the workforce reduces their ability to provide informal care and fill the traditional role of caregiver. The rising female employment rate contributes to the increasing need for funded home care. Men are beginning to fill the caregiver gap and are sharing in caregiving tasks more than in the past, but women still shoulder the major burden of care. Families with young children and dual careers may struggle to meet both obligations. Taking into account these scenarios, it is clear that the long-term care burdens on families and institutions will continue to increase substantially. Currently, there are more than 65 million Americans providing care to a loved one in need.[7]

## FIGURE 2-2

### Informal Care Providers

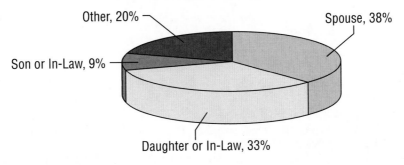

Source: National Care Planning Council, 2011

___

7. Akron General Medical Center, HEALTHY TIPS (Summer 2011).

Considering the future long-term care needs of the aging population, one will generally fall into one of three socioeconomic segments. For those with no meaningful financial assets relying primarily on Social Security, long-term care planning will have little impact because such individuals are not planning for themselves. How well this segment fares will be more a function of government programs and their personal health habits. Forty percent of the elder population with long-term care needs is impoverished, meaning their income is less than 150 percent of the federal poverty level ($14,710 annual income for a family of two[8]). Those with substantial assets typically are good financial planners whose plans emphasize minimizing estate taxes and maximizing inheritances. They still need to consider the risks of self-insuring. For those in the middle of the strata, approximately 50–60 percent of the population, traditional retirement planning is considered very important, and these individuals are likely to see a decline in economic status as they age. This segment will likely take increased personal responsibility for their retirement and will also have the financial means to transfer the risk of long-term care expenses to an insurance vehicle.

As the overall size of the older population rapidly increases in the coming decades, the number of disabled older Americans is expected to soar. Between the years 2000 and 2040, the number of older adults with disabilities is expected to more than double, increasing from about 10 million to about 21 million.[9]

The disabled older population will grow faster than the younger population, resulting in an increasing economic burden of long-term care. According to the most recent report from the American Association of Retired Persons (AARP), the 65 and older age group will increase 89 percent over the next 20 years, and the 85 and older age group will increase 74 percent during the same period. In 2040, it is expected that there will be only nine adults ages 25 to 64 to support each disabled older adult, down from 15 in 2000.[10] The future demand for long-term care depends heavily on how elder disability rates evolve over time. Current trends indicate that there have been recent health improvements at older ages; however, there is no guarantee that these trends will continue. Disability associated with the rising prevalence of diabetes and obesity in the younger population may offset the future decline in disability rates at older ages. Population aging, especially for those baby boomers reaching age 85 and beyond, signals a likely surge in the use of long-term care services.

---

8. American Association for Long-Term Care Insurance, http://www.aaltci.org/long-term-care-insurance/ (last visited Oct. 28, 2011).

9. RICHARD W. JOHNSON ET AL., URBAN INSTITUTE, MEETING THE LONG-TERM CARE NEEDS OF THE BABY BOOMERS, HOW CHANGING FAMILIES WILL AFFECT PAID HELPERS AND INSTITUTIONS (May 1, 2007).

10. *Id.*

**FIGURE 2-3**

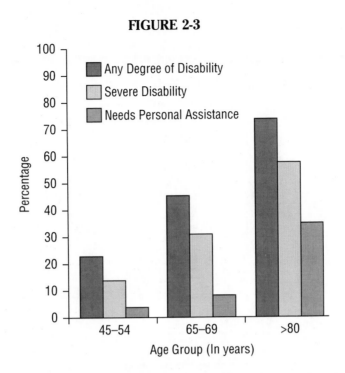

Source: American Academy of Family Physicians (AAFP) 2010 FP Comprehensive: a board preparation tool.

## Life Expectancy

Life expectancy has been on an upward trajectory for over 100 years. Greater longevity among the baby boomer generation will contribute to increased demand for long-term care services. Those surviving to age 65 can expect to live an average of 20 more years.[11] A complete table of single life expectancy is included in Appendix 1. Life expectancy has been dramatically affected by advances in diagnosing and treating illnesses. In particular, various forms of cancer (e.g., pancreatic and brain cancer) now show a higher survival rate than in the past.

The issue is not whether one will live a long life, but whether one will live a long life with a healthy quality of life. For those younger than age 85, the most current evidence suggests delayed onset of limitations and disabilities despite a coinciding increase in chronic diseases and conditions. This can be partly explained by early diagnosis and improved treatment of prevalent diseases, rendering them less disabling. As a result, people younger than 85 years old are living longer and are capable of managing their daily activities for a longer period of time than previous generations.

However, it is inevitable that increased life expectancy creates a greater need for long-term care services. The aging process ultimately exacts its toll. Forty-two

---

11. THE PRUDENTIAL INSURANCE COMPANY OF AMERICA, PRUDENTIAL RESEARCH REPORT: LONG-TERM CARE COST STUDY (2010).

percent of people age 65 and over reported a functional limitation, defined as a limitation of their typical daily activities—mobility, food preparation, driving, or personal hygiene, for example.[12] About 30 percent (1.5 million people) of the older population with long-term care needs have substantial limitations (defined as a loss of three or more activities of daily living or cognitive impairment). Of the 30 percent, 25 percent are age 85 and older, and 70 percent of this age group reported they are in fair to poor health.[13]

### FIGURE 2-4

### Health Worsens with Increasing Age

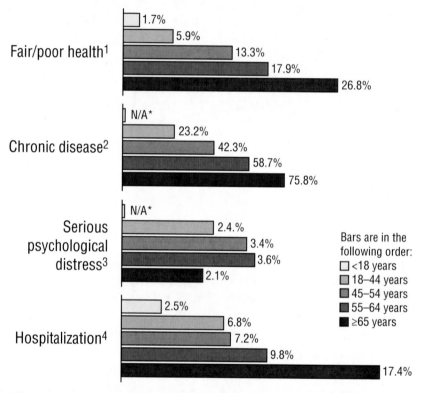

[1] Proportion (%) of survey respondents who described their health as fair or poor, 2007.

[2] Proportion (%) of adults age 18 and older who reported at least one of six chronic diseases—diabetes, cardiovascular disease, chronic obstructive pulmonary disease, asthma, cancer, and arthritis—2007.

[3] Proportion (%) of adults age 18 and older who reported serious psychological distress in the past 30 days, 2007.

[4] Proportion (%) of survey respondents who reported being hospitalized in the preceding year, 2007.

[*] Data for individuals under 18 years of age are unavailable for chronic disease and serious psychological distress.

Source: Center for Disease Control and Prevention, National Center for Health Statistics, National Health Interview Survey, 2007.

---

12. Health Status Report, 2010, http://www.agingstats.gov/Main_Site/Data/2010_Documents/docs/Health_Status.pdf.

13. THE HENRY J. KAISER FAMILY FOUNDATION, KAISER COMMISSION ON MEDICAID AND THE UNINSURED, LONG-TERM CARE: UNDERSTANDING MEDICAID'S ROLE FOR THE ELDERLY AND DISABLED (Nov. 2005).

The lifetime probability of being unable to perform at least two activities of daily living or being cognitively impaired is 68 percent for people age 65 and older.[14] By 2050, the number of individuals using paid long-term care services in any setting will likely double from the 13 million who used services in 2000 to 27 million people. This estimate is influenced by growth in the population of older people needing care. In addition to this growth, according to the U.S. Department of Health and Human Services (HHS) and the U.S. Department of Labor (DOL), 5.7 million to 6.5 million nurses, nurse aides, and home health and personal care workers will be needed to care for the 27 million Americans who will require some type of long-term care by 2050.[15]

Arguably, the increase in longevity is a result of support given to an increasing proportion of frail and ill individuals well into advanced ages. The substantial increase in longevity is concerning because it may have huge personal and societal implications. Conversely, once people experience a disease or injury requiring long-term care, the result is most often a decrease in life expectancy. Individuals living in institutional care, regardless of age, have significantly shorter life expectancies than contemporaries living independently. Mortality is driven not only by their condition but also by the impact of the significant change in environment. Intangible factors, such as one's will to live, and tangible factors, such as exposure to communicable diseases in a group environment, come together to reduce life expectancy. Until very recently, actuarial tables and life expectancy calculations have not taken this into account (**cf. Chapter 4, page 94**). However, this fact is becoming increasingly important as the population reaching the compression point increases. Excluding the death of a spouse, moving into an institutional care facility is possibly the single most disruptive event that one may experience. We must take into account that the population may be living longer and enjoying expectantly healthier lives; however, crossing the morbidity threshold dramatically changes one's outlook and has proven to decrease life expectancy.

## Medical Conditions and Advancing Technology

Despite significant advances in diagnoses, medical technology, and pharmaceutical remedies, the number of people with physical or functional impairments will likely grow significantly in the coming decades, along with the aging of the population. According to the American Association for Long-Term Care Insurance's 2009 Sourcebook, between 2000 and 2040, the number of older adults with disabilities will more than double, increasing from about 10 million to 21 million. The number of people in the United States facing barriers for employment, health

---

14. Mark A. Cohen et al., The AARP Public Policy Institute, Becoming Disabled After Age 65: The Expected Lifetime Costs of Independent Living (June 2005).

15. American Health Care Association, National Center for Assisted Living, www.ahcancal.org (last visited Oct. 28, 2011).

care, and independent living will no doubt escalate, as well as the number of individuals needing personal assistance from family members or paid caregivers.

The number of working adults who meet the eligibility requirements for Social Security Disability Income (SSDI) and are receiving SSDI benefits due to a qualifying disability has been steadily increasing, as seen in the following graph. In addition, this increase in SSDI claims is projected to continue, as evidenced by the Congressional Budget Office projections showing increasing caseloads from 6.7 million in 2000 to 10.4 million in 2015.[16] As the baby boomer population crosses the retirement threshold, the number of Social Security beneficiaries per covered worker is projected to increase, as well. The consequences of premature aging, defined as atypical aging due to a disability, and individuals with conditions that were once incompatible with long-term survival have been overlooked with respect to their potential impact on the SSDI program. Generally, analysts are now predicting that activities of daily living disabilities and work limitations among adults will increase, in part as a consequence of the growing prevalence of obesity and co-morbid related disorders.

## FIGURE 2-5

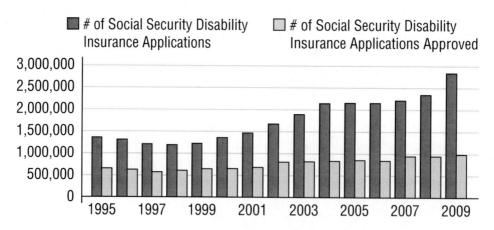

Source: U.S. Social Security Administration.

As a consequence to the longevity trend discussed previously, overall cancer incidence is rising as people live longer. Chronic diseases such as diabetes, cardiovascular disease, and arthritis are also increasing, but the mortality attributable to these diseases is decreasing. As a result, more people are living with chronic diseases. Other chronic debilitating diseases such as chronic obstructive pulmonary disease (COPD), congestive heart failure, and dementia are also resulting in decreased mortality yet increased morbidity.

With improved medical science, the probability of disability rather than premature death continues to increase, as shown in the following chart:

---

16. INSTITUTE OF MEDICINE COMMITTEE ON DISABILITY IN AMERICA, THE FUTURE OF DISABILITY IN AMERICA (Marilyn J. Field & Alan M. Jette, eds. 2007).

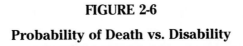

## FIGURE 2-6

## Probability of Death vs. Disability

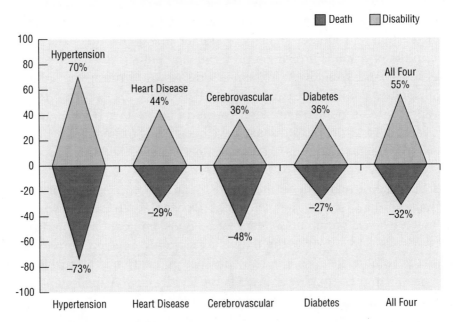

Source: National Underwriter, May 2002, obtained from The JHA Disability Fact Book 2003/2004, Need for Disability Insurance.

Dementia has become one of the fastest growing forms of disability in elder Americans, most often manifesting in Alzheimer's disease. Currently, it is estimated that over 5.4 million people in the United States suffer from Alzheimer's disease. Alzheimer's affects 10 to 20 percent of people age 65 and over, and the prevalence of Alzheimer's doubles roughly every 10 years after age 65. Studies indicate that as much as 10 to 20 percent of those age 65 and older have Mild Cognitive Impairment (MCI).[17] People whose MCI symptoms cause them enough concern to visit a physician appear to have a higher risk of developing dementia. It's estimated that as many as 15 percent of these individuals progress from MCI to dementia each year. From this estimate, it can be assumed that nearly half of all people who have visited a physician about MCI symptoms will develop dementia in three or four years.[18]

Alzheimer's destroys brain cells, and symptoms often include confusion, anger, mood swings, language breakdown, and long-term memory loss. Caring for

17. Alzheimer's Association, *2011 Alzheimer's Disease Facts and Figures*, 7 Alzheimer's & Dementia 2, at 208–44 (Mar. 2011); R.O. Roberts et al., *The Mayo Clinic Study of Aging: Design and Sampling, Participation, Baseline Measures and Sample Characteristics*, Neuroepidemiology, no. 30, 2008 at 58–69; T. Hanninen et al., *Prevalence of Mild Cognitive Impairment: A Population-Based Study in Elderly Subjects*, Acta Neurologica Scandinavica, no. 106, 2002 at 148–54.

18. Alzheimer's Association, *supra* note 17; R.C. Petersen et al., *Mild Cognitive Impairment: Clinical Characterization and Outcome*, Archives of Neurology, no. 56, 1999 at 303–08.

a person with Alzheimer's disease involves specialized services that differ from other types of senior accommodation.

According to the Society of Actuaries' *Long-Term Care News*, Alzheimer's claims are the most expensive, most frequent, and longest, and are trending higher.[19] Nervous system and mental claims are similar in expense to Alzheimer's, while cancer and injury claims are similar in frequency but shorter and less expensive. Besides the disabling effects of Alzheimer's disease, it is the sixth leading cause of all deaths in the United States and is the fifth leading cause of death in Americans age 65 and over. Although other major causes of death have been on the decrease, deaths caused by Alzheimer's disease have been rising dramatically. Between 2000 and 2008 (preliminary data), heart disease deaths decreased by 13 percent, stroke deaths by 20 percent, and prostate cancer-related deaths by 8 percent, whereas deaths because of Alzheimer's increased by 66 percent. Approximately 200,000 people age 65 and over with Alzheimer's disease comprise the younger onset Alzheimer's disease population. Every 69 seconds, someone in America develops Alzheimer's disease; by 2050, the time is expected to accelerate to every 33 seconds. In the coming decades, the baby boomer population is projected to add ten million people to these numbers. In 2050, the incidence of Alzheimer's diagnoses is expected to approach nearly one million people per year, with an estimated total of 11 to 16 million people living with the disease. Dramatic increases in the numbers of "oldest old" (those age 85 and older) across all racial and ethnic groups will also significantly affect the numbers of people living with Alzheimer's disease.

In 2010, nearly 15 million family and other unpaid caregivers provided an estimated 17 billion hours of care to people with Alzheimer's disease and other dementias, a contribution valued at more than $202 billion. Medicare payments for services to beneficiaries age 65 and older with Alzheimer's disease and other dementias are almost three times higher than for beneficiaries without these conditions. Total payments in 2011 for health care, long-term care, and hospice services for people age 65 and older with Alzheimer's disease and other dementias are expected to be $183 billion. This figure does not include the contributions of unpaid caregivers.[20]

Alzheimer's disease has a slow onset, beginning with mild memory difficulties and ending with severe brain damage. The course and pace vary from person to person. Alzheimer's patients live eight to ten years after they are diagnosed, although the disease can last for as many as 20 years.[21]

In conclusion, if the rate of activity and other limitations for those age 65 and over remains what it is today (roughly 40 percent), the number of older people with impairments or limitations will increase 100 percent by 2030.[22] Some estimates project the number of older adults with activity limitations will grow from

---

19. Society of Actuaries, LONG-TERM CARE NEWS, no. 22, Feb. 2009.
20. Alzheimer's Association, *supra* note 17.
21. TEXAS DEPARTMENT OF HEALTH SERVICES, ALZHEIMER'S DISEASE—QUESTIONS AND ANSWERS (Feb. 9, 2011).
22. INSTITUTE OF MEDICINE COMMITTEE ON DISABILITY IN AMERICA, *supra* note 16.

22 million in 2005 to 38 million by 2030. Because obesity has become more prevalent among the elderly, it is difficult for other social developments to counter its adverse health effects.

**FIGURE 2-7**

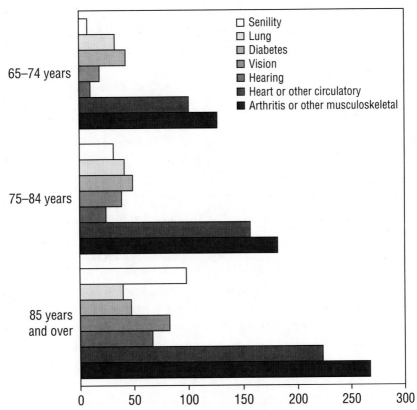

Number of persons with limitation of activity caused by selected chronic health conditions per 1,000 population

Source: Centers for Disease Control and Prevention, National Center for Health Statistics, National Health Interview Survey. Chartbook on Trends in the Health of Americans, 2006.

## Caregiving Facility Trends

Today's care options are moving from a strictly medical model to a more social model, while consumers are increasingly expecting and demanding more choices in care options. The industry is trending away from institutional, medical-based models to social, community-based, residential, or home-like settings, even for acute care. Aging baby boomers will undoubtedly increase the demand for a broad array of long-term care services and integrated options. Future planning includes the integration of long-term and acute care, a change from today's nursing home care versus home care model.

The preference for "aging in place" will direct the structure and architecture of future living options. Gradually, individuals are beginning to assume a more proactive role in the choice of service models and delivery of care. This trend is known as consumer-directed care. Remote monitoring technology is becoming more and more important. It has been shown to reduce emergency room visits and hospitalizations by significant numbers. As baby boomers age, residential developers will need to pay close attention to the physical design of homes because of the consumer's desire to age in place. With proper planning people could potentially remain in their homes for the rest of their lives.

As rapidly as the American population is aging, the supply of informal care-givers is declining. Current trends show that many of those who have been the traditional family caregivers are reentering the workplace in high numbers. Con-currently, families in general are having fewer children, thus reducing the num-ber of potential family caregivers. As stated earlier, many families are becoming increasingly geographically distant from one another, leading to the need for an increased pool of paid caregivers. In the future, the labor force in general will decline at the same time that the number of those needing long-term care services is increasing. Long-term care staffing shortages need to be addressed, as well as workforce development, to meet the anticipated growing need for caregivers.

In addition, the aging of the population is putting a strain on the already strained Medicaid system. Medicaid was originally intended as an acute medical care pro-gram for the impoverished population, not a long-term care planning tool.[23] Financial responsibility for long-term care continues to shift away from the federal govern-ment, placing more financial burden on states, individuals, and families. Congress has sent a clear message that the federal government has no intention of establish-ing new government-sponsored long-term care entitlement programs. The legisla-tion enacted to substantiate this stand will be discussed throughout later chapters.

Consumers need to think seriously about how to plan and pay for long-term care expenses. Current efforts to promote private long-term care insurance will create more funding for future long-term care services and increase the use of paid care. However, difficulties recruiting and retaining long-term care personnel could limit the availability of paid services and could potentially sharply increase the costs associated with long-term care. This concern merits increased attention from policymakers to ensure that the elder population receives high-quality care that is affordable to the recipient, their family, and society.

According to current estimates from the U.S. Census Bureau, more than 7.6 mil-lion Americans receive home care. The number is much greater when you consider that estimate does not include informal care—care that is provided by a family member or friend. Home care is generally defined as non-medical support services delivered in a residential setting with the intent to permit the aging resident to remain at home rather than enter an assisted living facility, nursing home, or other

---

23. Griepp & McCree, Attorneys at Law, *Your Long-Term Care: Medicare and Medicaid*, http://www
.griepplegal.com/articles/longterm_care/your_long_term_care_crisis_or.html (May 28, 2007).

type of facility. The graph below illustrates that the average care recipient has a need for assistance with multiple activities of daily living. It should be noted from the graph that over half of home care recipients are cognitively impaired. This typically means they need supervision to make sure they are not a danger to themselves or to others. In many cases, this supervision may be required on a 24-hour basis.

### FIGURE 2-8

### Functional and Cognitive Impairments of Care Recipients as Reported by Their Informal Caregivers

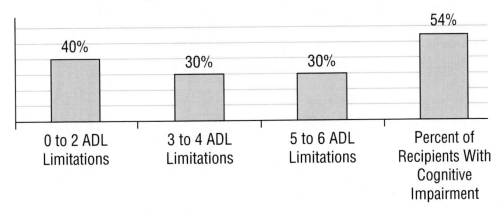

Source: National Care Planning Council. Putting Home Care in Perspective, June 25, 2009.

Providing respite for caregivers, or offering a solution for caregivers to reenter the workplace, adult day care centers and services provide medical, social, and therapeutic activities in a supportive group environment for individuals with physical or cognitive impairments. Some centers are independently operated; others are affiliated with a facility or organization such as a nursing home, assisted living community, senior center, or rehabilitation facility.

Care can be obtained in a social setting, medical setting, or specialized setting of adult day care services. A social setting program provides meals, recreation, and some basic health-related services. A medical setting program provides social activities as well as more intensive health and therapeutic services such as nursing services and rehabilitation therapy. A specialized setting program provides services relating only to specific diagnoses or needs, such as Alzheimer's disease or traumatic brain injury.

The general services offered by the majority of adult day care centers include

♦ social activities;
♦ health-related services;
♦ transportation;
♦ meals and snacks;
♦ personal care; and
♦ therapeutic activities.

Assisted living communities, or assisted living facilities (ALFs), help promote health, safety, and well-being among the residents. Assisted living was developed as a type of senior accommodation to provide housing, health care, and personal care services to seniors in need of assistance with activities of daily living in a more independent environment than a traditional nursing home. Among assisted living communities, there is wide variation in the level of care that may be provided. Some assisted living communities specialize in providing a supportive and safe environment for residents who are largely independent but need some minor periodic assistance with activities of daily living or medication management. Other ALFs have designed their services specifically for the very frail residents who need a high level of assistance on a daily basis. This particular type of facility has become a substitute for nursing homes and frequently provides many, though not all, of the same care services as a skilled nursing facility.

Residential care homes are known by different terms depending on the geographic location. In some areas they are called adult family homes; in other areas they may be referred to as personal care homes, adult foster homes, or board and care homes. Typically, they all have a common denominator: they provide care for adults in a home-like family setting. This type of setting is excellent for residents who do not want to live in a larger community locale but who still require a level of assistance similar to that offered in an assisted living community or nursing home. The personnel in a residential care home may assist with medications, hygiene, dressing, and many other daily tasks or activities of daily living. Because of the homes' intimate settings, proprietors can often specialize in particular resident requirements such as diabetes care, memory care, special dietary requirements, foreign languages, and religious or cultural requirements, as well as other needs. If this type of care setting is of importance to a client, it is important to verify that the long-term care insurance policy he or she is considering covers such a setting.

Retirement communities, also called senior independent living communities, are designed to accommodate independent seniors who have minor medical issues. Some retirement communities may have age restrictions, such as accepting only residents age 55 and older. Residents of retirement communities may have a variety of accommodation choices. While the majority of retirement communities cater to individuals, more communities are designing larger apartments and condominiums for retiring couples. Many communities have extensive activities and amenities available such as fitness facilities, golf and tennis facilities, monthly activities, and dining facilities.

Continuum of Care Retirement Communities (CCRC) are a fairly recent concept in the retirement living industry. As aging in place has become more important, developers, owners, and retirement communities have taken notice. In the 1990s, throughout the southeastern part of the United States, CCRC campuses began to emerge. CCRCs are usually divided into three living components housed on one campus: an independent living facility, an assisted living facility, and a skilled nursing home. Many CCRCs have options for seniors who vary from completely independent to completely dependent. Independent, healthy, and active retired individuals are able to find housing in senior apartments or condominiums with the option of aging in place. Assisted living facilities located on the campus provide for those who need a little more help in the way of medication reminders, assistance with hygiene, or housekeeping and meal preparation. When an illness or injury occurs, residents living within the continuum of care community may receive short-term rehabilitation or long-term convalescent care in the community's skilled nursing facility. Some campuses have home health components that provide assistance for short-care periods. Campuses often include wellness centers where the residents can have their blood pressure or blood sugar checked. Some communities include adult day care centers, Alzheimer's programs, and senior behavioral health centers with inpatient and outpatient services. The most appealing aspect of a continuum of care community is that a person gains stability and familiarity. Many losses and changes occur as a person ages or becomes frail. Being part of a community, making friends, developing relationships, and then being able to stay in that community when life changes is a comfort to both the residents and those who love them and care for them (**cf. Chapter 3, page 58**).

There are approximately 16,000 nursing homes in the United States.[24] Nursing homes, also known as skilled nursing facilities, are for those who require constant medical care and need significant assistance with their activities of daily living. The label "nursing home" has negative connotations for many people. Yet nursing homes provide an important component of long-term care housing options. A nursing home is normally the highest level of care for older adults outside of a hospital. Nursing homes also provide custodial care, including getting in and out of bed and providing assistance with feeding, hygiene, and dressing. However, nursing homes differ from other senior housing facilities in that they also provide a high level of medical care. A licensed physician supervises each resident's care, and a nurse or other medical professional is almost always on the premises. Skilled nursing care is available on site, usually 24 hours a day. Other medical professionals such as occupational or physical therapists are also available. This allows the delivery of medical procedures and therapies on site that would not be possible in other housing. The goal of care in a nursing home is to help individuals meet their daily physical, medical, social, and psychological needs. Nursing homes are generally standalone facilities, but some are operated within a hospital or a continuum of care community.

## Emerging Trends for Care

A number of key trends are emerging in long-term care related to financing, service delivery models, and shifts in consumer expectations and preferences. Changes

---

24. The Henry J. Kaiser Family Foundation, www.StateHealthFacts.org (last visited Oct. 28, 2012).

occurring in these areas point to a rapidly transforming long-term care landscape. Financing responsibility is shifting away from the federal government to states, individuals, and families. Providers are integrating and managing acute and long-term care services and adding new services to the continuum of care, and consumers are thinking more seriously about how to plan and pay for their future care needs, as well as how to independently navigate the long-term care system.

Policymakers, practitioners, and consumers recognize the dual and sometimes conflicting needs to address long-term care costs while maintaining and even improving quality of care. These two objectives have led to the emergence of several trends in the delivery of long-term care that have important implications as the aging of the baby boomers demands a broad array of long-term care services.

A number of initiatives at the federal, state, and provider levels are focusing on the management of acute and long-term care services through a range of integrated approaches. There is no consensus on the definition of integration. Some insist that to have an integrated system the funding as well as the delivery must be integrated. Others contend that the goal of integration is to ensure that all services are coordinated and managed at a point in time and across time to address the comprehensive needs of the individual and the family. Most would agree that the following elements are critical to achieving the goal of integration of services:

- Broad and flexible benefits, including primary, acute, and long-term care
- Extensive delivery systems that have the capacity and experience to go beyond traditional hospital, physician, and post-acute services to community-based long-term care, case management, and specialty providers
- Adoption of mechanisms for actually integrating care: care management and care planning protocols, interdisciplinary care teams, electronic medical records, and integrated information systems
- Overarching quality systems with a single point of accountability
- Flexible funding with incentives to align payers and minimize cost shifting

One of the primary barriers to integration of acute and long-term care is the fragmentation of funding sources, particularly Medicare and Medicaid. While a single source of financing is not essential to effective integration of services, it is difficult to reach that objective when providers do not have the financial incentive to develop a package of services across settings that best meets the needs of the elder population. Furthermore, Medicare and Medicaid have different eligibility requirements and coverage rules that impede the development of a rational plan of care for a person with acute and long-term care needs.

A second barrier is the concern about financial risk and the fear on the part of insurance carriers and providers to try to address the special challenges of integrating acute and long-term care for high-risk, high-cost people. There was an attempt to stimulate the Medicare-managed care market through the introduction of Medicare+Choice. There has, however, been little expansion in the availability and diversity of these managed care options. Evidence of this is seen with health maintenance organizations (HMOs) cutting back on attractive benefits such as no premiums and prescription drug coverage, and numerous reports of insurance carriers leaving many Medicare insurance markets. Given these trends, it is not likely that managed care plans will be offering long-term care benefits to their enrollees.

Perhaps the most overlooked barrier is the lack of knowledge, information, and training needed by health and long-term care providers to offer, coordinate, and manage services. There is no recognized authority in our current health care system for managing care across time, place, and profession, and little acknowledgment that individuals with chronic disabilities move back and forth between physicians, hospitals, nursing homes, and their own homes.[25] Acute and post-acute care providers historically have not communicated with long-term care providers, even though an elderly person may be getting services from both sectors. As technology advances, management information systems and patient databases that span time and place will expectantly drive the integration of acute and long-term care.

## Cost of Care

As stated before, long-term care includes a broad range of health and support services that people need as they age or if they are disabled. The vast majority of these services are personal care or assistance with activities of daily living that many families are able to provide for without a hard dollar cost. However, as care and support needs increase, paid care is usually required to supplement family-provided services or provide respite to family caregivers. Services from an assisted living facility or a nursing home become imperative as the need for care becomes more extensive and individuals can no longer be cared for in their homes.

Costs vary based on the type and amount of care needed, the providers used, and where a person lives. Home health and home care services, provided in two- to four-hour blocks of time, referred to as "visits," are generally more expensive for evenings, weekends, or holidays. The costs of services in some community programs, such as adult day care service programs, are often provided on a per day rate, but vary based on overhead and programming costs. Many care facilities charge extra for services provided beyond the basic room and board charge, although some have "all inclusive" fees. The trend in pricing among assisted living facilities has changed considerably. Over the last decade, assisted living facilities have continued to adapt to the wide range of care needs presented by our growing elder population. Many facilities now provide services to residents who

---

25. Robyn I. Stone, Long-Term Care for the Disabled Elderly: Current Policy, Emerging Trends and Implications for the 21st Century (Aug. 2000).

need continual care or supervision, while still providing a lower level of care to healthier individuals. As the range of services becomes broader, so does the range of monthly costs.

According to the 2011 MetLife Mature Market Institute Survey, the average costs in the United States are as follows:

**TABLE 2-1**    *2011*

| National Median | Level of Care |
|---|---|
| $19/hour | **Homemaker Services (Licensed)**—Provides "hands off" care such as helping with cooking and running errands. Often referred to as "Personal Care Assistants" or "Companions." This is the rate charged by a non-Medicare certified, licensed agency. |
| $21/hour | **Home Health Aide Services (Licensed)**—Provides "hands on" personal care, but not medical care, in the home, with activities such as bathing, dressing, and transferring. This is the rate charged by a non-Medicare certified, licensed agency. |
| $70/day | **Adult Day Health Care**—Provides social and other related support services in a community-based, protective setting during any part of a day, but less than 24-hour care. |
| $3,477/month | **Assisted Living Facility (One Bedroom/Single Occupancy)**—Provides "hands on" personal care as well as medical care for those who are not able to live by themselves. Additional assisted living costs may include fees for private transportation, off-site activities, medications, care assistance, meals, guest meals, and use of a guest apartment within the community. |
| $214/day | **Nursing Home (Semi-Private Room)**—Provides skilled nursing care 24 hours a day. |
| $239/day | **Nursing Home (Private Room)**—Provides skilled nursing care 24 hours a day. |

Understanding the cost associated with various levels of care can help families evaluate options and prudently plan for the potential cost of this type of care in their preferred location and setting. There are many resources for determining the cost of long-term care services, and most long-term care insurance companies provide comprehensive studies. For example, an independent study published by one of the foremost long-term care insurance providers, Genworth's 2011 Cost of Care Survey, conducted by CareScout, is one of the most comprehensive studies of its kind, covering nearly 15,500 long-term care providers in 437 regions nationwide. Additionally, Genworth's interactive website, www.genworth.com/costofcare, provides specific cost information by state and care type for 437 regions across the country. It allows someone to compare costs across four locations, which may include where one currently lives, where one's parents live, and where one might like to retire, and can calculate the estimated cost of care 10, 15, 20, 25, and 30 years in the future to assist in planning. These costs provide a benchmark to begin planning for wealth preservation.[26]

## Conclusions

Population aging, especially when baby boomers reach age 85 and older, signals a likely surge in the use of long-term care services. The quality of long-term care is often problematic, and a growing shortage of long-term care personnel will likely further threaten service delivery.

The key to having "quality of life" for older adults is functional ability—how well one is able to perform daily activities. Designing and implementing strategies and policies to promote healthiness and well-being for people with existing disabilities, and prevent the development and progression of potentially disabling conditions, needs to be a priority.

Planning, financing, and organizing long-term care services are essential in order to provide retirement security for Americans as they age. It is everyone's responsibility to share acquired knowledge and experience in order to help others more effectively manage the age wave in our society. All Americans will be affected.

---

26. This is not to be construed as an endorsement specifically for Genworth Financial, Inc.

# *Funding Options*  3

ONE OF THE MOST important factors to consider in planning for long-term care is how to pay for the care. According to the U.S. Department of Labor, long-term care expenses are the greatest uninsured risk Americans face today.[1] Because it is difficult to accurately predict if someone will need care, how much care one will need, where the care will be provided, and how much the care may cost, determining how to pay for long-term care can be complicated and challenging. Generally, people think of four basic ways to pay for long-term care: Medicare, Medicaid, self-funding, or private pay from a long-term care insurance policy.[2]

**FIGURE 3-1**

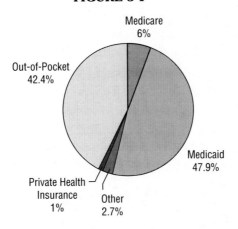

Source: Life Insurance Marketing Research Association International, Inc., 2009.

---

1. Advisory Council on Employee Welfare and Pension Benefits, U.S. Department of Labor (2008).

2. This chapter draws in part from HARLEY GORDON, CERTIFICATION IN LONG-TERM CARE COURSE HANDBOOK, Sections A, C, D (Releases 5.0, 8.0, 9.0, Corporation for Long-Term Care Certification 2003, 2009, 2011), and from HARLEY GORDON, IN SICKNESS & IN HEALTH: YOUR SICKNESS—YOUR FAMILY'S HEALTH, Chapters 4, 5, 8 (Financial Strategies Press 2007), and from HARLEY GORDON, WHY PLANNING WITH LIFE STAGE, PowerPoint presentation (2011).

Those considering relying on government programs administered by the Centers for Medicare and Medicaid Services (CMS)—Medicare or Medicaid—to provide long-term care services should consider the limitations of these programs. Typically Medicaid is used for care if functional eligibility criteria are met, there are very limited financial resources, or financial resources are depleted through transfer or paying for care. If skilled or recuperative care is needed for a short time, Medicare may pay for care. These programs provide very little or no choice in how, where, and by whom care will be delivered. More details on these programs will be provided later in this chapter.

For someone with sufficient income and assets, government-provided programs are not available; therefore long-term care expenses are funded from one's own private resources. Increasingly, people with means are utilizing private funding options to pay for long-term care if, and when, they need it. Private long-term care funding options include long-term care insurance, trusts, annuities, and home equity alternatives. Which option is best depends on many factors including age, health status, risk of needing long-term care, and personal financial situation. Specific circumstances will dictate the most appropriate plan for long-term care.

# Self-Funding

Once it is understood that a long-term care plan is critical to a family's financial and emotional well-being, the logical next step is to determine how the plan will be funded. Most people believe that life savings can be used for any number of things. If told that they may have to pay for care from life savings they may ask, "Do you think there is enough?" If told, however, that the only way to pay for care may be with funds from their retirement portfolio, the response may more likely be, "I am counting on that to fund my retirement." People with resources seek a certain lifestyle at retirement, and that lifestyle is not one of subsistence. The income from the portfolio is likely expected to support a certain lifestyle including life's passions. It is also used to fund continuing commitments to family and community. Can a person pay for care for an undetermined amount of time yet maintain his or her lifestyle and commitments? If yes, is that person really willing to pay out of his or her own pocket?

## Savings and Investments

When savings are considered as a source to self-insure long-term care, there are factors to consider. If one does not own a long-term care insurance policy, or prefers to pay out of personal resources, one of the most important questions to consider is, "Will retirement income and savings be able to cover all the costs of care?" Consideration must be given to the various financial resources one might have and how one feels about using these resources to pay for long-term care expenses.

Generally, when dealing with clients close to retirement, financial advisors will transition portfolios from assets that emphasize accumulation to those that focus on income (a so-called "asset accumulation to income distribution" model). Those investments are designated as an income portfolio. The portfolio may include

- bonds;
- annuities;
- tax-deferred (qualified) funds—401(k), defined benefit plan, individual retirement account (IRA);
- mutual funds that focus on generating income.

The remaining assets are typically referred to as an investment portfolio, in which the income from this portfolio tends to be reinvested. Included in this portfolio, among others, are

- investment properties;
- stocks; and
- mutual funds.

Other various sources of income may include Social Security, pensions, interest income, dividends from investments, cash, personal savings, and real estate.

Paying for care requires a reallocation of income and assets because assets do not pay for care, income pays for care. By definition, extended health care disrupts every plan the advisor and client have established to provide for a secure retirement:

- A plan to help ensure the financial viability of a surviving spouse
- A plan to help ensure financial viability during retirement
- A special-needs plan
- A well thought-out tax plan
- A charitable-giving plan
- A succession plan, because there may be no estate to pass on
- A plan to educate grandchildren
- A plan to hold assets separately in a second marriage

In addition, economic volatility over the last few years has demonstrated that a person's investment and financial circumstances can rapidly change. Many individuals and families are reexamining their investment strategies after experiencing sharp declines in portfolio values and real estate in a very short period of time. As such, advisors have found that many clients are revising their risk tolerance based on their experiences over the last few years. Those who have been confident that they would self-insure their long-term care risk are realizing that they are neither able nor willing to do so in an increasingly uncertain future.

Americans have also experienced rapidly rising health care costs that are outpacing inflation. The effect of this increase on personal income should be factored prominently into retirement and wealth preservation planning. For example, the latest research from the Employee Benefits Research Institute shows that a couple, both age 65 today, living to average life expectancy, could need as much as $295,000 to cover premiums for health insurance coverage and out-of-pocket expenses during retirement. A couple who lives to age 95 could need as a much as $550,000.[3] This figure does not include the cost of long-term care and most likely underestimates the amount of money needed when unexpected health care costs, longer life expectancies, and future reductions in Medicare benefits are included. Health and long-term care costs have the potential to significantly erode retirement savings and income and should be factored into the overall financial plan.

In essence, planning to pay with personal finances means a contingency fund should be established so that investments can quickly and easily be liquidated into cash to pay for long-term care. The fund can take the form of periodic investments over a specific length of time or available retirement assets accumulated in older ages. Examples of tangible assets people might use to produce income to fund their long-term care plan could include investment property, such as

- rentals;
- commercially leased property;
- land;
- a farm;
- a second home;
- a business.

However, there are complications associated with using retirement savings or tangible assets for long-term care services. One such concern is that, as people age, there is a tendency to accumulate cash rather than spend it. It is not unreasonable to assume that lifestyle expenses will closely match income. The need for long-term care services most likely will not change that approach. Consequently, a spouse will often try to cope with caregiving at home to avoid spending money. This is a precarious situation that can seriously deteriorate the physical and emotional health of the caregiver and his or her family. Often, family intervenes and ultimately spends the money anyway once the burden has become too much to handle. If for some reason a family is forced to spend retirement income for care, this will deplete resources needed by the surviving spouse after the care recipient deceases. Factors compounding the effect include

- lost investment opportunity;
- asset liquidation costs such as tax issues and market timing;
- rapidly escalating care cost demands, which could outpace investment returns.

---

3. Employee Benefit Research Institute, EBRI Issue Brief, No. 295 (July 2006).

Invariably, family income drops when a spouse deceases. Savings may be needed for the surviving spouse to maintain enough income to manage and retain their residence.

It is also challenging to determine the appropriate amount of money one needs to allocate or invest systematically in order to cover potential long-term care expenses. For example, if an amount equal to the insurance premiums over 20 years is invested, depending on the rate of return, only 5 to 12 percent of the potential insurance benefit may be available. Another consideration is timing and access to the funds. If long-term care is needed in the next five to ten years, or even later, the account will have insufficient time to grow.

The chart on page 42 is based on these factors:

- An annual investment of $2,025, contrasted with an annual long-term care insurance premium of $2,025 for a four-year plan (1,460 days) and a 5 percent compound benefit increase.

- $150 per day x 1460 days = $219,000, which is the initial "pool of money" available for care. If care is needed on day one of the policy, a total benefit amount of $219,000 is available. If care is needed in year ten, $339,741 is available, and the amount continues to grow while on claim, as specified in the long-term care insurance contract.

- In ten years, the same amount of money that would have been paid for insurance as investing ($2,025 x 10 years) = $20,250. Even with a 12.5 percent return on investment, the investment account would only have accumulated $36,407.

Interestingly, there is a real risk of outliving savings. Many risk-averse, affluent people prefer to limit exposure by transferring risk, spending pennies to protect dollars. Self-insuring requires large reserves to be set aside for the possibility of long-term care. Insurance is purchased to preserve assets. This is accomplished by leveraging premiums to buy significant coverage at affordable rates. Using interest earnings on retirement assets to pay for an insurance policy leaves the assets intact to be used for other purposes. Immediately upon purchasing a long-term care insurance policy, a pool of money is created and available to the insured that is not subject to risk like other assets. No matter what the risk, the total cost of premiums over a long period is usually a fraction of the cost of paying a claim from personal finances. Considering that the probability of experiencing a house fire is one in 1,200, the probability having a major automobile accident is one in 240, and the risk of needing long-term care is one in two,[4] long-term care insurance just makes good sense.

---

4. Arvin D. Pfefer, The Consumer Guide to Long Term Care Insurance (2006).

**FIGURE 3-2**

## "I'LL INVEST THE PREMIUMS INSTEAD."

This Table compares the growing Personal Benefit Account of a Long Term Care insurance plan with the investment of the premiums at various rates of interest.

| Year | Insurance Value | | Investment Account Value | | | | Cost of Care/Yr. |
|---|---|---|---|---|---|---|---|
| | Daily Benefit | Personal Benefit Acct. | Invest @ 5.0% | Invest @ 7.5% | Invest @ 10.0% | Invest @ 12.5% | |
| 1 | $150 | $219,000 | $2,025 | $2,025 | $2,025 | $2,025 | $54,750 |
| 2 | $158 | $229,950 | $4,151 | $4,202 | $4,253 | $4,303 | $57,488 |
| 3 | $165 | $241,448 | $6,384 | $6,542 | $6,703 | $6,866 | $60,362 |
| 4 | $174 | $253,520 | $8,728 | $9,058 | $9,398 | $9,749 | $63,380 |
| 5 | $182 | $266,196 | $11,189 | $11,762 | $12,363 | $12,993 | $66,549 |
| 6 | $191 | $279,506 | $13,774 | $14,669 | $15,624 | $16,642 | $69,876 |
| 7 | $201 | $293,481 | $16,488 | $17,794 | $19,212 | $20,747 | $73,370 |
| 8 | $211 | $308,155 | $19,337 | $21,154 | $23,158 | $25,366 | $77,039 |
| 9 | $222 | $323,563 | $22,329 | $24,765 | $27,498 | $30,561 | $80,891 |
| 10 | $233 | $339,741 | $25,470 | $28,648 | $32,273 | $36,407 | $84,935 |
| 11 | $244 | $356,728 | $28,769 | $32,821 | $37,526 | $42,982 | $89,182 |
| 12 | $257 | $374,564 | $32,232 | $37,308 | $43,303 | $50,380 | $93,641 |
| 13 | $269 | $393,293 | $35,869 | $42,131 | $49,658 | $58,703 | $98,323 |
| 14 | $283 | $412,957 | $39,687 | $47,316 | $56,649 | $68,066 | $103,239 |
| 15 | $297 | $433,605 | $43,697 | $52,890 | $64,339 | $78,599 | $108,401 |
| 16 | $312 | $455,285 | $47,906 | $58,881 | $72,798 | $90,449 | $113,821 |
| 17 | $327 | $478,050 | $52,327 | $65,323 | $82,103 | $103,780 | $119,512 |
| 18 | $344 | $501,952 | $56,968 | $72,247 | $92,338 | $118,777 | $125,488 |
| 19 | $361 | $527,050 | $61,841 | $79,690 | $103,597 | $135,649 | $131,762 |
| 20 | $379 | $553,402 | $66,959 | $87,692 | $115,982 | $154,631 | $138,351 |
| 21 | $398 | $581,072 | $72,331 | $96,294 | $129,605 | $175,984 | $145,268 |
| 22 | $418 | $610,126 | $77,973 | $105,541 | $144,591 | $200,007 | $152,531 |
| 23 | $439 | $640,632 | $83,897 | $115,481 | $161,075 | $227,033 | $160,158 |
| 24 | $461 | $672,664 | $90,117 | $126,168 | $179,207 | $257,437 | $168,166 |
| 25 | $484 | $706,297 | $96,647 | $137,655 | $199,153 | $291,642 | $176,574 |
| 26 | $508 | $741,612 | $103,505 | $150,004 | $221,093 | $330,122 | $185,403 |
| 27 | $533 | $778,692 | $110,705 | $163,280 | $245,227 | $373,413 | $194,673 |
| 28 | $560 | $817,627 | $118,265 | $177,551 | $271,775 | $422,114 | $204,407 |
| 29 | $588 | $858,508 | $126,203 | $192,892 | $300,978 | $476,904 | $214,627 |
| 30 | $617 | $901,434 | $134,539 | $209,384 | $333,100 | $538,542 | $225,358 |

**\*\*NOTE\*\***

A gray box above indicates the point in time at which the value of the Investment Account equals, or exceeds, the expected cost of one year of care.

Source: http://www.guidetolongtermcare.com/privacy.html.

FIGURE 3-3

**70% of clients age 65 or older will need some form of LTC**

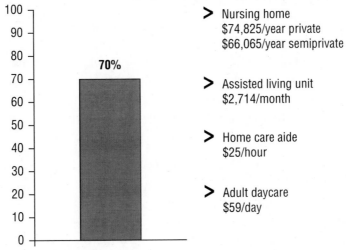

Source: U.S. Department of Health and Human Services—National Clearinghouse for LTC Information. "2007 Average National Costs," www.longtermcare.gov., March 26, 2008. ©2009 Lincoln National. 2010 Genworth Cost of Care Survey

Even if a client is unable to qualify for a traditionally designed long-term care insurance policy due to adverse health, there are various alternate insurance vehicles available.

# Social Insurance

The terms "Medicare" and "Medicaid" are often confused. Medicaid was established by the same federal laws that created Medicare in 1965. Although the two are quite different, both exist to provide health care coverage, and both are government-funded.

There is an abundance of information available on the government programs offered. A non-exhaustive list of resources is located in Appendix 2. Extensive research is required if serious consideration is being given to these as a plan of care.

## *Medicare*

Medicare is a federal health program financed through payroll taxes. States do not contribute to the program. It is called an entitlement program because people are entitled to benefits, regardless of assets and income, by paying into the program during their working years.

There are four parts to Medicare:

- ◆ Medicare Part A, Hospital Insurance
- ◆ Medicare Part B, Medical Insurance

- Medicare Part C (Medicare Advantage), which was formerly known as Medicare+Choice
- Medicare Part D, prescription drug coverage

Generally, people who are over age 65 and receiving Social Security benefits automatically qualify for Medicare Parts A and B. So do people who have been receiving disability benefits for two years, people who have amyotrophic lateral sclerosis (Lou Gehrig's disease) and receive disability benefits, and people who have permanent kidney failure and receive maintenance dialysis or a kidney transplant.

Someone can be eligible for Part A at age 65 without having to pay premiums if he or she

- already receives retirement benefits from Social Security or the Railroad Retirement Board;
- is eligible to receive Social Security or Railroad benefits but has not yet filed for them; and
- is a beneficiary or has a spouse with Medicare-covered government employment.

Some can be eligible for Part A under age 65 without having to pay premiums if he or she

- receives Social Security or Railroad Retirement Board disability benefits for 24 months; or
- has end-stage renal disease and meets certain requirements.

While premium payment is not required for Part A if one of these conditions is met, a beneficiary who wants Part B must pay for it.

Part A is paid for by a portion of Social Security tax. It helps pay for inpatient hospital care, skilled nursing care, hospice care, and other services. Part B is paid for by the monthly premiums of people enrolled and by general funds from the U.S. Treasury. It helps pay for doctors' fees, outpatient hospital visits, and other medical services and supplies that are not covered by Part A. Part C (Medicare Advantage) plans allow beneficiaries to choose to receive all of their health care services through a provider organization. These plans may help lower costs of receiving medical services or may provide extra benefits for an additional monthly fee. A beneficiary must have both Parts A and B to enroll in Part C. Part D (prescription drug coverage) is voluntary, and the costs are paid for by the monthly premiums of enrollees and Medicare. Unlike Part B, which allows for automatic enrollment and requires opting out if not wanted, with Part D, once eligible, one has to opt in by filling out a form and enrolling in an approved plan.

Many people incorrectly assume that Medicare will pay for long-term care. Medicare is designed to cover acute medical care, not chronic care or disabilities in older ages. It only covers medically necessary care, focusing on medically acute care such as hospital stays and doctors' visits, or short-term care such as rehabilitative services, as long as the medical condition is expected to improve. In a care setting, the patient must show progress toward recovery, as Medicare does not pay for chronic conditions. Because of its availability, almost everyone age 65 and over has coverage through Medicare. There are over 47 million Medicare beneficiaries in the United States, which includes beneficiaries from all territories (including 3,513 beneficiaries from American Samoa) and those who presently live in another country.[5]

Generally, Medicare does not pay for most long-term care nor for personal or custodial care, which is the most prevalent type of long-term care service.[6] Medicare will pay for a limited skilled nursing facility stay, hospice care, or home health care if certain criteria are met. Skilled nursing facility care is defined as a semi-private room, meals, skilled nursing and rehabilitative services, and other services and supplies (after a related three-day hospital stay). Medicare Part A covers expenses up to 100 days of skilled care rehabilitation. The first 20 days are covered at 100 percent; the subsequent 80 days are covered based upon a copayment rate. The patient must have a qualifying hospital stay prior to the skilled rehabilitation; a qualifying hospital stay is defined as an inpatient hospital stay of three consecutive days (three midnights) or more that starts the day the patient is admitted as an inpatient (does not cover days in for observation nor the day of discharge).

The skilled nursing care is prescribed by a physician. If all these conditions are met, Medicare will pay a portion of the cost up to 100 days. The benefit amount payable by Medicare is an indexed figure that has historically increased on an annual basis. For the first 20 days, Medicare will pay 100 percent of the skilled nursing facility cost. For days 21 to 100, expenses are personally paid up to a specified amount. Medicare then pays the balance up to 100 days. The insured is responsible for 100 percent of the cost of care for each day after 100 days. However, Medicare often stops paying before the 100th day if the medical condition is not improving. There is a misconception that Medicare automatically covers up to 100 days of most nursing home expenses. Even though a large number of nursing home admissions come from hospitals, not all of these receive Medicare reimbursement. Many patients are younger than age 65 and not on Medicare. For those age 65 and over, a hospital stay resulting in nursing home care does not automatically qualify for Medicare coverage. Medicare will not pay for custodial care in the absence of a skilled care plan. However, if a Medicare beneficiary meets all of the qualified criteria, Medicare will pay for custodial care in a skilled care setting for which it provides payment. Care included in the skilled care services plan consists of assistance with bathing, dressing, ambulating, toileting, incontinence, feeding, and administering medication. Medicare will not exclude the custodial services if they are a necessary part of the skilled care plan in a nursing home.

All nursing homes, whether they meet the definition of a Medicare skilled nursing facility or not, provide services from a nurse, physician, or therapist. Therefore, they meet the medical definition of skilled care. However, to be a certified Medicare nursing home and receive payments from Medicare, a nursing home must meet the

---

5. The Henry J. Kaiser Family Foundation, www.statehealthfacts.org (last visited Oct. 28, 2012).
6. www.Medicare.gov (last visited Oct. 28, 2012).

Medicare definition of a skilled nursing facility: there must be registered nurses on duty 24 hours a day, a physician on call at all times, and an ambulance service to a local hospital. Medicare may also require additional staffing and facility arrangements to qualify for certification. Many states have adopted the same federal criteria for licensing their nursing homes. In some states the skilled criteria are used to define a nursing home. Other states, whose nursing home facilities offer lesser services, may offer tiered licensing classes and include a tier known as intermediate care.

Prior to 1997, Medicare reimbursements to nursing homes were based on actual costs submitted on each patient. The Balanced Budget Act of 1996 forced Medicare to phase in a prospective payment system of reimbursement, which is currently now fully implemented. Payments are still made for each patient but are based on pricing formulas determined by the intensity of care needed as well as the number of anticipated days of care multiplied by a rate factor derived from 1998 historic costs in that geographic area. This is prospective payment. As a rule, nursing homes claim they are losing money with this payment system.

Medicare is the principal provider of home health care and hospice care under Medicare Part B. However, there is a growing trend for Medicaid to provide more home care than Medicare.[7] Home health care is defined by Medicare as part-time skilled nursing care, physical therapy, occupational therapy, speech-language therapy, home health aide services, medical social services, durable medical equipment (such as wheelchairs, hospital beds, oxygen, and walkers) and medical supplies, and other health-related services. For Medicare qualification, home health care must be under a physician's plan of care, requiring frequent visits by a therapist, licensed practical nurse (LPN), or registered nurse (RN). As part of the plan of care, aides may also provide assistance with bathing, dressing, ambulating, toileting, incontinence, and feeding. The beneficiary must be homebound, meaning it is very difficult to leave the home during the period of recovery. However, a recent ruling now allows Medicare home care recipients to leave their homes for therapy or treatment and still receive benefits.[8] In addition, Medicare Part B may also cover the cost of durable medical equipment. This equipment must meet certain criteria to be covered. Medicare usually pays 80 percent of the Medicare-approved amount for certain pieces of medical equipment, such as a wheelchair or walker.

Medicare was never intended to pay for chronic, long-term home care. In 1996, Congress passed the Balanced Budget Act (BBA), along with the Health Insurance Portability and Accountability Act of 1996. These acts restricted access to Medicare home health care and reaffirmed the government's intent of only covering rehabilitating, acute care. Medicare pays for home care services on a limited basis to help the homebound Medicare beneficiary recover from an injury or medical condition through a home health care agency. Medicare pays the Medicare-certified home health agency one payment for covered services received during

---

7. National Care Planning Council (2011).

8. U.S. Department of Health and Human Services, Centers for Medicare and Medicaid Services, Medicare and Home Health Care, http://www.medicare.gov/publications/pubs/pdf/10969.pdf (2010).

a 60-day period. This 60-day period is called an "episode of care." The payment is based on the medical condition and care needs. If the recipient fails to respond to care through improvement, deteriorates, or is not improving in any way, Medicare will no longer cover the cost of care.

In 1997, under the BBA, Medicare adopted an interim payment system based on a projected 1999 implementation of the Prospective Payment System (PPS) for home care. PPS greatly restricted eligibility and reimbursements for homebound recipients. Under PPS, a home health care agency is only reimbursed per patient for each 60-day episode. This does not mean care cannot be less or more than 60 days because the agency can schedule visits until the prospective payment runs out. There are provisions to cut off reimbursement if the patient recovers early, or to extend payment if the condition worsens. Recent complaints from the home health industry indicate that PPS is not covering actual care given. Recently, because of pressure from home health agencies, Congress passed legislation to restore some funding to home care. Even with such legislation, though, Medicare is not a source of help for chronic, non-improving, and homebound long-term care recipients.

Medicare is a social insurance program that provides health insurance coverage to over 47 million Americans—almost everyone over age 65 and recipients of Social Security disability benefits. Pressure to curb health care spending, the projected insolvency of the Hospital Insurance Trust Fund, and concerns about gaps in coverage that leave beneficiaries exposed to significant health care costs will shape the evolution of the Medicare program.

**FIGURE 3-4**

**Distribution of Out-of-Pocket Expenses for Medicare Beneficiaries in 2006**

Total Out-of-Pocket Spending for Medicare Beneficiaries: $191 Billion
Average Total Out-of-Pocket Expenses per Beneficiary: $4,241

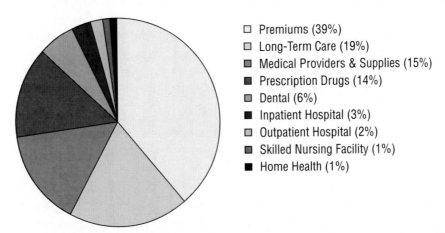

- □ Premiums (39%)
- ▨ Long-Term Care (19%)
- ▨ Medical Providers & Supplies (15%)
- ■ Prescription Drugs (14%)
- ▨ Dental (6%)
- ■ Inpatient Hospital (3%)
- □ Outpatient Hospital (2%)
- ▨ Skilled Nursing Facility (1%)
- ■ Home Health (1%)

Source: Kaiser Family Foundation analysis of the CMS Medicare Current Beneficiary Survey Cost and Use File, 2006. Reproduced by Morningstar with Permission.

Notes: Includes Medicare Advantage enrolles, and institutionalized and non-institutionalized beneficiaries. Premium spending includes Medicare A, B, C, and D and private health insurance premiums.

## *Medicaid*

Medicaid is a joint federal- and state-financed program that helps low-income individuals and families pay for the costs associated with long-term medical and custodial care, provided they qualify. Although largely funded by the federal government, Medicaid is administered by the individual states, where coverage may vary.

In many states, nursing home stays for non-skilled, custodial care are all that is covered, meaning staying at home and receiving skilled medical care is not always an option. In addition, Medicaid is not accepted by all nursing homes, nor will it cover recreational activities or any other forms of non-medical care.

Increasingly, Medicaid is also paying for home services for those who are Medicaid qualified. People receiving Medicaid assistance may receive benefits for services such as nursing home and home health care if they meet the eligibility requirements set forth by Medicaid. Most often, eligibility is based on income and personal financial resources, but for long-term care Medicaid coverage, certain health and functional criteria must be met as well. States are now considering more Medicaid funding for home care and assisted living. To receive a Medicaid waiver for alternative community services, the patient must first be evaluated for 90 days in a nursing home.

The best source for information on the criteria, because they are state-specific, is the state's Medical Assistance office and the state's Medicaid agency's website. In addition, local area Agencies on Aging in conjunction with Medicaid will often pay for home repairs, transportation, and maintenance tasks such as snow removal for low-income recipients. Many low-income people can receive rent subsidies and assistance with utility bills from federal and local government programs. The local Agency on Aging can furnish information on such programs.

Medicaid programs are restricted to the financially indigent; therefore, assets must be spent down before one qualifies for Medicaid. Medicaid has limitations on the amount of assets one can own and the amount of income received each month. Before qualifying for Medicaid benefits, current law requires individuals applying for Medicaid long-term care services to divest all but a minimum level of assets. The only exception is if one has a state partnership long-term care insurance policy, one may retain a portion of one's assets. This will be further explained later in this chapter. Countable assets include savings accounts and investments but exclude the primary residence with limitations, one automobile with limitations, life insurance with a face amount of $1,500 or less, and certain other items such as wedding rings, personal belongings, and durable medical equipment. The face amount of life insurance for Medicaid purposes is defined as the amount of the basic death benefit contracted for at the time the policy is purchased. If the total face amount is more than $1,500, then the total cash surrender value is a countable resource. Policies, such as term insurance, with no cash surrender value are exempt for Medicaid eligibility purposes. Special rules allow a community spouse (the spouse who remains in the community) of a nursing home resident to keep a portion of the couple's income and assets to prevent impoverishment. Also, there are restrictions on transferring assets to others in order to qualify for Medicaid.

There are two ways to make assets inaccessible to Medicaid, and therefore protect them from being spent on care: put them in a trust or give them away outright. This strategy is called *Medicaid planning* and is subject to a look-back period. The look-back period is a span of time that a state Medicaid program examines for financial transactions to see if the applicant made gifts to reduce their assets sufficiently to qualify for Medicaid benefits.

More than half the states employ a "spend down" program in which the Medicaid beneficiary's monthly income goes to the nursing home, with Medicaid making up any difference in cost of care. There is a condition that the monthly income must be less than the private cost of a room in the facility.

The remaining states that do not stipulate a spend down program, known as "income cap" states, are[9] Alabama, Alaska, Arizona, Arkansas, Colorado, Delaware, Florida, Idaho, Iowa, Louisiana, Mississippi, Nevada, New Jersey, New Mexico, Oklahoma, Oregon, South Carolina, South Dakota, Texas, and Wyoming. New Jersey waives the income cap for applicants already admitted to skilled nursing facilities.

Eligibility for Medicaid is granted only if the monthly income of the applicant is at or less than a cap, which is adjusted annually. Those whose income exceeds the cap, even by a penny, do not qualify for Medicaid unless they establish a qualified income trust, commonly called a "Miller trust," into which all income is deposited and from which distributions under the cap may be made.[10] A Medicaid applicant's income still has to be spent on his or her care in an income cap state, even if it is under the cap; the cap only determines eligibility. The Miller trust can be used to qualify a Medicaid applicant with income in excess of the eligibility limit for long-term care assistance from Medicaid. Such a trust is not really a "special needs" trust, as it is not funded with the beneficiary's assets. The Miller trust can be named as recipient of the individual's income from a pension plan, Social Security, or other source.

The rules that allow states to set a cap also provide a means to circumvent it. A Medicaid applicant's family is allowed to establish a Miller trust.[11] Established either by the family of the applicant or the nursing facility, the trust must provide that the

- ◆ beneficiary (the applicant) is the Medicaid applicant;
- ◆ beneficiary's income will be paid into the trust;
- ◆ beneficiary receives a monthly personal-needs allowance;

---

9. 42 U.S.C. § 1396a(a)(10)(ii)(V).
10. 42 U.S.C. § 1396p(d)(4)(B); *see also* Miller v. Ibarra, 746 F. Supp. 19 (D. Colo. 1990).
11. 42 U.S.C. § 1396r-5(d)(1).

♦ beneficiary's spouse, if applicable, will be paid a sum equal to the minimum monthly maintenance needs allowance (MMMNA); the community spouse is allowed to keep a MMMNA; and

♦ trustee distributes to the nursing home, to pay for the applicant's care, an amount less than the current cap. The balance remains in trust, and at the death of the applicant, the trust turns the balance over to the state.

The Miller trust is significant only in those states that impose an income cap on Medicaid long-term care eligibility. There are additional existing strategies through Medicaid estate planning that are beyond the scope of this book.

On February 8, 2006, the Deficit Reduction Act of 2005 (DRA) was signed into law.

## Deficit Reduction Act of 2005 (DRA)

This legislation affects many aspects of domestic entitlement programs, including both Medicare and Medicaid. Prior to this legislation the look-back period was three or five years, depending on the nature of the property transfer. Transfers under this law are now minimally a five-year look-back. Transfers for less than adequate consideration, gifts to family members, or transfers into or out of a trust trigger a period of ineligibility for benefits based on the amount of the transfer and commencing on the date of application for benefits. The beginning date for the penalty period is now the later of the date the person enters a nursing home or begins a Medicaid-waivered care program, or the date the person applies for Medicaid. What this boils down to is that the penalty period will not begin until the nursing home resident is virtually destitute. In every state, this period equals the value of the assets transferred divided by the average monthly cost of nursing home care for a semi-private room in that state. Furthermore, the DRA legislation requires annuities to be disclosed and states to be named a beneficiary for cost of Medicaid assistance.

One purpose of the new legislation is to prevent the use of Medicaid as an inheritance protection program for the middle class. However, gifts made in the most innocent manner could jeopardize someone's eligibility for Medicaid even if it is legitimately needed. In addition, the perception that many affluent Americans transfer assets to gain Medicaid coverage for nursing home care is an issue that has consumed considerable public policy interest in recent years. The thought is that an individual's assets should be used to pay privately for nursing home care instead of being transferred to relatives, because Medicaid was intended to be a safety net only for the indigent. Asset transfer practices are thought to distort the intent of the Medicaid program and unnecessarily inflate public spending.

In response to such concerns, and as an attempt to reduce spending, the DRA included provisions for tightening the Medicaid eligibility rules related to asset transfers and nursing home care. The DRA also altered the role of Medicaid with regard to private long-term care insurance by creating new incentives and opportunities for states to refocus Medicaid long-term care services delivery systems away from nursing homes to a greater community orientation. A core component of the DRA allowed for the expansion of the State Partnership Long-Term Care Insurance Programs. It lifted the moratorium on states expanding new partnership programs to increase the role of private long-term care insurance in financing long-term services; requires programs to adopt National Association of Insurance Commissioners (NAIC) model regulations; and requires the Secretary of Health and Human Services to develop standards for making policies portable across states. The State Partnership Long-Term Care Insurance Programs will be covered in extensive detail in Chapters 4 and 5.

These considerable policy changes are intended to ensure that federal and state financing obligations are more limited. The reforms are aimed at promoting community-based care and limiting access to institutional care. The ultimate impact of these changes remains to be determined by how states and other stakeholders respond.

Many nursing homes now claim that Medicaid reimbursement is not paying their actual costs. Medicaid reimbursement is carried out at a state level. Generally, the states employ some rather convoluted and arcane rules to reimburse nursing homes. Most states reimburse with a prospective payment system like Medicare, but a few states reimburse actual costs up to certain predetermined statewide maximum amounts. Some states pay directly; others pay through privately contracted managed care administrators. Medicaid reimbursement to nursing homes is not uniform from state to state. Some state nursing home associations claim that 85 percent of their member nursing homes are not meeting costs with Medicaid. In other states nursing homes may be faring better.[12]

Medicare and Medicaid reimbursement have a direct impact on the daily rates of private pay residents. These are residents who are paying out of pocket for their own care. They may be spending money from their own income and assets, or their family may be assisting in the financing through personal resources as well. Many of these people are going through Medicaid spend down, depleting assets until they qualify for Medicaid. If the nursing home is losing money on government reimbursement, it may be charging private pay residents higher daily rates to make up the difference. But one should not assume this is always the case. Currently, at least two states, Minnesota and North Dakota, prohibit nursing homes from charging more than the Medicaid reimbursement rate. In addition, not all homes lose money on government reimbursement. These facilities may be charging the same for all residents.

---

12. Thomas Day, About Nursing Homes, http://www.longtermcarelink.net/eldercare/nursing _home.htm.

Medicaid planning situations are all unique. Therefore it is important to obtain more detailed information from the state Medical Assistance office as well as consult with an attorney.

## Veterans Benefits

The U.S. Department of Veterans Affairs (VA) provides three types of long-term care benefits for veterans. The first type is benefits provided to veterans who have service-connected disabilities. These medically necessary services include home care, hospice, respite care, assisted living, home health care, geriatric assessments, and nursing home care. In order to receive the services, a veteran must be enrolled in VA's health care system. Veterans with service-connected disabilities have priority for health care enrollment acceptance.

Some of these services may be offered to veterans in the health care system who do not have service-connected disabilities but who may qualify because of low income or because they are receiving pension income from VA. These recipients may have to pay out-of-pocket copayments, or the services may only be available if the regional hospital has funds to cover them.

Currently, veterans desiring to join the health care system may be refused application because their income is too high or they do not qualify under other enrollment criteria. Increased demand in recent years for services and lack of congressional funding have forced VA to allow only certain classes of veterans to join the health care system.

The second type of VA long-term care benefit is state veterans' homes. The Veterans Administration in conjunction with the states helps build and support state veterans' homes. Money is provided by the federal government to help with construction, and a small subsidy is provided for each veteran using these nursing homes. These homes are generally available for any veteran, and sometimes the non-veteran spouse, and are run by the states, often with the help of contract management. There may be waiting lists in some states.

Most state homes offer nursing home care, but some may offer assisted living, domiciliary (a form of supported independent living), and adult day care. State veterans homes are not free but are subsidized, and the cost could be significantly less than a comparable facility in the private sector. Some of these homes can accept Medicaid payments. For a complete list of state veterans' homes, please visit http://www.longtermcarelink.net/ref_state_veterans_va_nursing_homes.htm.

The third type of benefits for veterans is disability payments. These include compensation, pension, and survivors' death benefits associated with compensation and pension. Compensation is designed to award the veteran a certain amount of monthly income to compensate for potential loss of income in the private sector due to a disability, injury, or illness incurred in the service. In order to receive compensation a veteran has to have evidence of a service-connected disability. Most veterans who are receiving this benefit are awarded an amount based on a percentage of disability when they left the service.

However, some veterans may have a record of being exposed to extreme cold, having an in-service non-disabling injury, having tropical diseases or tuberculosis, or other incidents or exposures that at the time may not have caused any disability but years later resulted in medical problems. In addition, some veterans may be receiving compensation but their condition has worsened, and they may qualify for a higher disability rating. Veterans mentioned above may qualify for a first-time benefit or receive an increase in compensation amount. Applications should be submitted to see if they can receive an award. There is no income or asset test for compensation, and the benefit is non-taxable.

Pension is available to all active-duty veterans who served at least 90 days during a period of war. There is no need to have a service-connected disability to receive pension. To be eligible, the applicant must be totally disabled if he or she is younger than 65. Proof of disability is not required for applicants age 65 or over. Apparently, being old is evidence in itself of disability. The purpose of this benefit is to provide supplemental income to disabled or older veterans who have a low income. If the veteran's income exceeds the pension amount, then there is no award. However, income can be adjusted for unreimbursed medical expenses, and this allows veterans with household income larger than the pension amount to qualify for a monthly benefit.

Compensation and pension claims are submitted on the same form, and VA will consider paying either benefit. Generally, for applications associated with the cost of home care, assisted living care, or nursing home care, the pension benefit is a better option.

All active-duty veterans who served at least 90 days during a period of war are eligible for pension and additional disability allowances, aid and attendance, or housebound allowances. Surviving single spouses of these veterans are also eligible for lesser benefits and for the allowances. Veterans' service includes World War II, the Korean Conflict, the Vietnam Conflict Period, and the Gulf War Conflict. Pension can pay a monthly amount to help offset the costs associated with home care, assisted living, nursing homes, and other unreimbursed medical expenses. The amount of payment varies with the type of care, recipient income, and the marital status of the recipient. There are income and asset tests to qualify. VA claims this benefit is only for low-income veterans, but a quirk in the way the benefit is calculated for recurring medical expenses and long-term care costs associated with home care, assisted living, or nursing homes could allow veteran households earning between $2,500 and $5,000 or more a month to qualify. Estimates are that up to 30 percent of all

Americans over the age of 65 might be eligible for a pension benefit under the right circumstances.[13]

## Federal Long-Term Care Insurance Program

In 2001, the federal government, through the Office of Personnel Management, created the Federal Long Term Care Insurance Program (FLTCIP) to provide long-term care insurance for its enrollees: federal and U.S. Postal Service employees and annuitants, active and retired members of the uniformed services, and their qualified relatives.

The creation of long-term care insurance for federal employees and military personnel underscores the reality that the federal government and VA are primarily health care providers through Medicare and VA medical benefits.

FLTCIP policies are simple to understand and offer benefits tailored to their targeted audience. Policies are sold directly through highly trained, non-commission-based staff that understand how long-term care insurance works and how to recommend long-term care insurance coverage. Federal employees and their families are advised to investigate this program.[14] This program, similar to other long-term care insurance programs, is subject to rate increases. The program experienced its first rate increase in 2010. For more information on the program, please visit the FLTCIP website at http://www.ltcfeds.com/.

The following chart provides the reasons why federal employees purchase an FLTCIP long-term care insurance policy:

**FIGURE 3-5**

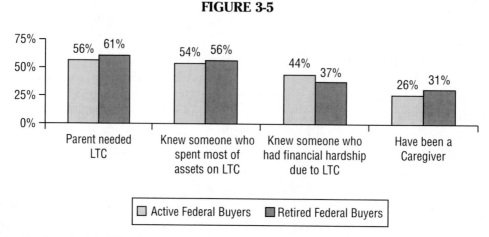

Source: U.S. Department of Health and Human Services, 2004.

---

13. Veterans Long-Term Care Benefits, Law for Life, GosselinLaw; 2011.

14. The Federal Long-Term Care Insurance Program, http://www.ltcfeds.com (last visited Oct. 28, 2012); U.S Office of Personnel Management, *Federal Long-Term Care Insurance Program*, http://www.opm.gov/insure/ltc/index.asp (last visited Oct. 28, 2012).

# Other Funding Considerations

It is important to consider that some methods of funding long-term care require a health screening, which necessitates the applicant being in relatively good health, not currently needing or receiving long-term care services, and not having a debilitating, chronic condition such as Parkinson's disease. In contrast, some options are only available if someone is in poor health, such as a long-term care single-premium immediate annuity. However, if one is in relatively good health, a long-term care insurance policy and a continuing care retirement community are an option for a plan of care. Conversely, if one is terminally ill, an accelerated death benefit could be an option. There are plans of care that utilize options not predicated on health considerations such as annuities, home equity loans, reverse mortgages, trusts, or life settlements.

## *Options for the Uninsurable*

### Long-Term Care Annuities

In addition to the options mentioned above, a long-term care annuity is a possible solution to pay for long-term care expenses. People whose medical conditions have disqualified them from obtaining traditional long-term care insurance may be able to qualify for a long-term care annuity.

This type of annuity allows an individual to purchase a long-term care insurance policy that usually has a benefit pool equal to the annuity purchased. The underwriting is greatly simplified because the annuity owner is required to use the annuity first to pay any long-term care expenses. The insurance company begins paying benefits from the long-term care insurance fund once the annuity fund is exhausted.

### Long-Term Care Trusts

Another option for an uninsurable client is a long-term care trust. Such an instrument can be used to provide funding for someone who may need long-term care now or in the future. The trust may be designed however the client chooses; it can be as complex or as simple as the client desires. It can be drawn up as testamentary or living, as revocable or irrevocable, as a spousal trust or a special needs trust, having special needs language or not, or being restrictive in its use or not at all restrictive. The trust can be structured similar to a long-term care insurance policy or not at all like one. A long-term care trust can allow for care by family members and friends, travel expenses, and incidentals, for example. Using a life insurance policy to fund the trust provides a tax-free cash benefit pool of money for use by an uninsurable spouse after the insurable spouse deceases. Amounts distributed from the trust for care can vary. For instance, at the onset of needing care a small amount can be distributed, and then as care increases larger amounts can be distributed. Upon death of the uninsurable client, the remaining trust assets can pass to other family members or a charity, if desired.

## Supplemental Health-Related Insurance Benefits

### Critical Illness Insurance

Critical illness insurance, or critical illness coverage, is an insurance product where the insurer is contracted to typically make a lump-sum cash payment if the policyholder is diagnosed with one of the critical illnesses listed in the insurance policy. Common illnesses included in critical illness insurance policies are cancer, heart attack, and stroke. The policy may also be structured to pay out regular income, and the payout may also be on the policyholder undergoing a surgical procedure, for example, having a heart bypass operation. The policy may require the policyholder to survive a minimum number of days, known as the survival period, from when the illness was first diagnosed. The survival period used varies from company to company; however, 28 days and 30 days are the most common survival periods used.

The insurance contract terms contain specific rules that define when a diagnosis of a critical illness is considered valid. They may state that the diagnosis needs to be made by a physician who specializes in that illness or condition, or they may name specific tests that confirm the diagnosis. There are forms of critical illness insurance other than the lump-sum cash payment model. These critical illness insurance policies directly pay health providers for the treatment costs of critical and life-threatening illnesses covered by the policyholder's insurance policy, including the fee of specialists and procedures at a select group of high-ranking hospitals, up to a certain amount per episode of treatment as set out in the policy.

Because critical illness insurance is designed to help alleviate concerns about potentially devastating expenses brought on by serious medical problems, it is beneficial to have it as a supplemental insurance to long-term care insurance, but it should not be considered as a replacement or substitute to long-term care insurance. Critical illness insurance

- usually provides a lump-sum benefit to pay costs not covered by other insurance; typically, policy face amounts range from $5,000 to $500,000;
- has benefits that are not restricted; it can pay for housekeeping expenses, modifications to a home or car to accommodate a disability, child care expenses, and other costs associated with critical illness;
- that is offered as an employee benefit in a company setting provides important benefits such as policy discounts, guaranteed issues, simplified underwriting, and premium payment via payroll deduction.

### Cancer Insurance

Cancer insurance conceptually is very simple. Benefits are paid directly to the policyholder regardless of any other insurance in force. The benefits can then be used to help pay for all of the extra costs associated with cancer treatment.

There are medical and non-medical expenses associated with cancer. Examples of medical expenses are physician and hospital charges, medications, surgery, and treatment costs. Examples of non-medical expenses are loss of income, transportation, lodging, child care, and increased living expenses. Most health insurance plans cover only the medical expenses associated with cancer. Cancer insurance benefits can be used for medical and non-medical expenses. Cancer insurance policies are designed to supplement existing health insurance policies or income.

Similar to critical illness insurance, which generally includes cancer as one of the covered illnesses in the contract, cancer insurance should be considered as a supplement to a long-term care insurance policy, but not a replacement nor a standalone product for funding long-term care expenses.

## Accident Insurance

Accident insurance covers injury or death due to an accident. This type of insurance does not usually cover negligence, acts of God, or natural disasters, and the policy may include restrictions such as caps on total payouts or restrictions on payouts for activities deemed risky.

Accident insurance policies have payouts that vary depending on the severity of the injuries. Some include very specific language about amounts that will be paid out in the event of losing particular extremities, for example. The payout is designed to cover medical care along with pain and suffering. If an accident causes permanent disability, the payment may be structured to provide income for the accident victim. In the event of a death, the benefits are paid out to the named beneficiary on the policy.

This type of insurance policy can be purchased as a standalone policy or bundled into an existing insurance policy. Accident insurance is often offered along with cancer insurance on a payroll deduction basis to employer groups as part of an employee benefit program. The premiums for payroll deduction policies become cost-prohibitive for older workers and are more difficult to qualify for if medical underwriting is involved in the application process.

As with critical illness and cancer insurance, because of the specified situations that are covered in these policies, accident insurance should be considered as supplemental insurance and not as a replacement or substitute to funding long-term care expenses.

## Medicare Supplement Insurance (Medigap)

Medicare supplement insurance, also known as Medigap, is a private health insurance plan designed to supplement the coverage provided under governmental programs such as Medicare. Its purpose is to fill the gaps in coverage of a person's original Medicare plan.

Medigap policies can help pay your share (coinsurance, copayments, or deductibles) of the costs of Medicare-covered services. Some Medigap policies also cover certain benefits original Medicare does not cover. Medigap policies do not cover the share of the costs under other types of health coverage, including Medicare Advantage Plans, standalone Medicare Prescription Drug Plans, employer/union group health coverage, Medicaid, VA benefits, or TRICARE. Insurance companies generally cannot sell a Medigap policy if coverage is provided through Medicaid or a Medicare Advantage Plan.

Depending on which standardized Medigap plan is purchased, the remaining out-of-pocket balance for the 80 days of Medicare coverage for skilled nursing facilities may be covered (**cf. page 45**). If Medicare ceases payments prior to the 100-day maximum, the Medigap policy ceases paying benefits because these policies are designed to pick up a portion of Medicare-covered expenses, up to the Medicare benefit limitations.

## Medical Insurance

Medical insurance does not provide coverage for long-term care expenses. It behooves the advisor to review a client's personal medical insurance policy as part of the long-term care funding analysis, as medical insurance may provide some short-term care coverage and can provide a basis for strategizing the long-term care insurance policy design.

## Continuum (Continuing) Care Retirement Communities (CCRC)

As reviewed in Chapter 2, a continuum care retirement community (CCRC) is a community living arrangement, typically on a single campus, that provides residential living, health care, and social services, usually for the elder population. CCRCs offer various levels of care ranging from independent living to skilled nursing care.

Depending on the type of CCRC, it can be a financing option for long-term care services, as well as a living arrangement to access long-term care services on a more suitable basis. If and when one needs care, he or she would move from the independent living residence to the assisted living or nursing home residence, depending on the extent of care required.

Probable expenses to consider when investigating CCRCs in the long-term care funding analysis are

- ◆ monthly fee;
- ◆ one-time entrance fee; and
- ◆ additional fee when transferring from one facility to another on the campus.

There is a possibility that the monthly fee is included in the total cost and does not increase even if the residential living setting changes due to more advanced care necessity.

Additional expenses could be incurred because many CCRCs provide care in the assisted living or nursing home but may provide little or no care in the independent living setting. Some CCRCs allow residents to hire their own home health care service while living in the independent living setting. Other CCRCs require one to be fully independent to remain in such setting. Health screenings are often required and may or may not be covered by personal medical insurance.

Because CCRC costs are not subject to outside regulation, there can be a lot of variation in CCRC expenditures. A number of factors influence CCRC costs, and understanding these factors can help determine what your client will be paying if he or she moves into a CCRC.

Many nonprofit CCRCs provide financial assistance to qualifying individuals to help pay entrance fees and/or monthly fees. Some nonprofit communities will also subsidize residents who run out of money. Providing financial aid helps these communities maintain their tax-exempt status as a charitable organization. Ask about the community's particular policies if they are not stated in the contract.

Regarding monthly fees, CCRC costs can vary greatly depending upon the cost structure. However, most communities, regardless of the type of contract offered, require residents to pay an entrance fee as well as ongoing monthly fees. Monthly fees can be as low as $500 at some communities, escalating up to $3,000 or more depending on the contract type and service plan.

Entrance fees start as low as $20,000 for a non-purchase (rental) agreement, and buy-in fees are among the most expensive CCRC costs, ranging up to $500,000 or more depending on the size and location of the unit as well as the community.[15] Many people incorrectly believe the entrance and buy-in fees are the total cost, whereas it is a base cost; there are ongoing costs over and above such fees.

Other factors that affect CCRC costs include

- whether the resident will rent or own the unit;
- the size and location of the unit;
- the services and amenities not covered by the contract;
- whether accommodations are shared or private;
- current health status; and
- the type of contract signed.

There are various types of CCRC contracts to consider. Contract type is the most significant factor when it comes to CCRC costs. The three basic types of CCRC contracts are associated with varying levels of risk; generally, the lower the risk, the higher upfront CCRC costs:

- Extensive contracts provide a lifetime guarantee of housing and all the care that is needed (low risk, highest upfront costs).
- Modified contracts are similar to extensive contracts, except that care coverage is limited to a specified number of days, beyond which services are paid for out of pocket (medium risk, mid-level cost).

---

15. *CCRC Costs: How Much Will You Pay?*, SENIORHOMES.COM, http://www.seniorhomes.com/p/ccrc -costs/ (last visited Oct. 28, 2012).

♦ Fee-for-service contracts allow for payment only for the services that are used (highest risk, lowest upfront costs).

Another major factor that affects CCRC costs is medical insurance, which can help bring down the share of the costs. Medicare and Medicaid pay for some skilled nursing care and medical costs for eligible residents at certified facilities. Before moving in, some communities may stipulate that the prospective resident agree to apply for Medicaid or Supplemental Security Income (SSI) in the event that the resident depletes his or her own resources and needs extra funding assistance. This is a preventative measure to ensure that the CCRC will still be paid for the services utilized. It may also be required that the resident enroll in Medicare Part A or Part B and/or have a Medigap policy for supplemental health insurance.

Rarely, yet it does occur, a CCRC may require applicants to obtain long-term care insurance prior to moving in. If a prospective resident already has an existing policy, he or she needs to check it to see whether it covers some of the CCRC fees. If a resident purchases a long-term care insurance policy through a company recommended by the CCRC, it's possible that the premiums could be incorporated into the monthly fees. If an applicant is found to be uninsurable, he or she would have to make other arrangements, or seek another CCRC. This is a protective action on the part of the CCRC so that they are assured of payment for their facility costs and care services. While CCRC costs may seem higher than other types of long-term care at first, they can actually be lower overall when spread out over a lifetime.

## Home Equity

The equity in a home can be substantial, especially if the house was purchased many years earlier and the mortgage is paid off. This can potentially be a valuable source of funds to cover long-term care expenses, but there are important factors to consider. The two ways to tap into a client's home equity as a long-term care funding source are

♦ home equity loans (significant drawbacks limit their appeal; for example, future income to pay the loan back, or the spouse whose income was intended to be used to repay the loan deceases prior to loan repayment); and
♦ home equity conversion mortgages (HECM), also referred to as reverse mortgages.

Reverse mortgages allow homeowners to tap into the equity in their home without the need to pay it back during their lifetime. Whatever is borrowed accrues interest to be paid back along with the principal at either death or the sale of the home. The program can be useful in generating income to pay for long-term care insurance, or, if one does not qualify for insurance, to pay for care.

Reverse mortgages can be used by homeowners who are age 62 and older. Borrowers may choose one of five payment options:

- Monthly income for life
- Monthly income for a fixed period of time
- A line of credit
- A combination of lifetime income and a line of credit
- A combination of income for a fixed period of time with a line of credit

The borrower remains the owner of the home and may sell it and move at any time, keeping the proceeds that exceed the mortgage balance. The homeowner cannot be forced to sell the home to pay off the mortgage, even if the mortgage balance grows to exceed the value of the property. If the loan exceeds the value of the property when it is paid, the borrower or his or her heirs will owe no more than the value of the property. Federal Housing Administration (FHA) insurance will cover any balance due the lender.

As part of the HECM program, the federal Department of Housing and Urban Development (HUD) provides free reverse mortgage counseling for those considering using such a mechanism. The toll-free telephone line is 1-888-466-3487 and the website is http://portal.hud.gov/hudportal/HUD?src=/program_offices /housing/sfh/hecm/hecmhome.

One important factor to consider is the economic trend of the housing market. Long-term care insurance protects income. It therefore gives the family the opportunity to allow the equity lost to recover from a down market.

## Life Insurance and Annuities

Most people associate life insurance with death, not long-term care; however, some life insurance policies and annuities can be an important source of personal funds for long-term care. Permanent life insurance in any form (whole life, universal life, and variable life) creates a cash value that may be used to pay for long-term care expenses, in the form of accelerated benefits.

Many policies today also include a living benefit provision that authorizes payment of the policy's face amount, or a portion of it, in the event of the policyholder's permanent confinement in a long-term care facility.

Some insurance companies offer policyholders the right to accelerate benefits. Generally, companies

- allow only a portion of the death benefit to be drawn on, and may apply interest;
- pay less than 50 percent of the death benefit;
- still lapse policies whose policyholders do not continue to pay premiums.

The use of life insurance and annuities combined with long-term care riders, known as linked products, is addressed in detail in Chapter 4.

## Life Settlements

Some life insurance policies that are no longer needed may be sold for more money than would be received by surrendering the policy to the insurance company. This transaction, in which the assignment of the life insurance owner's death benefit is exchanged for a lump-sum payout, is known as a life settlement. There are some general guidelines for life settlements. The policyholder

- has a life expectancy of 12 years or less;
- is over age 55;
- owns a policy with a cash surrender value and a face value above a certain minimum, usually at least $100,000.

The cash generated from a life settlement can be used to pay for long-term care expenses, but rather than tie up the cash proceeds for care, a portion of the proceeds can be used to purchase a lump-sum premium-paid long-term care insurance policy, or the proceeds can be deposited into an interest-bearing vehicle and withdrawals can be made from such vehicle for the ongoing premium of a long-term care insurance policy.

## Long-Term Care Insurance

Long-term care insurance (LTCI) is a long-term care planning option for individuals who may need to pay for long-term care expenses in the future, not only providing payment for care but also providing control, choice, and financial independence. LTCI was specifically developed to cover the costs of a large variety of long-term care services in a wide variety of settings, most of which are not covered by traditional medical insurance and other forms of insurance. Such services include care in one's home such as custodial care or assistance with activities of daily living, as well as care in a variety of skilled facilities and even community settings. Long-term care insurance is an excellent way to leverage a small portion of assets one has spent a lifetime accumulating to protect and execute one's estate plan as intended.

LTCI provides a benefit payment for covered expenses up to the benefit amount set forth in the policy. Not only does the policy provide benefits for a wide variety of settings, but it may also offer care options and additional support services not found or provided by any other funding vehicle.

There are many factors to consider in obtaining adequate LTCI coverage. There is a great deal of choice and flexibility in LTCI policies. A range of care options and benefits allow one to obtain the services needed in the setting that best suits one's needs and lifestyle.

The cost of a LTCI policy is based on benefit amounts, the benefit period, the type and amount of services chosen to be covered, the attained age when the policy is purchased, the health history of the insured, and optional benefits such as inflation growth protection. If health history is a concern or long-term care services are currently being received, most likely the applicant will not qualify for individual long-term care insurance. However, there may be the option to purchase a limited amount of coverage, pay a higher, non-standard premium, purchase group long-term care insurance coverage through an employer, or purchase an alternative type of long-term care insurance policy such as a linked product (**cf. Chapter 4, page 83**).

According to the 2011 Long-Term Care Insurance Price Index, a 55-year-old couple purchasing LTCI protection can expect to pay $2,350 per year (combined) for about $338,000 of current benefits ($169,000 each), which will grow to about $800,000 of combined coverage for the couple when they turn age 80. This data comes from the 2011 Long-Term Care Insurance Price Index published by the American Association for Long-Term Care Insurance (http://www.aaltci.org), which analyzed rates for 11 LTCI policies. According to the association report, a 55-year-old single individual pays $1,480 annually for comparable coverage. If the 55-year-old couple did not qualify for preferred health discounts, their cost would increase by $325 annually.

LTCI policies offer a specific benefit amount with a specific premium amount that can be factored into one's overall financial plan. Typically, LTCI premiums are waived while receiving benefits. Policies that are currently available cover skilled, intermediate, and custodial care in state-licensed care settings. Most policies also cover home care services such as skilled or non-skilled nursing care, physical therapy, homemaking services, and home health aides provided by state-licensed or Medicare-certified home health agencies. Many policies allow, as an optional benefit, care to be provided informally by a family member or friend.

Planning involves making decisions based on known facts and unknown assumptions regarding future events and circumstances. When considering LTCI as a planning option, one should assess the client's needs and risk tolerance, then test several feasible plan configurations to create a suitable plan, based on specific personal values, finances, and concerns. Policy provisions and their practical significance should be thoroughly understood in order to evaluate the economic value of long-term care insurance as an asset protection and risk-transfer vehicle. To make a sound long-term care insurance purchase decision, focus on evaluating features of policies to determine what is critical versus what is optional and comparing cost versus value.

There are six major reasons why people buy long-term care insurance:

1. The most common reason for buying long-term care insurance is the buyers witnessing someone they love have a long-term care event and realizing firsthand the *emotional and financial toll* such an event can take on a family.
2. To maintain their *independence* and not have to rely on family members.
3. To *protect their assets* against the high costs of long-term care and to preserve their children's inheritance.
4. To *make long-term care services affordable*, such as home health care and custodial care.
5. To provide themselves with *more options* than just nursing home care, and to pay for nursing home care if it is needed.
6. To *preserve their standard of living.*[16]

---

16. AssistGuide Information Services, *Top Five Reasons to Buy Long Term Care Insurance*, http://www.agis.com/Document/4498/top-five-reasons-to-buy-long-term-care-insurance.aspx (2008).

It is not surprising that a new trend among baby boomers is purchasing long-term care insurance for their parents. This is frequently accomplished to protect not only their parents' estate but their own future. Oftentimes several siblings will split the cost of the insurance premium, although the coordination of care typically falls on one sibling.

Without an LTCI policy, the effect of long-term care costs on retirement assets can be significant, even for relatively short-term situations. A LTCI policy transfers the risk and pays for the high cost of long-term care services while preserving assets and preventing new income debt.

The essence of the product, the value proposition that is impossible to attach a dollar figure to, can be thought of in this way:

♦ It allows your client's loved ones to supervise care, not provide it.
♦ It becomes a second gift of life to children.
♦ And it keeps those children together . . . by keeping them apart.

LTCI provides a stream of income that funds the long-term care plan. That income stream is used to pay for care, as stated above, which allows those whom the client loves to supervise, rather than provide, care. That income stream allows for the retirement income to continue to be used to fulfill financial commitments. Because the retirement portfolio never has to be liquidated, the estate plan executes properly.

## Conclusions

A client's individual circumstances must be considered before choosing a funding option for his or her long-term care planning.

Table 3-1 provides a brief summary of the various funding options for long-term care planning. Professional insurance advisors can provide more detailed information, including associated costs and fees as they pertain to each alternative, as each option is evaluated for appropriateness.

A more detailed explanation of programs and their applications in long-term care funding can be found at the National Clearinghouse for Long-Term Care Information website, which was developed by the U.S. Department of Health and Human Services (HHS) to provide information and resources for long-term care planning, http://www.longtermcare.gov/LTC/.

Procrastinating on long-term care planning is prevalent. Often, people first learn about long-term care when they or a loved one needs care. People do not want to think about a time when they might need care, but when it does happen, the options are often limited by lack of information, the immediate need for services, and insufficient resources to pay for preferred care. Planning ahead allows more control over the future. The plan is to allow clients to remain safe and in the community for as long as possible, while preserving the emotional, physical, and financial well-being of those

**TABLE 3-1**
**Long-Term Care Funding Options**

| Option | Advantages | Disadvantages |
|---|---|---|
| **Personal savings** CDs, mutual funds, individual stocks and bonds | • Ability to obtain the long-term care one prefers | • Need to accurately estimate future costs of long-term care and set aside enough money to cover those costs for several years |
| **Retirement income** 401(k), 403(b), pension plan | • If it will cover long-term costs, assets will not have to be spent down | • It may not be enough to cover long-term care costs, especially if a married couple is living on one income and one spouse requires long-term care |
| **Long-term care insurance** Specific medical expense coverage related to long-term care | • May not have to spend down any of retirement assets<br>• Optional return of premium benefits is available<br>• Some policies offer indemnity and cash benefits<br>• Indexing of benefits for inflation growth | • Ongoing premiums vary depending on benefits and benefit periods<br>• If long-term care is never needed, the premiums may not be returnable<br>• One may have to pay for some care up front and then be reimbursed by the insurance company<br>• Non-guaranteed premiums |
| **Linked or accelerated benefit life insurance** Accelerates policy's death benefit to reimburse qualified long-term care expenses | • Some policies allow one-time premium<br>• Some policies offer return of premium riders<br>• More money may be available to pay for long-term care than the actual premium paid<br>• Use of no-lapse guarantee products to provide premium guarantees | • Any loans, withdrawals, or benefits paid will reduce the amount of any premiums returned<br>• Returned premiums may have tax implications<br>• May have to pay for care up front, then be reimbursed by the insurance company |

Source: Lincoln National Corporation 2009 and contributing editor.

they love. The goal is to place the family back to where they were before the event occurred. Without proper planning, someone's life is going to be drastically affected.

- The time to protect a client's wealth from unreimbursed medical expenses is now.
- Failure to do so could have a dramatic impact on a client's financial situation.
- Not planning ahead could affect not only a client but his or her children and grandchildren as well.
- Not planning ahead could cost a client control of his or her own care.
- Waiting to plan impacts one's ability to qualify for insurance protection.
- Waiting to plan significantly impacts the purchasing price of insurance.
- Not planning ahead forfeits the ability to have the protection in case of a claim.

Preparation for a long-term care occurrence must be done before any need arises. It is important to establish a funding source, a stream of income that pays for care and for potential long-term care expenses in the most cost-effective manner. It is a professional advisor's responsibility to be the family's advocate, educating the client about how severe the consequences will be if such an event occurs. Once a client is educated on the consequences of what long-term care does to his or her family, the client is obligated to make a decision on what his or her plan for care will be.

# *Long-Term Care Insurance* 4

RELYING ON SELF-FUNDING social programs, such as Medicare and Medicaid, or the VA to pay for long-term care (LTC) presents serious challenges. Our attention now turns to long-term care insurance (LTCI), a product specifically designed for the purpose of paying for care over an extended period of time. However, as with life and disability income insurance, the importance of long-term care insurance is not in how it works, its extrinsic value, but what it ensures, its intrinsic value.[1] Consider what long-term care insurance ensures:

- It preserves the emotional and physical well-being of one's spouse during an illness or injury by allowing the spouse to supervise the care rather than being forced to provide the care.
- It allows children to maintain a relationship with their parent as children supervising care, not children who are forced to reorient their lives to provide care.
- For a single person with no children, it preserves the emotional and physical well-being of those one deeply cares about during an illness or injury by allowing those loved ones to supervise care rather than being forced to provide the care.

---

1. This chapter draws in part from HARLEY GORDON, CERTIFICATION IN LONG-TERM CARE COURSE HANDBOOK, Sections A, C, D, E (Releases 5.0, 8.0, 9.0, Corporation for Long-Term Care Certification 2003, 2009, 2011), and from HARLEY GORDON IN SICKNESS & IN HEALTH: YOUR SICKNESS—YOUR FAMILY'S HEALTH, Chapters 6, 7 (Financial Strategies Press 2007).

Long-term care insurance ensures more control of assets by

♦ providing a stream of income that can be used to pay for care;
♦ protecting the client's primary source of income generated from tax-deferred (qualified) funds, annuities, bonds, and other investments in the income portfolio;
♦ allowing the client's lifestyle to continue; and
♦ ultimately, allowing the investment portfolio to execute for the purpose intended. That is, to
  ○ minimize or eliminate taxes; and
  ○ pass assets on to the surviving spouse and family.

An advisor can utilize a portion of the clients' investments to protect all of the clients' investments and assets. Ultimately, long-term care insurance is no different from life and disability income insurance, assuming it is now understood that it protects retirement income.

**TABLE 4-1**

| Life Insurance | Annuities | Disability Income Insurance | Long-Term Care Insurance |
|---|---|---|---|
| Guarantees income, | Guarantee income, | Guarantees income, | Guarantees retirement income by paying for care, |
| which preserves lifestyle and family | which preserves lifestyle and family | which preserves lifestyle and family | which preserves lifestyle and family |

The concept of long-term care insurance is reasonably straightforward. As stated in previous chapters, it provides payment for those who need long-term care in a wide variety of settings including the home, hospice centers, adult day care centers, assisted living facilities, and skilled nursing facilities. It provides long-term care insurance purchasers peace of mind that they will be able to afford the type of care they want and that they are protecting their families. Long-term care insurance allows families to provide care in a less demanding way. They can secure care on their own schedule utilizing other resources to do the rest.

# History and Evolution of Long-Term Care Insurance

Long-term care insurance is one of the newer types of insurance to enter the marketplace for a very good reason: it was not as necessary in earlier years. Historically, very few people put their relatives in nursing homes. In the early part of the 20th century, someone who was poor and had no family went to live in a state "almshouse," or "poorhouse." Changes to caring for family members in the home occurred when women became a prominent part of the workforce and were unavailable to help care for elderly family members. Nursing home care demanded reform by the 1970s and 1980s when it became apparent that some facilities offered less than standard care. Even though Medicare, which began in 1965, was expected to pay for some care, the ability to select a nursing home became important.

Early long-term care insurance, which debuted in the 1970s, used the basic design of Medicare. If a long-term care insurance policyholder was moved from a hospital and required skilled care, the long-term care insurance policy paid the bill for skilled care. These policies became far more popular in the 1980s when hospitals began discharging people earlier than they had in the past. The reason for the shorter hospital stays stemmed from the change in the reimbursement system of Medicare. Instead of paying for services rendered, Medicare began paying a lump sum based on a predetermined amount for a specific illness. As well, Medicare then paid for 21 days in a nursing home, the amount extending to 100 days when insureds had Medicare supplemental insurance. After 100 days, insureds were on their own to pay their bills. If skilled care was not necessary, Medicare and the supplement insurance policy paid nothing. It became apparent that the nursing home costs for stays longer than allowed by Medicare and supplemental insurance required additional coverage. The early policies were designed to provide payment for expenses after Medicare rehabilitation ended on the 100th day. To be compatible with Medicare, the policies included a three-day hospital stay requirement and other similar contractual language that paralleled Medicare regarding skilled care. These long-term care insurance policies were very different from the comprehensive benefits in currently offered policies. While nursing homes have been in existence for many years, the concepts of home care and adult day care were unfamiliar to most people. However, as longevity increased with the advancement of medical technology and pharmacology, new forms of caregiving facilities began to emerge.

Historically, many nursing home residents do not require a skilled level of care. They do not need a skilled nurse to administer medications, but rather need a nurse's aide to help them dress or perform other tasks. In the 1980s, many insurance companies addressed this issue and offered policies that covered skilled, intermediate, and custodial care. They evaluated the need for custodial care by using activities of daily living (ADLs) or cognitive impairment as the trigger for benefits. Long-term care insurance policies defined the need for custodial care as the inability to perform activities of daily living without assistance. The activities included bathing, dressing, eating, toileting, transferring from bed to chair, and maintaining continence. As the competition for business grew, insurance companies lowered the number of activities necessary to qualify for benefit payment. Relatively speaking, in comparison to other insurance products, there were only a small number of insurance companies offering long-term care insurance policies.

It was not until the late 1980s and early 1990s that the market for long-term care insurance began to develop. Many people still wanted other alternatives;

options for home care benefits began to appear. The coverage was either a stand-alone home health care insurance policy or a rider on a nursing home insurance policy. The payment was typically half the daily benefit amount selected for nursing home daily benefit amount if it was part of a long-term care nursing home insurance policy. Eventually, policies offered payment for assisted care, adult day care, homemaker's services, personal care, home health care, hospice care, and even respite care for a family member taking care of the insured. As assisted living facilities became more popular, long waiting lists ensued caused by an insufficient amount of facilities to meet the demand. Eventually, more facilities were established as the development of assisted living evolved. Facilities began offering graduated care, where one could live in a facility and receive varied degrees of care. If and when a person needed more care, he or she could simply add on services for an additional fee. As nursing homes recognized the value of that concept, many converted an area, a "wing" as it is known, of the facility to accommodate those residents who needed only occasional services, offering the option to increase services when more care became necessary. However, traditional medical insurance generally did not, and still does not, cover these types of expenses, and long-term care insurance was still in its relative infancy.

As home care and adult day care became more popular, more insurance companies saw the opportunity to offer long-term care insurance as part of their product portfolio. The next generation of long-term care insurance policies in the late 1980s recognized the need for home health care benefits, and additional benefits began to emerge in the policies that were being marketed. These additional benefits were offered as riders; optional benefits were offered for additional premium. The most prevalent rider in this era of policies was the home health care benefit.

Over time, long-term care insurance policies were no longer tied to the Medicare standard. Instead, benefit payment was, and still is, triggered by the insured's inability to perform defined ADLs and cognitive impairment. The early 1990s saw the first major insurance companies define the benefits in terms of a *pool of money* and the integration of contracts to include all types of care settings: home health care, adult day care, assisted living facilities, and nursing home facilities. These policies were basically site-neutral, meaning insureds had the choice to receive care in any setting and location they chose.

Today's long-term care insurance policies integrate numerous long-term care services. In addition to the choice of settings, policy benefits may include

- cash benefit options;
- indemnity or reimbursement model for payment of benefits;
- daily or monthly benefits, inflation riders;
- survivor benefits;
- shared benefits between multiple policyholders;
- return of premiums paid upon death;
- waiver of premiums while during a claim period;

- restoration of benefits after a claim period;
- non-forfeiture benefits;
- informal caregiving;
- homemaker services;
- respite care;
- international benefits;
- alternate plans of care; and
- premium payment options.

After reviewing this list, it's clear that long-term care insurance policies have become quite complicated and continue to evolve. Most policies currently offered may provide up to 16 different features and options from which to select, with each option offering two to four choices. Benefit amount choices alone may offer up to 30 alternatives from which to choose. These result in hundreds of benefit combinations under the same product, which then generate hundreds of different premium scenarios. Because of this complexity, it is vital to work with an insurance advisor who specializes in this area of planning. In addition, to help consumers better understand the product, the National Association of Insurance Commissioners (NAIC) developed *The Shopper's Guide to Long-Term Care Insurance*, which presents potential purchasers with valuable information in a consumer-friendly, easy-to-read format. The guide contains an overview of long-term care insurance, as well as planning and purchasing options, worksheets, shopping tips, and various samples of policies and benefits available. As well, it includes an extensive explanation of the various aspects of long-term care insurance products. The guide also contains a comprehensive contact list for every state insurance department. Most states require this guide to be provided to consumers by employers and insurance advisors when presenting long-term care insurance products.

To understand today's products, it is helpful to look at how long-term care insurance has evolved over the past 20 years (Table 4-2). Understanding the origins and evolution of long-term care insurance will help an advisor and client gain a better perspective on where these policies stand today.

In addition to long-term care products evolving, the marketing of long-term care insurance has evolved as well. Offering policies on a group basis as part of an employee benefit program began in 1989. Purchasing long-term care insurance in this manner has become quite prevalent. The most notable group long-term care insurance program is the Federal Long-Term Care Insurance Program (FLTCIP). It was expected that implementation of the FLTCIP would spur additional interest and growth in the long-term care insurance market. The program began in earnest in July 2002. It is considered one of the largest long-term care insurance educational campaigns ever. More than one million people requested enrollment kits. As of July 31, 2011, 270,861 applications were received. About 64 percent of enrollees were active employees and spouses, 31 percent were annuitants and their spouses, and another

**TABLE 4-2**
**Early and Current Long-Term Care Insurance Policies**

| Early Policies (pre-1993) | Current Policies |
| --- | --- |
| Did not cover Alzheimer's disease | Cover Alzheimer's and related dementia |
| Required a prior hospitalization for benefits to begin | Do not require prior hospitalization for benefits to begin |
| Required care to be "medically necessary" | Require care to be the result of a disability or a cognitive impairment and sometimes a medical necessity |
| Required need for skilled care before paying for custodial care | Do not require prior need for skilled care to pay for custodial care |
| Could be cancelled by insurance companies | Are guaranteed renewable |
| Covered home health care only at the skilled level | Cover custodial, as well as skilled, home care |
| Required prior nursing home stay to pay for home care | Do not require prior nursing home stay to pay for home care |
| Policy language was unclear and vague | Policy triggers and benefits are clearly spelled out |
| No state or government standards for long-term care policies | NAIC model policy and state regulations |
| Post-claim underwriting used to deny claims | Upfront underwriting used to eliminate post-claim underwriting |

Source: HARLEY GORDON, CERTIFICATION IN LONG-TERM CARE COURSE HANDBOOK, Section D (Release 8.0, Corporation for Long-Term Care Certification 2009).

5 percent were surviving spouses, parents/in-laws, and adult children. Thus, in relatively short order, the FLTCIP became the largest group long-term care insurance program in the United States. In part, this was due to the significant marketing and enrollment activities, including more than 2,100 educational meetings, briefings to human resources staff, and outreach programs to affinity groups. The large number of enrollments affords a unique opportunity to better understand the attitudes and perspectives of both working and retired individuals regarding long-term care concerns, the importance of planning, and the role that insurance can have in meeting the needs of disabled individuals. An examination of such attitudes can assist policymakers as well as insurance companies in seeking to better understand marketplace opportunities and barriers and devise strategies to encourage growth in the market.[2]

---

2. DEPARTMENT OF HEALTH & HUMAN SERVICES, FEDERAL LONG-TERM CARE INSURANCE BUYERS/NON-BUYERS OFFICE OF ASSISTANT SECRETARY FOR POLICY & EVALUATION DATA BRIEF, No. 1 (Aug. 2004).

**FIGURE 4-1**

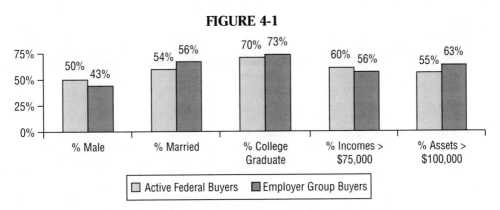

Source: Analysis of Buyer Data from Federal Long-Term Care Insurance Program 2004.

It has been found that when it comes to buying long-term care insurance protection, there are some significant differences between those purchasing employer-sponsored (group) coverage and those purchasing on an individual basis through an insurance professional. According to the annual study conducted by the American Association for Long-Term Care Insurance (AALTCI), one of the industry's professional trade organizations, group insurance buyers tend to be younger, select longer coverage, and also file claims at younger ages.

Summarized study data for 2008 from the *2009 LTCI Sourcebook* of the American Association for Long-Term Care Insurance in Table 4-3 shows a comparison of group and individual purchasers.

The Association analyzed data on 95,000 buyers of employer-sponsored long-term care insurance protection and over 200,000 individual buyers. Some 8.2 million Americans currently have long-term care insurance protection, and about 400,000 new policies or group certificates are issued annually. Individuals continue to purchase protection at younger ages, but that is especially true for those buying coverage in the workplace, according to AALTCI. In 2008, some 24 percent of buyers purchasing coverage through an employer-sponsored program were between ages 35 and 44. Another 36 percent were between ages 45 and 54, and 23 percent were between ages 55 and 64. The Association's study of individual buyers found that 5 percent were between ages 35 and 44, 24 percent were between ages 45 and 54, and 53 percent were between ages 55 and 64. For the first time, the study examined initial premiums paid by employees purchasing protection under a group program. One of the largest misperceptions is that long-term care insurance protection is expensive. The Association's study revealed a significant spread between the low and high premium amounts paid per employee. For example, for those between ages 45 and 55, the low premium was $430 per year while the high premium was $985. The average for this age band was $690. The study also looked at claims being paid to those covered by an employer-sponsored long-term care insurance program. Because many employer-sponsored plans offer some form of simplified underwriting or even guaranteed issue, the expectation is that more people will qualify for benefits at younger ages. Indeed, the Association's research found that 13 percent of new claims opened during 2008 were for

**TABLE 4-3**

| Age of Buyers | Group LTCI | Individual LTCI |
|---|---|---|
| Under 45 | 36% | 7% |
| 45 to 54 | 36% | 24% |
| 55 to 64 | 23% | 53% |
| 65 and Over | 5% | 16% |

| Daily Benefit | Group LTCI | Individual LTCI |
|---|---|---|
| Less than $100 | 9.0% | 6.5% |
| $100 to $149 | 33.0% | 31.5% |
| $150 to $199 | 25% | 35% |
| $200 and Over | 33% | 27% |

| Premium Paid (Group Long-Term Care Insurance) | | | |
|---|---|---|---|
| Age | Low | High | Average |
| 35 – 44 | $230 | $650 | $435 |
| 45 – 54 | $430 | $985 | $690 |
| 55 – 64 | $750 | $1,400 | $1,120 |
| 65 and Over | $1,520 | $2,535 | $1,925 |

| New Claims | Group LTCI | Individual LTCI |
|---|---|---|
| Under 50 | 3% | 0.4% |
| 50 to 59 | 10% | 1.5% |
| 60 to 69 | 22% | 7.0% |
| 70 to 79 | 33% | 30.5% |
| Age 80 and over | 32% | 60.6% |

New Claims are defined as those claims that began being paid in 2008. This is more relevant than looking at the overall block of all claims (some of which have been open for many years).

individuals younger than age 60. Some 11.5 percent of new group long-term care insurance claimants file their claim during the fourth or fifth year of their coverage. The largest open claim under a group program exceeds $490,000, and the individual has been on claim for over nine years.[3]

Significant efforts have been made to encourage people to purchase long-term care insurance policies. The federal government began allowing a tax deduction for long-term care insurance premiums paid beginning in 1997. The tax treatment for qualified long-term care services and long-term care insurance contracts was clarified in the Health Insurance Portability and Accountability Act of 1996 (HIPAA), Public Law (Pub. L.) No. 104-191, which included standards that applied to policies

---

3. AMERICAN ASSOCIATION FOR LONG-TERM CARE INSURANCE, 2009 LTCI SOURCEBOOK (2009).

sold in 1997 and later in order to qualify for tax subsidies. Nearly all policies sold today are tax-qualified (**cf. Chapter 5, page 104, and Chapter 6, page 112**).

Another government incentive to purchase long-term care insurance was the birth of the state government-instituted partnership programs. In a 1992 pilot program in four states, Medicaid formed a partnership with long-term care insurance companies to provide for easier access to Medicaid benefits for those who had purchased long-term care insurance policies. The exact rules differed by state, but under the program people who purchased a long-term care insurance policy but exhausted their benefits could apply for Medicaid assistance without being subject to the same asset spend down restrictions as those who had not first paid for care through private insurance. The Partnership for Long-Term Care, or LTC Partnership Program, as it was called, was limited to selected insurance companies and approved policies offered by those companies.

The idea was to encourage citizens to purchase a limited, and therefore more affordable, amount of long-term care insurance coverage, with the assurance that they could receive additional long-term care services through the Medicaid program. In addition, participants could access Medicaid without having to "spend down" all of their assets, although income must be devoted to long-term care levels typically required to meet Medicaid eligibility requirements. A unique insurance model was developed in the 1980s with support from the Robert Wood Johnson Foundation (RWJF). RWJF sponsored an initiative to examine whether combining public and private resources would help balance the financing of LTC.[4] The result of the RWJF initiative was the creation of the LTC Partnership Program, which combined a specially designed private insurance product with Medicaid coverage. The creators of the partnership program were aiming to promote private insurance for long-term care, which could improve access to care and limit the financial exposure to high costs. They also were hoping that, by increasing the number of people financing at least part of their care through private insurance, they could reduce Medicaid expenditures. Not only would the insurance limit the spend down to qualify for Medicaid, but it would, in theory, also reduce the incentive for individuals to undertake asset transfers in order to appear to be eligible for Medicaid. Some asset transfers were legal, such as transfers that occurred outside a state's look-back threshold. Most states were concerned, though, that incentives existed for people to transfer assets to become eligible for Medicaid. As the states began implementing their RWJF Partnership demonstrations, several criticisms were leveled at the program, which prevented further expansion. First, policymakers were troubled that a public program like Medicaid would endorse private insurance products, which they believed to be beyond the mission of the program and which could inappropriately promote products with limited value.[5]

---

4. M.R. Meiners et al., *National Program Office, in* Who Will Pay for Long Term Care: Insights from the Partnership Programs 49–64 (N. McCall, ed. 2001).

5. M.R. Meiners et al., *Reflections of a Partnership Insider on Long Term Care Financing, in* Who Will Pay for Long Term Care: Insights from the Partnership Programs, *supra* note 4, at 289–99.

Others were concerned that the partnership would increase Medicaid spending rather than reduce it. It was thought that the aspect of this program that allowed individuals to retain their own assets could inadvertently qualify wealthy individuals to participate in Medicaid services, which are intended for low-income Americans. As a result of these concerns, Congress included a provision in the Omnibus Budget Reconciliation Act of 1993 (OBRA 1993) that effectively prevented new states from developing partnership programs. OBRA 1993 amended section 1917(b)(1)(C) of the Social Security Act; it requires states to perform estate recovery actions against Medicaid beneficiaries upon their death. Beneficiaries participating in established or approved partnership programs as of that date were exempted from this requirement. This provision would not allow any new programs to offer asset protection, without which there was little incentive to participate. Upon death, the partnership program participants' assets would be taken by the state even though they were protected when they were alive.

Through legislative proposals and the growing concern of long-term care expenditures, the Deficit Reduction Act of 2005 (DRA) was signed into law on February 8, 2006 (**cf. Chapter 3, page 50 and Chapter 5, page 104**). The DRA lifted the technical barriers Congress had imposed on such programs, allowing for the expansion of the partnership program to other states across the country. Under the DRA, all states can implement LTC Partnership Programs through an approved state plan amendment if specific requirements are met. The DRA requires programs to include certain consumer protections, most notably provisions of the National Association of Insurance Commissioners' Model LTC regulations. The DRA also requires that partnership polices include inflation protection when purchased by a person under age 76.

Since the DRA was passed, the long-term care insurance market has experienced an exodus of insurance companies, particularly in the past five years, as 15 insurance companies have sold their long-term care insurance block of business and are no longer in the market. Currently, six companies control over 80 percent of the market.[6] Comprehensive, standalone policies represent the majority of long-term care insurance sold today. The policies sold currently are designed to cover as many different care scenarios as possible.

Thought leaders are uniformly optimistic about the future of the long-term care insurance market; views range from cautious optimism to unreserved optimism for a variety of reasons:[7]

- ♦ There's no alternative in sight for the baby boomers.
- ♦ Fantasies of early retirement and self-funding are gone.
- ♦ Record budget deficits make social insurance improbable.
- ♦ Medicaid is in deep trouble.

6. AMERICAN ASSOCIATION FOR LONG-TERM CARE INSURANCE, THE 2011 SOURCEBOOK FOR LONG-TERM CARE INSURANCE INFORMATION (2011).

7. THE FORBES CONSULTING GROUP, LONG-TERM CARE INSURANCE THOUGHT LEADER REPORT (2003).

- Consumer awareness has nowhere to go but up.
- Personal responsibility messages will continue to get out to the public.
- Pricing has become more rational.

In addition to legislation that has influenced the progression of long-term care awareness, there have been public awareness campaigns to address the need to plan for long-term care. Most notably is the *Own Your Future* awareness campaign, which is a joint federal-state effort to raise awareness of long-term care and the need for planning. Each year since 2005, the U.S. Department of Health and Human Services (HHS) has partnered with selected states to conduct campaigns that included a letter signed by the state's governor and mailed to all households with members age 45 and older. The content of the letter offers information about the importance of planning for long-term care and includes a free planning kit that can be obtained by reply mail or a toll-free telephone number, or downloaded from the National Clearinghouse for Long-Term Care Information website at www .longtermcare.gov. Some states offer the opportunity to attend regional forums. The states that have already adopted long-term care insurance partnership programs include information on their programs as well. Funding for the clearinghouse and the *Own Your Future* campaign was included in the Deficit Reduction Act of 2005. The Administration of Aging (AoA), the Office of the Assistant Secretary for Planning and Evaluation (ASPE) of the HHS, and the Centers for Medicare and Medicaid Services (CMS) are partners in the clearinghouse website and the campaign.

Due to the complicated nature of long-term care insurance products, consumer education is critical to expanding coverage. Consumers often have difficulty understanding how the products work, when and whether they should purchase coverage, how coverage is accessed, and how premiums are determined.

## Long-Term Care Insurance versus Disability Income Insurance

The advisor who works with clients in the area of disability income planning is accustomed to working with a concept that must be sold, not bought. The disability income planning advisor is also already motivating healthy people to think about an unhealthy future. A critical task for an advisor is to help the client understand that long-term care insurance protects the client from a need that is separate and distinct from a need caused by a disability.

Disability income insurance, like life insurance, is used to protect future earnings. It is an insurance product that provides income replacement through a specified benefit in the event of an illness or injury resulting in a disability that prevents the insured from working in his or her occupation. Benefits are usually provided on a monthly basis so that the individual can maintain his or her standard of living and continue to pay regular expenses. While most people are prepared for the medical costs of a severe injury or illness through their medical insurance, without disability income insurance they are not prepared for the loss in earnings that accompanies such a calamity. People who rely on their occupations to pay their living expenses should seriously consider disability income insurance to protect such earnings.

While disability income insurance provides income replacement in the event of a disabling injury or illness, long-term care insurance provides income for the cost of care resulting from a disabling injury or illness. In addition, long-term care insurance provides wealth protection, care coordination, caregiver support, and discounted provider services. In short, disability insurance protects one's income while long-term care insurance protects one's accumulated wealth.

The life and disability income insurance industries have not based their marketing efforts on the risk of dying or becoming disabled, but rather on educating the client about the consequences to those he or she loves if these unexpected events ever occur. In fact, insurance advisors do not focus on the need to buy a product, but rather on the need to create a plan to mitigate those consequences. Once the plan is created, an insurance product is suggested as a funding solution. Financial planners and advisors do not use the risk of the client not having money to pay for a child's education or to fund a secure retirement, because the client believes he or she will have that money. Rather, the focus is on educating the client about the severe consequences for loved ones if the client does not create a plan for these contingencies. Investments are then positioned as a funding solution. Once the plan is in place, long-term care insurance will be positioned, not as a product that protects the client, but as a funding source for the plan.

In the current insurance market, there are disability income insurance policies that offer long-term care features, so that in the event of a severe disability or cognitive impairment that results in a loss of activities of daily living, an additional benefit amount is paid to assist with long-term care expenses. This benefit is payable if there is a loss of two ADLs. Some disability income policies offer long-term care insurance conversion riders, which allow an insured to convert the disability income insurance policy to a long-term care insurance policy as the retirement age nears. Generally, a base long-term care benefit amount is offered, but the benefit amount can be increased for additional premium at the time of original application for disability income insurance. Not only are disability income insurance products now addressing the need to plan for long-term care, but a more diversified approach in the life insurance and annuity market has been occurring, as well. This will be addressed later in this chapter.

## Tax-Qualified versus Non-Tax-Qualified Insurance Policies

While the NAIC Model Regulation initiated the definition of today's long-term care insurance policies, it is the Health Insurance Portability and Accountability Act of 1996 (HIPAA) that standardized the product and focused consumers' minds on its value. Passage of this bill demonstrated a clear consensus that insurance would, and should, become a key means of financing long-term care.

Tax-qualified long-term care insurance policies offer their policyholders certain tax advantages, including deductibility of premiums, tax-free benefits, and preferential treatment by many states. Such policies must meet certain standards, many of which were originally outlined in the 1993 NAIC Long-Term Care Insurance Model Regulation.

The Internal Revenue Code defines a qualified long-term care insurance contract as one that[8]

- does not have a medical necessity trigger;
- covers only qualified long-term care services;
- does not pay or reimburse expenses that are reimbursable by Medicare, either entirely or by covering a deductible or coinsurance, except when Medicare is a secondary payor or the policy pays on an indemnity or cash benefit basis;[9]
- is guaranteed renewable;
- does not provide a cash surrender value or other money that can be paid, assigned, pledged as collateral for a loan, or borrowed, except any refund on the death of the insured or on a complete surrender or cancellation of the contract; such a refund cannot exceed the aggregate premiums paid for the contract;
- includes in gross income any refund on a complete surrender or cancellation to the extent that premiums had been deducted or excluded from taxable income;[10]
- applies all refunds of premiums, and all policyholder dividends or similar amounts, as reductions in future premiums or to increase future benefits;
- satisfies certain consumer protection standards. Tax-qualified contracts must satisfy all of the following standards. Non-tax-qualified contracts may or may not satisfy them.
    - Policies must be guaranteed renewable (as long as the policyholder pays the required premium). Insurance companies may not cancel or refuse to renew a policy because of the insured's age, health deterioration, or claims history. They may raise premiums, but only on all policies of that class, regardless of individual claims experience.
    - Policies must offer an inflation protection option. Advisors who sell tax-qualified policies must also offer and explain this option in their sales presentation.
    - Policies must be offered with an optional non-forfeiture benefit, but it may not be a cash surrender value. A premium refund benefit in the

---

8. I.R.C. § 7702B(b)(1).

9. *Id.*

10. I.R.C. § 7702B(b)(2)(C).

form of reduction of future premiums is permitted. This requires the insured to pay an additional premium, and to receive a reduced maximum benefit, to be able to cancel the policy after a period of time, usually three years. The selection of this option may not alter the policy's coverage elements, eligibility, or benefit triggers. If the non-forfeiture option is not selected, the insurer must provide a contingent benefit upon lapse, also called contingent non-forfeiture.

○ Policies must include an unintentional lapse provision, permitting a policyholder who misses a premium payment because of his cognitive or physical impairment to reinstate the policy up to five months later.

○ Policies sold to replace existing long-term care insurance policies, qualified or otherwise, may not impose any pre-existing condition restrictions or probationary periods that existed in the original policy and were satisfied.

Furthermore, tax-qualified long-term care insurance contracts may not impose unreasonable benefit limits or exclusions. The law specifically requires them to comply with certain provisions of the NAIC Long-Term Care Model Regulation pertaining to prohibitions on limitations and exclusions, extension of benefits, disclosure, and other standards. Especially noteworthy are these provisions:

♦ Policies may not condition coverage of a level of care upon prior need for a higher level of care or hospitalization.

♦ Insurance companies may not practice post-claim underwriting. They must conduct proper and complete underwriting, including the use of medical questions, prior to issuing the policy. Post-claim underwriting is the practice of "underwriting" a policy after a claim is submitted. This method's rationale was to cut down on underwriting costs by underwriting only those policies on which claims were submitted, but policyholders are generally disconcerted by the uncertainty that their claims will be honored.

Rarely mentioned in discussions of HIPAA, but very important nonetheless, is the elimination of the hands-on assistance requirement to receive benefits that was prevalent in earlier policies. Such language meant that a claim would not be paid unless the policyholder needed assistance involving direct physical contact. The new term used is standby assistance, which means that supervisory assistance is sufficient; this might be, for example, someone's presence nearby to provide help with balance when necessary. Other terms associated with standby assistance are directional and verbal cuing. A majority of policies employ standby assistance as the criterion for payment.

Additional definitions applicable to tax-qualified long-term care insurance policies include the following:

♦ Qualified long-term care services: necessary diagnostic, preventative, therapeutic, curing, treating, mitigating, and rehabilitative services and maintenance or personal care services that are required by a chronically ill individual and are provided pursuant to a plan of care prescribed by a licensed health care practitioner.[11]

♦ Chronically ill individual: any individual who has, in the preceding 12 months, been certified by a licensed health care practitioner as:
  o being unable to perform, without substantial assistance, either hands-on or standby, from another individual, at least two activities of daily living for a period of at least 90 days due to a loss of functional capacity;
  o having a similar level of disability; or
  o requiring supervision to protect him or her from threats to health and safety due to severe cognitive impairment.

♦ Activities of daily living (ADLs):[12]
  o Eating
  o Toileting
  o Transferring
  o Bathing
  o Dressing
  o Continence
  o To be tax-qualified, a long-term care insurance contract must use at least five of these six ADLs in determining whether the insured is chronically ill.

♦ Licensed health care practitioner: any physician (as defined in Section 1861(r)(1) of the Social Security Act) and any registered professional nurse, licensed social worker, or other individual who meets such requirements as prescribed by the Treasury.[13]

All long-term care insurance policies that were issued before HIPAA took effect on January 1, 1997, are grandfathered. They are recognized as tax-qualified policies if they met the long-term care insurance requirements of the states in which they were issued on their dates of issue.[14] Group plans are also recognized if their group certificates were established prior to that date; their enrollees are deemed to hold tax-qualified policies even if they enrolled later. This rule means that policies issued before 1997 are considered tax qualified even if they contain

---

11. I.R.C. § 7702B(c)(1).

12. I.R.C. § 7702B(c)(2)(B).

13. I.R.C. § 7702B(c)(4).

14. Pub. L. No. 104-191, § 321(f) (1996). The requirements that a grandfathered policy must meet are those of its state of issue's statutes and regulations that regulate long-term care insurance, as defined by the National Association of Insurance Commissioners (NAIC)'s Long-Term Care Insurance Model Act, § 4, as in effect on August 21, 1996, regardless of the terminology used by the state in describing the insurance coverage. Treas. Reg. § 1.7702(B)(2).

provisions that are prohibited in new tax-qualified policies, such as the use of medical necessity as a benefit trigger. Grandfathered policies remain tax qualified so long as no material changes are made to them. In this context, a material change is generally a policy upgrade, such as the addition of an inflation rider; it will render the policy non-tax qualified. The following changes are permitted and are not considered material changes:

♦ Premium model changes
♦ Class rate increases or decreases
♦ Discounts added after the issue date because other family members, such as a spouse, purchase a policy, or household discounts
♦ Premium decreases due to reduction in coverage
♦ Provision of alternate forms of benefits that do not increase the premium
♦ Deletions of riders that prohibit benefit coordination with Medicare

Tax-qualified long-term care insurance coverage may be provided as a rider on a life insurance contract. In tax years starting in 2010,[15] long-term care insurance riders on certain annuity contracts are also to be deemed tax qualified. The portion of such a contract providing long-term care insurance coverage is treated as a separate contract.[16]

Non-taxed-qualified (NTQ) long-term care insurance policies can contain a medical necessity trigger that allows benefits to be paid if the insured requires medical attention. These types of policies do not require the insured to be chronically ill to receive benefits. Policyholders qualify for benefits by showing that they need assistance with two or more ADLs, or that they require supervision due to a cognitive impairment.

Less than 1 percent of new individual long-term care insurance premiums sold last year were NTQ. Approximately five insurance companies are providing NTQ policies in the market. As of this writing there are no NTQ group insurance contracts offered, only individual insurance contracts. Some insurance companies will probably continue to offer NTQ policies in the foreseeable future; most likely, it will be due to them being a career agency distributor, which writes the most NTQ policies today. With so little NTQ business being sold currently, administering tax-qualified and non-tax-qualified policies tends to be expensive.[17]

When advising a client on whether to purchase a tax-qualified or non-tax-qualified policy, the general advice should be to purchase a tax-qualified policy for the following reasons:

♦ The premiums for tax-qualified policies are initially 4 to 12 percent less expensive than premiums for non-tax-qualified policies.

---

15. Pub. L. No. 109-280, § 844 (2006).
16. I.R.C. § 7702B(e)(1).
17. Email from Mike Skiens, MasterCare Solutions Inc. (Aug. 14, 2011).

- Because non-tax-qualified policies make it easier to qualify for benefits, the premiums are more likely to be subjected to premium increases.
- More than 99 percent of the new long-term care insurance policies issued are tax qualified.
- It is becoming increasingly more difficult to find non-tax-qualified policies.[18]
- Only tax-qualified policies will qualify for DRA state LTC Partnership Program status.

# Linked Products (Hybrid Long-Term Care Insurance) Overview

The provisions of the Pension Protection Act (PPA) of 2006 provide new tax benefits for what are often referred to as long-term care "linked products," combination products, asset-based plans, or hybrid products. These new benefits apply to life insurance policies and annuity contracts. PPA permits tax-free distribution of life insurance or annuity cash value to pay for long-term care, beginning in 2010. As a result, now consumers have multiple financial vehicles to choose from to fund their long-term care planning. Linked products are also available on an individual basis or, increasingly, through a plan offered by an employer.

These linked products address one of the common objections consumers have to standalone long-term care insurance: the concern that the client may never use the benefits of a standalone policy, with nothing to show for the premium paid. It is worth noting that if that is of real concern to the client, the benefit design of a standalone policy can include a return of premium option that allows for a full refund of the premium.

The PPA contains a section that allows for more favorable tax treatment for these linked products, so new opportunities are emerging for the life insurance and annuity industry. The legislation includes provisions that clarify and enhance the tax treatment of linked products, improving upon previously vague language, which left room for interpretation by tax advisors. Detailed information on the favorable tax treatment will be provided in Chapter 6.

A long-term care linked product will work best for clients whose financial plans call for life insurance or an annuity in addition to long-term care coverage. The first consideration is whether it is better to purchase a standalone long-term care insurance policy with a separate standalone life insurance policy or annuity. Factors to consider for this to be the appropriate choice include the following:

- Clients seek more choice in the design of their policy, including the maximum benefit period, benefit amount, modes of premium payments, elimination period, inflation features, and optional benefits.

---

18. Broker World Magazine, 2010 Broker World Long-Term Care Insurance Survey (July 2010).

- The need for life insurance is separate and distinct from the need for long-term care insurance, and the client wishes the benefits to remain independent of each other.
- Underwriting considerations—linked products may provide more favorable underwriting than standalone long-term care insurance products.
- Clients to whom the tax-deductibility of premiums is appealing. The tax laws on deductions for standalone long-term care insurance premiums are much clearer than they are for linked long-term care benefits or riders.[19]

In the current market, linked products generally fall into the following product combinations:

- Life insurance with a long-term care benefit
- Life insurance with a long-term care rider
- Life insurance with an accelerated benefit rider
- Annuity with a long-term care rider
- Annuity with a long-term care benefit
- Annuity, life insurance with a long-term care benefit

## Life Insurance with Long-Term Care Benefits

The base life insurance plan is most often a whole life, universal life, or variable universal life insurance policy. The product combinations of life insurance with long-term care products accelerate the life insurance policy's death benefit to cover qualifying long-term care expenses, typically after an elimination period of 60, 90, or 100 days, after having a loss of the ability to perform qualifying ADLs.

The policy may offer the ability to elect an "extension of benefits" option for an additional premium cost. Such a policy is underwritten using a flexible premium universal life insurance policy product. The benefit purchased can extend the long-term care coverage up to several times the life insurance death benefit. For example, the option could extend a $100,000 death benefit so that the insured may receive up to an additional $200,000 in long-term care benefits. This product design utilizes a long-term care benefit model, whereas a policy using a long-term care rider does not allow the long-term care benefit amount to exceed the life insurance death benefit. This second type adds an optional rider to the policy. The client is purchasing a base policy of permanent life insurance, and the option to receive long-term care benefits is provided through an optional rider added to the policy. Many of these policies are sold on a recurring premium basis.

Factors that may make a life insurance policy with long-term care benefits an appropriate choice to purchase include the following:

---

19. Matt Pressler & Angela Turk, M Financial Group, "A Case Study of Long-Term Care Product Alternatives" (Dec. 2010).

- Client is adverse to ongoing premium payments and would like a single-premium life and long-term care solution.
- Client desires to have a cash value element to the policy.
- Client desires to have funds available as a death benefit if long-term care is not needed, and life insurance needs are secondary to long-term care needs.
- Client desires the simplicity of having only one insurance policy.[20]

Partial withdrawals and policy loans taken from a modified endowment contract (MEC) are taxable under federal income tax law to the extent that there is any gain in the policy. An additional tax of 10 percent of the taxable amount may be payable unless the policyholder is age 59½ or satisfies another exemption from payment of the additional tax.[21]

Some universal life (UL) and variable universal life (VUL) insurance policies now offer optional riders that help prevent erosion of retirement assets due to long-term care costs. Available for an additional fee, the riders allow acceleration of VUL death benefit, in certain circumstances, to pay for qualified long-term care services. The death benefit is reduced by the amount accelerated. If long-term care is never needed, the full death benefit is paid to the beneficiaries. For clients in need of life insurance, a VUL policy with an optional long-term care rider offers an attractive, potentially more affordable option to buying separate life insurance and long-term care insurance policies. As many discovered in recent years, relying only on stocks for retirement and estate planning can be uncertain. Clients who experienced broad market losses will appreciate how a VUL policy with an equity stabilization account can help mitigate equity risks within an overall investment portfolio. The ability to direct premiums after insurance costs into a stabilized account helps smooth the impact of volatility on the portion of the VUL cash value, calming policyholder concerns and enhancing the potential for long-term returns. Knowing the stabilized account reduces or eliminates losses can give policyholders the comfort needed to remain invested, even during periods of extreme volatility, and the confidence to allocate remaining premiums more aggressively. Gains from other policy investment portfolios can be swept into the stabilized account, without triggering a tax event.[22]

Factors that may make a life insurance policy with a long-term care rider an appropriate choice to purchase include the following:

- Client is most interested in life insurance, and long-term care insurance needs are somewhat secondary.
- Client seeks flexible funding options.

---

20. *Id.*
21. Internal Revenue Service, http://www.irs.gov/publications/p575/ar02.html (2011).
22. Robert Bucky Wright, *VUL Could Be Coming Back*, 114 National Underwriter 1 (Jan. 4, 2010).

- Clients understands the need for long-term care protection but is concerned he or she may never use the benefit. Funds not used for long-term care benefits translate into death benefit for heirs.
- Client desires to add long-term care coverage after the policy is issued.
- Client seeks an indemnity-style rider.[23]

The linked product life insurance policies offered in today's market contain many of the policy features and optional riders found in standalone long-term care insurance policies. The policies are available as a single-premium or flexible-premium payment. Generally, if single-premium payment is chosen, a minimum single premium amount is required.

Life insurance can be customized with an accelerated benefits rider, which can provide access to the death benefit in the event the insured is diagnosed with a chronic illness. Use of accelerated benefits will reduce the policy's cash value and death benefit. There is no restriction placed on the use of the benefit received. It is a rider on a whole life or universal life insurance policy. The long-term care benefits are paid from the death benefit. Other than its source of funding, a policy of this type is identical to a standalone long-term care insurance policy. The policy can pay one of two ways:

1. A monthly percentage of the death benefit
2. A monthly payment determined by dividing the death benefit by a number of months provided in the contract, usually 24, 36, or 48 months

The apparent advantage of this structure is that the insured receives the face value of the policy one way or the other. However, because the underwriting for the two types of insurance is very different—mortality for life insurance and morbidity for long-term care insurance—the death benefit at the same premium is likely to be smaller than in a standalone life insurance policy.

Unlike a linked product, a life insurance policy with an accelerated death benefit does not contain a long-term care insurance rider. Rather, it permits the policyholder to accelerate the death benefit and receive part or all of it while still alive by drawing the benefit down to pay for long-term care expenses.

## Annuity with Long-Term Care Insurance Benefits

In considering an annuity with a long-term care benefit or rider product, there are two types of linked annuity with long-term care benefit products available:

- Deferred long-term care annuity
- Immediate long-term care annuity

The annuity product with a long-term care rider links long-term care benefits to a single-premium deferred annuity. This type of annuity is generally available to individuals up to age 85 with simplified or guaranteed insurability. This product begins

---

23. Pressler, *supra* note 19.

as an annuity with either a lump-sum deposit or periodic deposits made over time. It combines long-term asset growth with long-term care protection. With these types of policies, an optional benefit rider offers additional benefit amount guarantees. Depending on the product, benefit payments for long-term care can be payable on a reimbursement or indemnity basis. If no care is needed, the annuity gains interest like any other fixed annuity. But if the owner annuitant needs care, a formula will be used to determine the amount of the monthly benefit available to the client.

### FIGURE 4-2

### Annuity Sample Case

## WITH AND WITHOUT LTC RIDER

✓ **The customer:** Age 60, deposits $100,000 into an annuity; at age 80, needs 24 months of accelerated LTC benefits and another 24 months of tail benefits.

✓ **Without a LTC rider:** At age 80, she cashes out $219,000 from the annuity (assuming 4% annual growth), pays $36,000 of taxes on the gain (assuming a 30% tax rate), netting $183,000 after tax.

✓ **With a LTC rider:** This particular rider pays out up to 200% of account value, with 65 basis points per year assessed against the account value for the LTC insurance charges. At age 80, the annuity has grown to $193,000 (assuming a net crediting rate of 3.35%— i.e, the 4% crediting rate minus the 65 bp charge). Over the course of the LTC claim, it pays out $386,000 tax-free to the customer. (Note: This ignores potential tax benefits of itemized deductions for un-reimbursed LTC medical expenses, which might dampen some of the above differentials for many insureds.)

Source: Carl A. Friedrich, Milliman Inc., Chicago.

An alternative to the annuity product with long-term care rider is the annuity product with long-term care benefits, which functions exactly like a fixed annuity, but has a long-term care multiplier built into the policy. There is no premium rider attached to this medically underwritten annuity policy. Instead, a portion of the internal return in the contract is used to pay for the long-term care benefit. Long-term care coverage is calculated based on the amount of coverage selected when the policy is purchased. The annuity is a series of regular payments over a specified and defined period of time. The funds for the annuity come from a single premium payment that the individual makes at the outset. The insurance company offers a payout of 200 or 300 percent of the aggregate policy value over two or three years after the annuity account value is depleted. For example, a policyholder with a $100,000 annuity who had selected an aggregate benefit limit of 300 percent and a two-year benefit period would have an additional $200,000 available for long-term care expenses after the initial $100,000 policy value was depleted. The policyholder would spend down the $100,000 annuity value over a two-year period and then receive the additional $200,000 over a four-year period or longer. In this example the contract pays $50,000 a year for a minimum of six years, but care will last longer if less benefit is needed. Again, if long-term care is never needed, the annuity value would be paid out in a lump sum to any named beneficiary.

With an immediate annuity with long-term care benefits, a single-premium payment is made to the insurance company and a specified monthly income is received. It is available without regard to a client's health, so if clients do not qualify for long-term care insurance because of age or health or if they are already receiving long-term care, they can still purchase this type of long-term care annuity. The single-premium payment is converted to a monthly income stream that is guaranteed either for a specified period of time or for the life of the individual receiving the payments. The payout schedule varies based on the amount of the initial premium, age, and gender. Generally, because of their longer life expectancy, females receive a smaller monthly payment over a longer period of time than males of the same age.

Important considerations to factor in long-term care annuity planning include the following:

◆ The annuity amount received may not be enough to pay for long-term care expenses.
◆ Inflation may make the monthly income received from the annuity less than what is needed.

Many clients who reach the required minimum distribution (RMD) age of 70½ have accumulated a significant amount of qualified assets. They may realize some of it will not be needed for income purposes. Most traditional retirement accounts (401(k), IRA) are extremely inefficient for wealth transfer because they are often subject to two levels of tax (estate and income), which can wipe out 75–80 percent of their value. An annuity or life insurance with long-term care benefits can utilize these excess tax-deferred (qualified) funds for long-term care protection, while at the same time liquidating these funds in a tax advantageous way for wealth transfer. Such products allow the insurance advisor to reposition the client's qualified money into an individual retirement arrangement (IRA) annuity. Through systematic taxable annual withdrawals, a joint or single 20-pay whole life insurance policy, for example, is funded. Long-term care benefits are available from both the annuity cash value and the life insurance policy death benefit. This planning, though medically underwritten, allows for

- better estate liquidity for heirs—a tax-free life insurance death benefit can help pay taxes on any remaining IRA balance;
- access to the annuity cash value and life insurance death benefit for qualifying long-term care expenses;
- a guarantee of required minimum distributions to be satisfied annually from the IRA annuity after the client reaches age 70½.

As part of the suitability review, it is important to consider whether a linked product is a viable option for the client. The next step is to determine the value of the client's assets and the best source for funding the insurance policy. Because income and assets vary widely by client, no single model can determine suitability; however, here is a non-exhaustive list of assets to consider:

- home ownership
- normal annual expenditures such as housing, medical, charity, automobile, travel and leisure, and gifts
- portion of income that may come from Social Security and qualified benefit plans
- value of qualified defined contribution plan assets
- value of other types of assets

After identifying the assets available, the advisor then needs to determine which assets are to be liquidated first. In addition, when evaluating linked products—both life insurance and annuities with long-term care coverage—it is important to consider the following:

- surrenders and withdrawal penalties and fees from assets
- interest rates of current assets
- interest rates of linked products
- surrender charge duration
- long-term care coverage options
- minimum funding requirements
- underwriting requirements
- issue age limitations

Once a linked product policy is in place, if clients need coverage for long-term care, they have it. If their need for care is minimal or non-existent, the cash outlay for life insurance or an annuity will provide a benefit for them or their beneficiaries through the death benefit proceeds.

# Long-Term Care Insurance Cost Considerations

Insurance companies assume the risk associated with annuities and insurance policies and assign premiums to be paid for the policies. In the policy, the insurance company states the length and conditions of the agreement, exactly which losses it will provide compensation for, and how much will be awarded. The premium charged for the policy is based primarily on the amount to be awarded in case of loss and the likelihood that the insurance company will actually have to pay. In order to be able to compensate policyholders for their losses, insurance companies invest the premiums they receive, building up a portfolio of financial assets and income-producing real estate, which can then be used to pay future claims. There are two basic types of insurance companies: primary and reinsurance. Primary companies are responsible for the initial underwriting of insurance policies and annuities, while reinsurance companies assume all or part of the risk associated with the existing insurance policies originally underwritten by other insurance companies.

## Persistency

It is important to understand how long-term care insurance premiums are established. Before an insurance company can determine a premium for long-term care insurance, it must first make assumptions in five major categories:

1. Persistency—the percentage of policies sold that will remain in force each future year
2. Utilization—the use of long-term care services in each future year
3. Expenses—the expenses incurred in marketing and administering in-force policies, and in processing claims
4. Interest—the interest earned on policy reserves
5. Risk—the risk and profit margin necessary to maintain solvency under adverse experience and to generate a profit for the insurance company

Estimates in the first two areas have proven especially difficult because of the short history and rapid evolution of long-term care insurance. Although long-term care insurance may appear to resemble medical insurance, its premiums are established very differently. Medical insurance premiums paid during a year cover average expected claim costs for the insured during the same year. With medical insurance, the premium charged to a 40-year-old reflects the annual average medical costs for a 40-year-old, the premium for a 50-year-old reflects average medical costs for a 50-year-old, and so on. In contrast, premiums for long-term care insurance policies are set with the assumption that the insured will continue to pay premiums into future years that will create a pool of money that will be available as the potential need for long-term care services increases with age. Therefore, long-term care insurance works much like life insurance in that the premium solvency depends on the long-term accumulation and investment of premiums to meet future cost. Similar to life insurance, the cost of the long-term care insurance policy depends on how early in life one obtains the coverage. Younger people are expected to pay into the insurance pool for a longer period, and the likelihood of needing services in the near future is lower than that of an older purchaser of coverage.

**TABLE 4-4**

| Age | Average Annual Premium amounts paid in 2007—averaged for all ages and for specific age groups (2008 LIMRA International, Inc.) |
| --- | --- |
| All ages | $2,207 |
| Under age 40 | $881 |
| 40 to 49 | $1,781 |
| 50 to 59 | $1,982 |
| 60 to 64 | $2,249 |
| 65 to 69 | $2,539 |
| Age 70 and older | $3,026 |

## Premium Stability

In theory, the premium for long-term care insurance is expected to be fixed or level for the life of the policy. Some insurance advisors, inadequately disclosing the risk of premium rate increases, have caused immense misconceptions about long-term care insurance premiums. When a new policy premium is approved by state insurance departments, it is expected to remain stable throughout the life of a policy. Typically, policyholders make the same payment annually for the amount of time required by the policy, which is known as a level premium. "Level premium" does not mean that the premium cannot increase. Both initial premiums and premium increases on open or closed blocks of business must be approved by state insurance departments. A company may seek the state insurance department's approval of a premium change on a class basis. A premium increase on a class basis means that a person cannot be singled out for his or her own premium increase. For example, the insurance company cannot arbitrarily raise the policy premium due to increasing age or change in health. An increase could be approved for all persons who have a particular policy if actual claims experience differed significantly from respect to the original assumptions made for that policy.

Additionally, for a number of reasons, an insurance company may decide to stop selling a certain policy to new applicants. Policies that have been issued to this point are known as a closed block of business. Existing policyholders are allowed to retain their policy, but because new, healthy people are not being added to the policy block, some policyholders may become concerned that this will result in a premium increase. When an insurance department approves the initial premium of a policy, the policy must be shown to be self-supporting. This means increases should be unnecessary through the life of the insured pool provided the assumptions in the original pricing are correct. Insurance companies may still request approval of a premium rate increase on a closed block of business due to unanticipated factors arising after the original pricing.

Regulators understand that the relative lack of long-term care claims experience makes it difficult to predict future claims. The current intent of insurance regulators, the NAIC, is to promote rate stability in the long-term care insurance industry, similar to the rate stability in the life insurance market. It is difficult to identify companies that may have to file for future premium increases, as companies with the lowest premiums may not always be the ones who file for increases. Two resources that can provide helpful information regarding company premium solvency are the *Long-Term Care Experience Report* published annually by the NAIC, and the *Guidance Manual for Rating Aspects of The Long-Term Care Insurance Model Regulation*, also published by the NAIC[24] (**cf. Chapter 4**).

An additional indication of rate stability is the insurance company's underwriting philosophy. In the Long-Term Care Experience Report, companies with high loss ratios may be more likely to need future rate increases; however this is not always an accurate indicator. The more useful indicator is in the underwriting of the policy. Because many group long-term care insurance plans are not medically underwritten, underwriting can be evaluated from the insurance company's approach to obtaining request for proposal (RFP) information, its benefits offered, and how aggressively it seeks participation in the program. For individually underwritten policies, insurance companies vary on their medical history and other underwriting protocols. Accordingly, claim experience is in relation to how the policy is underwritten. As a rule, underwriting philosophy combined with loss ratio is a good indicator for future premium rate increases.

Companies new to selling long-term care insurance require additional capital to build distribution channels and to staff administrative and claims departments. Many of these companies report, year after year, underwriting losses on their long-term care insurance business. This is not a business for small, poorly rated, or undercapitalized companies. Nor is it a business for companies not committed to years of loss in order to build an eventual profitable book of business. Companies that play the middle ground and sell few policies will likely exit the market due to high overhead and adverse selection from stagnant sales of long-term care insurance. In the past five years, 15 major companies have sold their long-term care insurance books of business, and three insurance companies have stopped selling new policies. Of all factors involved in setting premium rates, underwriting has proven to have the greatest effect of all on rate stability.[25]

24. National Association of Insurance Commissioners, *NAIC Store*, http://www.naic.org/store_home.htm (last visited Oct. 28, 2012).

25. National Care Planning Council, *Long Term Care Insurance*, http://www.longtermcarelink.net/eldercare/long_term_care_insurance.htm (last visited Oct. 28, 2012).

## Voluntary Lapse Rates

- Policy persistency is proving to be a concern to the long-term care insurance industry in that persistency continues to improve (with individual business persistency improving more than group business persistency). The Society of Actuaries reports that voluntary lapse rates continue to decrease (persistency improvement), with overall results, all policy years combined, for the 2005–2007 experience study at 3.8 percent versus 5.2 percent from the 2002–2004 period.[26]

- The overall individual long-term care insurance voluntary lapse rate in the current study is 2.7 percent, a noteworthy improvement from 4.3 percent and 4.2 percent for the 2002–2004 and 2000–2001 experience studies.

- Voluntary lapse rates for employer-sponsored business also improved, 6.4 percent for the current study compared to 7.5 percent for the 2002–2004 experience study. Note that, consistent with prior studies, the results for group business are based on a small number of companies.

- In general, policies with lower annual premiums exhibit higher rates of voluntary lapse than those with greater annual cost.

- Policies with marital discounts continue to exhibit lower rates of voluntary lapse than those without these discounts.

- For total termination rates, including voluntary lapses and deaths, the individual and group long-term care insurance business continues to show different patterns by policy year. Group plans experience higher rates of termination in the early policy years, corresponding to their higher voluntary lapse rates, than individual plans. However, in later policy years, this trend reverses as deaths become a more significant part of total termination rates for the older individual policyholders.[27]

## Long-Term Care Utilization

The pricing of long-term care insurance involves the projection of future benefit payments, expenses, and premium payments. Key to the projection of these amounts is an estimate of how long policyholders will retain their policies. A low persistency rate increases premiums. The need for long-term care services is modest for someone age 60, but significantly increases for those reaching age 75 and older. If an insurance company sells coverage to a group of 65-year-olds, it can anticipate that some of these individuals will not submit a claim due to death

---

26. U.S. Long-Term Care Insurance Persistency, A Joint Study Sponsored by LIMRA and The Society of Actuaries (2010).

27. *Id.* For purposes of this report, voluntary lapse includes termination for any reason other than death. This includes termination for non-payment of premium, expiration of benefits, conversion, and, in most cases, terminations for an unknown reason. This is consistent with the definition of voluntary lapse applied to past LIMRA and Society of Actuaries long-term care insurance experience studies, and allows for better comparison of results over time.

before needing long-term care services, while others will voluntarily cease to pay premiums at some point in their lives, therefore allowing the policy to terminate. The premiums paid by these former policyholders remain in a premium pool and are available to fund future claims for policies that remain in force. In effect, those who drop out of the pool subsidize those who remain in the pool.

## Mortality Table Discussion

One of the reasons that some early long-term care insurance policies were under-priced is that insurance companies used mortality tables with high death rates and assumed unrealistically high lapse rates. This was due partly to an inappropriate reliance on experience with other types of insurance. One such table used early in the long-term care insurance industry was the 1958 Commissioner's Standard Ordinary (1958 CSO) Mortality Table. Some insurance companies used this mortality table for pricing long-term care insurance, but it was designed for pricing only life insurance. The 1958 CSO Table is the mortality table developed by the Society of Actuaries Special Committee on new Mortality Tables, incorporated in the NAIC Model Standard Non-Forfeiture Law for Life Insurance. These mortality rates were increased in order to produce conservatively higher reserves to pay claims if the life insurance policyholders deceased sooner than expected. However, for long-term care insurance, the conservative assumption is that fewer policyholders will decease and more policyholders will live to use long-term care services. Thus, a more appropriate mortality table is a table used in pricing annuities, for which the conservative assumption is that policyholders will live longer and thus receive larger payouts. A paper published by the Society of Actuaries in 1995 recommended the use of the 1983 Group Annuity Mortality (1983 GAM) Table for the calculation of reserves. Regulators and many insurance companies then switched to this more appropriate table. However, this table is still proving to not be conservative enough. The Long-Term Care Experience Committee of the Society of Actuaries completed an intercompany study of the long-term care experience between 1984 and 1993, to include several insurance companies, which showed that mortality rates for long-term care policyholders dropped significantly during the period of the study, and were actually lower than the rates in the 1983 GAM Table. A more recent annuity mortality table, the 1984 GAM Table, has been published by the Society of Actuaries and shows lower mortality rates than the 1983 table. This most current annuity mortality table has not yet been adopted by the NAIC for calculating long-term care insurance reserves. A study, not yet completed as of this writing, by the Society of Actuaries entitled LTC Morbidity Improvement Study (HP171) analyzes the changes in long-term care morbidity and the impact of those changes on lifetime disability.[28] Morbidity is defined as the rate of incidence of a disease.

In addition, many insurance companies initially relied on their experience with other methods to determine their estimated lapse rates. Medical insurance

---

28. The Society of Actuaries, http://www.soa.org/files/research/projects/current-research -projects.pdf (Jan. 2011).

demographics, in particular Medicare supplement (Medigap) policyholders, were one such population used in the determination. Lapse rates for these products are often very high, especially in the first few years after purchase of the policy. It is not uncommon for 20 percent of the Medigap insurance policyholders to lapse coverage in a given year. Early experience in long-term care insurance showed a similar pattern. First, many policyholders did not understand that their premiums were building a large reserve for future costs that would be forfeited if they dropped their coverage. Secondly, there was a high degree of replacement of policies, to obtain improved benefits and policy features. Today, a reasonably conservative insurance company assumes that ultimate lapse rates will be only 2 percent or less. As companies lower their lapse rate assumptions, initial premiums will likely be higher, but the likelihood that premiums will need to be further increased will hopefully be reduced significantly.[29]

## Claim Statistics

The long-term care insurance industry has seen its share of challenges and continues to evolve. The NAIC and its member states have worked to protect consumers by instituting regulations to address issues encountered in the insurance market and to keep consumers abreast of the changes in the industry. The NAIC is an organization of the state insurance regulators from each state whose purpose is to help state legislators coordinate and share information when developing laws and regulations in the insurance industry. The NAIC functions as an advisory body as well as a service provider for the state insurance departments. Commissioners use the NAIC to pool scarce resources, to discuss issues of common concern, and to align their oversight of the industry. Each state, however, ultimately determines what actions it will take. One such example of the NAIC's involvement is The Long-Term Care Insurance Model Act and Regulation, which is a state model law that was developed by the NAIC. In 1987, the NAIC adopted the Long-Term Care Insurance Model Act followed by the Long-Term Care Insurance Model Regulation in 1988. These models were adopted to assist states in developing a regulatory structure for the oversight of long-term care insurance. In the 1990s, state regulators witnessed a period of adjustment in the market as insurance companies refined their assumptions and adjusted the premiums accordingly. Many states saw insurance companies impose significant rate increases, and the result was that many policyholders could not afford to retain the policies, resulting in lapsed insurance policies.[30] Although insurance companies need to charge sufficient premiums to remain solvent and to pay claims, state regulators seek to make

---

29. Allen Schmitz & Daniel Nitz, Long-Term Care Insurance Valuation: An Industry Survey of Assumptions and Methodologies (Dec. 2009).

30. *Long-Term Care Insurance: An Evolving Industry, S. Spec. Comm. on Aging and the S. Comm. on Homeland Security and Government Affairs, Subcomm. on Oversight of Government Management, The Federal Workforce, and the District of Columbia* (Oct. 14, 2009) (testimony of Mary Beth Senkewicz, Deputy Insurance Commissioner, Life & Health Florida Office of Insurance Regulation).

sure that consumers are treated fairly in the pricing of the policies. Federal law subsequently required that consumer protections contained in the NAIC models be applied to tax-qualified long-term care insurance policies beginning in 1996. Since then, numerous improvements to the models have been made to address the unique challenges in the long-term care insurance industry, to include

+ rate stability;
+ suitability of products;
+ loss ratio requirements; and
+ consumer disclosures.

## National Association of Insurance Commissioners (NAIC) Long-Term Care Insurance Model Act and Regulation

In an attempt to prevent the continuation of sizable rate increases and to mitigate the need for future rate increases, the NAIC developed and adopted rate stabilization standards in 2000 as part of revisions to the NAIC LTC Insurance Model Regulation, which

+ added supplemental requirements for consumer disclosures;
+ changed the minimum loss ratio requirement from 60 percent to 58 percent of the original premiums filed; and
+ established 85 percent loss ratios for rate increases.

To further explain the loss ratio changes, prior to 2000, long-term care insurance companies were required to meet a minimum loss ratio of 60 percent, meaning that 60 percent of the total premium had to be applied toward payment of claims. In 2000, the NAIC changed this requirement to 58 percent of the original premiums filed; however, if a company increases the premium, it will then need to meet an 85 percent loss ratio. This was intended to create a strong disincentive for companies to underprice their products initially to gain market share. Following each premium rate increase, the company is required to file subsequent experience with the state insurance commissioner for three years. If the increase appears excessive, the commissioner may require the insurance company to reduce premiums or adopt other measures, such as reducing its administrative costs to minimize the cost to policyholders. If premiums increase above a given level for a majority of a policyholder class based on their age, the company is required to file a plan for improved administration and claims processing, or demonstrate that appropriate claims processing procedures are in effect.

In summary, the NAIC Long-Term Care Insurance Model Act and Regulation sought to better protect consumers from rate instability in several ways. As amended in August of 2000, the model act and regulation financially penalizes insurance companies that intentionally underprice policies and, furthermore, allows state regulators to prohibit insurers that repeatedly engage in such behavior from selling policies in their state. In addition, the new model requires greater disclosure of premium increases and provides policyholders more options when their premiums are increased. These changes were applied prospectively, with more than half of the states and several insurance companies adopting the new standards.[31]

More recently, the NAIC developed the NAIC Guidance Manual for Rating Aspects of the Long-Term Care Insurance Model Regulation in 2009. This manual provides regulators additional information and interpretation of the 2000 Model Act and Regulations. While it is not a legally binding document, the "purpose" section of the guidance manual states that "it is anticipated that insurers will review this material in order that they make the filing process as expeditious as possible."[32] Actuaries may refer to the guidance manual as appropriate in preparing the "actuarial certification" for the long-term care products they are filing. The 2000 Model Act and Regulation presents a significant departure from the traditional rate regulations associated with long-term care insurance. Most significant is the departure from loss ratio requirements applied to the insurance company's policy form and certified by the actuary at the time of initial filing. In place of loss ratio requirements, the actuary is now required to provide a written certification that several conditions have been met. Another significant departure from previous premium rate regulation was in the requirements the actuary must satisfy at the time of a request for a premium increase on in-force business subject to Section 20 of the 2000 Model Act and Regulation. The requirements are different for business being sold under the original Model Act and Regulation, the single lifetime loss ratio requirement, and the 2000 Model Act and Regulation.[33] These new requirements include an actuarial certification, a supporting actuarial memorandum, stating that the revised premiums are sufficient under moderately adverse conditions and no further in-force premium increases are anticipated. In addition to the certification, the actuary must provide several other requirements, including

- ♦ a requirement to justify the in-force premium increase through projections of claims and premiums;
- ♦ disclosure of the original assumptions that were not met therefore causing the premium rate increase request, as well as other disclosures; and
- ♦ certification that the new premium schedule meets a loss ratio requirement on both the original and increased premiums.

Premium instability causes problems for insurance departments, insurance companies, and advisors. Many actuaries, particularly those that work for an insurance department, feel that rate stabilization should be the top priority during the design of a long-term care insurance product, if for no other reason than that many consumers are on fixed incomes and cannot afford rate increases. While

31. The Society of Actuaries, Annual Health Meeting (June 29, 2010).

32. National Association of Insurance Commissioners, Guidance Manual for Rating Aspects of The Long-Term Care Insurance Model Regulation (2009).

33. American Academy of Actuaries, Health Practice Council Practice Note, http://www.actuary .org/pdf/practnotes/health_ltci_03.pdf (May 2003).

this may sound good to the consumers, the simple fact remains that overall claim experience to base premium rates is underdeveloped. With the increasing longevity and the growing number of older Americans in the population, it could be a long time before there is more significant continuity and stability in long-term care insurance premiums.

The NAIC continues to be an advocate for the consumer. In 2010, the NAIC developed a claim review process that gives claimants access to a helpful advocate if the insurance company denies a claim.

## Conclusions

Long-term care insurance helps pay for the medical expenses that no other source of insurance addresses. It can avoid depleting both income and assets. It is often the best choice for many consumers. Simply stated, the policyholder pays a budgeted premium today for a long-term care insurance plan that can provide payment for expenses when needed.

- The client sets aside dollars today and transfers the larger liability to a third party, an insurance company.
- Health buys the insurance; money pays the premiums.
- The longer the client lives, the higher the chance it will be needed.
- The best time to buy is before it is needed.

Even though it is one of the newer insurance products on the market, long-term care insurance provides

- flexibility and choice;
- control;
- independence;
- security;
- wealth care;
- wealth protection;
- legacy;
- tax protection; and
- a shield for family members.
    - It allows family members to maintain control of the type and quality of care being delivered.
    - Family members can be part of the caregiving plan on their own terms.
    - Long-term care insurance is sold to families.

# Legislation Affecting Long-Term Care Insurance

**5**

THE RESPONSIBILITY OF PROVIDING long-term care has fallen primarily on either family members who provide unpaid care or on the government's means-tested entitlement program, Medicaid. With funding split between the federal government and tax revenue from each state, Medicaid is the largest single payment source for professional long-term care services in America.[1]

## FIGURE 5-1

### Distribution of Medicaid Enrollees

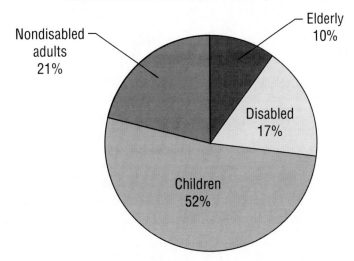

Source: Levin-Scherz, Jeff, http://managinghealthcarecosts.blogspot.com, and The Henry J. Kaiser Family Foundation, 2011.

---

1. Kaiser Commission on Medicaid and the Uninsured, The Henry J. Kaiser Family Foundation (Nov. 2006), http://www.kff.org/about/kcmu.cfm.

Long-term care consumers are a diverse population whose spending and enrollment patterns vary widely across different types of service settings. These differences reflect a number of factors including use of long-term services and the balance between institutional and community-based care, the manner in which acute and other supportive services are used, and whether Medicaid enrollees also have Medicare coverage. The second largest payment source is Medicare, which only pays in certain limited circumstances and has well-known fiscal pressures of its own.[2]

Longevity is increasing, baby boomers are reaching retirement age, and government programs such as Medicaid, Medicare, and Social Security are being challenged by difficult economic realities. Twenty-seven percent of all Medicaid spending is on the elderly and disabled, 55 percent of all Medicaid spending is on long-term care facilities, and Medicaid pays for almost half of all nursing home care in the country.[3] Awareness of the significance of long-term care planning and creating a plan is of unsurpassed importance.[4]

## FIGURE 5-2

### Medicaid Spending
(Billions)

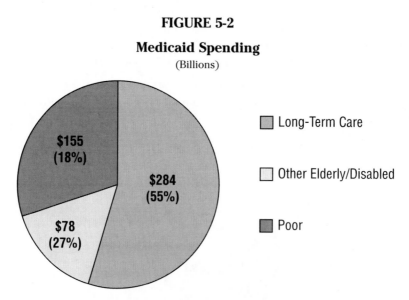

Source: Levin-Scherz, Jeff, http://managinghealthcarecosts.blogspot.com, and The Henry J. Kaiser Family Foundation, 2011.

The potential addition of baby boomers to the increasing number of Medicaid beneficiaries, due to the growing ranks of uninsured Americans and those with disabilities, has presented financing issues for state Medicaid programs. States that currently spend the least on long-term care are facing the greatest increase

---

2. National LTC Network, Guide to CLASS and Long Term Care Planning, http://www.comfortltc.com/Portals/2/CLASS-Guide-1st-ed%5B1%5D.pdf (2010).

3. Kaiser Family Foundation, Medicaid Resource Book (2003).

4. This chapter draws in part from Harley Gordon, Certification in Long-Term Care Course Handbook, Sections C, D (Release 8.0, Corporation for Long-Term Care Certification 2009), and from Harley Gordon, In Sickness & In Health: Your Sickness—Your Family's Health, Chapters 5, 6 (Financial Strategies Press 2007).

in demand.[5] While it may be reasoned that cutting benefits and reducing the federal government's commitment to Medicaid will ease the financial burden of this expansion, this action could in fact undermine the needed benefits for individuals with significant health care needs—those individuals who really need financial assistance and have minimal assets.

Private long-term care insurance has been of particular interest to legislators as a way of curbing expenditures or dependence on Medicaid and the loss of assets that often occurs in the event of a long-term care need. Favorable long-term care insurance legislation is expected to encourage more people to purchase long-term care insurance, either individually or through their employers. Active legislation, proposed and enacted, encourages individuals to finance their health care needs prior to needing long-term care. This is anticipated to lower the number of future Medicaid enrollees and allow people to stretch their own financial resources.

## Legislative Issues

The following is a historical timeline of legislative action concerning long-term care insurance:

1965—Pub. L. No. 89-97, Social Security Act of 1965: Established Medicare benefits.

1980—Medicare Secondary Payer Act of 1980: Established to reduce the costs associated with the Medicare system.

1980s–1993—Long-Term Care Insurance Model Act and Regulation: Developed to promote the availability of coverage, protect applicants from unfair or deceptive sales or enrollment practices, facilitate public understanding and comparison of coverage, and facilitate flexibility and innovation in the development of long-term care insurance.

1985—Medicare Catastrophic Coverage Act: Added a drug benefit to Medicare and limited out-of-pocket expenses. The Act was repealed in 1989.

1988—Pub. L. No. 100-360, Medicare Catastrophic Coverage Act of 1988: Represents the first significant regulation of Medicaid. Asset and trust transfers became more stringently defined.

1989—Pub. L. No. 101-234, Medicare Catastrophic Coverage Repeal Act of 1989: Repealed Medicare Catastrophic Coverage Act.

---

5. J. Holahan & A. Ghosh, *Understanding the Recent Growth in Medicaid Spending, 2000–2003*, HEALTH AFFAIRS (Jan. 26, 2005).

1993—Pub. L. No. 103-66, Omnibus Reconciliation Act of 1993: Created stricter asset and trust look-back period and allowed four states to offer the first LTC Partnership pilot programs in the nation.

1996—Pub. L. No. 104-191, Health Insurance Portability and Accountability Act: Defined long-term care insurance triggers for benefits to be payable as a loss of two of six activities of daily living (ADLs) due to physical or cognitive impairment, and enacted tax-qualified policy status allowing favorable tax treatment of long-term care insurance.

1997—Pub. L. No. 105-33, Balanced Budget Act of 1997: Enacted to reduce Medicare spending. Reduced payments to health service providers such as hospitals, doctors, and nurse practitioners. However, some of those changes to payments were restored by subsequent legislation in 1999 and 2000.

2000—National Association of Insurance Commissioners Model LTC Regulations Act: Adopted a new regulatory approach intended to encourage stronger state legal protections, expanded the authority of regulators, and guided state regulators in overseeing rates.

2003—Pub. L. No. 108-173, Medicare Prescription Drug, Improvement, and Modernization Act: Allowed for a standalone Medicare prescription drug program and a pilot program for national and state background checks on "direct patient access" employees of long-term care facilities or providers.

2005—Pub. L. No. 109-171, Deficit Reduction Act of 2005: Created more restrictive asset transfer rules for Medicaid and allowed LTC Partnership program to expand to any state. Established new rules for the treatment of annuities, including a requirement that the state be named as the remainder beneficiary. Allowed Continuing Care Retirement Communities (CCRCs) to require residents to spend down their declared resources before applying for medical assistance. Set forth rules under which an individual's CCRC entrance fee is considered an available resource. Required all states to apply the "income first" rule to community spouses who appeal for an increased resource allowance based on their need for more funds invested to meet their minimum income requirements. Authorized states to include home and community-based services as an optional Medicaid benefit. Previously, states had to obtain a waiver to provide such services.

2006—Pub. L. No. 109-280, Patient Protection Act of 2006: Excluded from gross income (i) any charge against the cash value of an annuity contract, or (ii) the cash surrender value of a life insurance contract made as payment for coverage under a qualified long-term care insurance contract that is part of, or a rider on, such annuity or life insurance contract if the investment in the contract is reduced, but not below zero. Excluded from gross income direct distributions from governmental retirement plans to pay for health and long-term care insurance premiums for retired public safety officers.

2010—Pub. L. No. 111-152, Community Living Assistance Services and Support Provisions in the Patient Protection and Affordable Care Act and Health Care and Education Reconciliation Act of 2010: Created a voluntary, federally administered, consumer-financed program. This program was never launched due to financial design flaws.

## Health Insurance Portability and Accountability Act of 1996 (HIPAA)

As previously introduced in Chapter 4, the Health Insurance Portability and Accountability Act of 1996 (HIPAA) changed the way the health care industry and medical insurance were administered, providing the first nationally recognized regulations for the use and disclosure of an individual's health information. HIPAA legislation affects long-term care facilities and medical treatment of disabled individuals by including provision for administrative simplification that requires the development of standards for the electronic exchange of health care information. Administrative simplification also requires rules to protect the privacy of personal health information, the establishment of security requirements to protect personal health information, and the development of standard identifiers. The three main areas of HIPAA compliance for health care providers are:

- ♦ Electronic Data Interchange (EDI)—Requires common format and data structure be used when exchanging specific transaction types, code sets, and identifiers electronically.
- ♦ Patient Privacy—Requires covered entities to have formal policies and plans regarding who has the right to access patient identifiable health information.
- ♦ Security—Requires covered entities that maintain or transmit patient identifiable data to develop formal methods to safeguard the integrity, confidentiality, and availability of electronic data.

According to the Center for Medicare and Medicaid Services (CMS) website, covered entities are those businesses that furnish, bill, or receive payment for health care in the normal course of business and conduct covered transactions transmitted in electronic form such as by fax or electronic submission. In addition, those involved with an individual's Personal Health Information (PHI), and also involved in the health care community, such as insurance agencies and insurance companies, must comply with HIPAA.

HIPAA's impact on long-term care insurance is explained throughout this guide. HIPAA standardized long-term care insurance with enhanced consumer protection and rate stabilization features. The legislation set standards for a long-term care insurance policy to be considered federally qualified. HIPAA established insurance carrier rules that, for example, guaranteed renewability of insurance policies, defined the scope of coverage, and set criteria individuals must meet before benefits can be paid. It also established the tax treatment of employer and employee expenditures on federally qualified insurance policy premiums.[6] Passage of this bill demonstrated government's clear consensus that insurance would, and should, become a key means of financing long-term care. HIPAA's focus on insurance was revolutionary. Just six years earlier, the political process was seriously considering long-term care coverage through national health insurance. Less than a decade before its passage, Congress held hearings in which it criticized long-term care insurance. After much controversy over a national health insurance plan, Congress compromised. It decided that any discussion of future long-term care financing must include the insurance industry. It looked at the patchwork of benefits, triggers for benefits, and contractual language, and concluded that more standardization would be best. Its debate was similar to the efforts a decade earlier to standardize Medicare supplements.

A thorough explanation of the standards set forth in the legislation can be found in Chapter 4 under the section Tax-Qualified versus Non-Tax-Qualified Insurance Policies. The favorable tax treatment of tax-qualified long-term care insurance policies will be reviewed in Chapter 6.

## Deficit Reduction Act of 2005 (DRA)

As described in Chapters 3 and 4, the Deficit Reduction Act of 2005 (DRA) was enacted with the intent to generate massive federal entitlement reductions, in particular to the Medicaid system. Medicaid offers an important safety net for people with disabilities and others who do not have access to private insurance to cover their health care needs. Provisions in the DRA related to Medicaid premiums and cost sharing, benefits, and asset transfers make up about half of the savings expected from the DRA and have the most significant implications for beneficiaries.

Specifically related to long-term care insurance planning, the DRA lifted the 1993 moratorium on expanding state partnership long-term care insurance policies. The objective of the Long-Term Care Partnership Program, as it is officially called, is to use Medicaid's safety net as an incentive for middle income Americans

---

6. Enid Kassner, *Long-Term Care Insurance and the New Tax Law*, http://research.aarp.org/health /fs7r_ltclaw.html (Feb. 1998); Stephan R. Leimberg & John J. McFadden, Tools and Techniques of Employee Benefit and Retirement Planning 365–66 (7th ed. 2001).

to purchase long-term care insurance and, by doing so, encourage them to financially prepare for the risk of needing long-term care. This, in turn, is expected to help delay or avoid the potential need for Medicaid to be burdened with paying for the policyholder's long-term care expenses. In the partnership program, states guarantee that if benefits in a partnership policy do not sufficiently cover the cost of care, the policyholder will qualify for Medicaid under modified eligibility rules that allow a pre-specified amount of assets to be disregarded from the Medicaid asset test. However, the policyholder must meet the other Medicaid eligibility rules. This is generally referred to as "asset protection" in the context of the partnership program.

"Partnership-qualified" long-term care insurance policies must meet special requirements that differ somewhat from state to state. Most states require partnership policies to offer comprehensive benefits, cover institutional and home care services, be tax-qualified, provide certain specific consumer protections, and include state-specific provisions for inflation protection. Often the only difference between a partnership-qualified policy and other long-term care insurance policies sold in a state is the amount and type of inflation protection required by the state. The pricing may vary between partnership-qualified and non-partnership policies from state to state. Some states do not charge a different premium for a partnership-qualified policy, whereas other states may charge more or less for a partnership-qualified policy.

Partnership policies must be certified by the state as meeting the specific requirements for the Long-Term Care Partnership Program. State insurance departments are responsible for ensuring that individuals who sell partnership policies are trained and understand how these policies relate to public and private coverage options.

The expansion of the Long-Term Care Partnership Program made possible by the DRA does not, for the most part, call for alterations in how Medicaid is administered. However, there are key aspects of Medicaid eligibility rules that states must consider when adopting a partnership program. For the purposes of this guide, we will briefly review aspects an advisor needs to consider with regard to partnership policies and Medicaid planning. For more comprehensive information, we recommend the reader consult with an elder law attorney who specializes in this discipline.

### Asset Protection

The asset protection feature of the partnership program is an incentive for potential insurance policy purchasers, as stated previously, because it allows policyholders to retain a pre-specified amount of assets and still be eligible for Medicaid benefits if, and when, additional long-term care coverage is needed. Medicaid would begin providing benefits beyond what the insurance policy provided. Without the asset protection provision of the partnership program, a person with limited means may not choose to purchase a long-term care insurance policy.

The dollar-for-dollar asset protection provision specified by the DRA is based on the practices from the original partnership states: California, Connecticut, Indiana, and New York. Under those state programs a policyholder was, and still is, allowed to keep an amount of assets equal to the amount the insurance policy pays toward the policyholder's long-term care expenses. To provide an example, if a policyholder has a partnership-qualified long-term care insurance policy and receives $100,000 in benefits while on claim, and applies for and is eligible for Medicaid, the policyholder is able to retain $100,000 worth of assets over and above the state's Medicaid asset threshold. Without a partnership-qualified long-term care insurance policy in force, in most states, the asset threshold is $2,000 for a single person. Asset thresholds for married couples are typically more generous.[7] The assets protected are over and above any other asset that would normally be exempt, or non-countable, in the Medicaid eligibility determination process. Because these policies must include inflation protection, the amount of the benefits received can be higher than the amount of insurance protection originally purchased.

## Asset Transfers

Because of the DRA, the rules for transferring assets to gain Medicaid eligibility extended the look-back period from three to five years, and adjusted the start date for the penalty period to the date of the Medicaid application. As a result, it became more difficult and costly for an individual to transfer assets in order to gain Medicaid eligibility. This can be especially important for an advisor who is considering Medicaid planning as part of the long-term care plan. If a person transfers assets, then he or she must pay out of pocket an amount equal to the amount he or she transferred, thus defeating the purpose of the transfer.

The DRA added new rules regarding annuities that applicants for Medicaid-covered long-term care services must meet in order to obtain Medicaid eligibility. Applicants are defined as persons applying for nursing facility care, a level of care in any institution equivalent to that of nursing facility services, and home and community-based services furnished under section 1915(c) or (d) waivers. The law requires individuals, spouses, or their representatives to provide a disclosure and description of any interest the applicant or the community spouse may have in an annuity, regardless of whether the annuity is irrevocable or is treated as an asset.[8]

## Home Equity

The DRA designates anyone with home equity value above $500,000 disqualified for Medicaid eligibility. Each state, however, is given the ability to increase the

---

7. U.S. Department of Health and Human Services, National Clearinghouse for Long Term Care Information, Medicaid Eligibility Requirements (Apr. 1, 2011), http://www.longtermcare.gov/LTC/Main_Site/index.aspx.

8. CONGRESSIONAL RESEARCH SERVICE, MEDICAID COVERAGE FOR LONG-TERM CARE: ELIGIBILITY, ASSET TRANSFERS, AND ESTATE RECOVERY, http://aging.senate.gov/crs/medicaid18.pdf (Jan. 31, 2008).

amount of permitted home equity to an amount not in excess of $750,000. Additionally, homeowners have the ability to reduce their equity through a reverse mortgage or home equity loan. The goal of this provision is to encourage the use of home equity to pay for needed care. It is also intended to motivate people with significant home equity to purchase long-term care insurance so their home is not at risk if care is needed.

The Medicaid entitlement program is not uniform from state to state. It is not possible to predict what the program will look like in the future. It does, however, represent a safety net needed by those with low income or those who are unable to afford the cost of long-term care services. This latter, broader constituency includes many people who in fact could cover their own long-term care expenses but do not have enough resources to guarantee never needing the Medicaid safety net. The Long-Term Care Partnership Program offers consumers a way to financially prepare for their long-term care expenses while still having the assurance that the safety net will be there for them if needed. The risk of impoverishment is greatly reduced because those with a qualified long-term care partnership insurance policy can have confidence that their assets will not need to be totally depleted before such assistance is available. Partnership programs help both individuals and the states. For individuals, it allows them to receive and pay for services they need without having to spend all of their assets. For the state, it can decrease the amount of Medicaid dollars used for long-term care services.

Some important factors to consider when analyzing qualified long-term care partnership insurance policies include the following:

♦ It is important to know if the long-term care insurance policy is a partnership-qualified policy or not, because they can be the same as non-partnership policies. A partnership-qualified policy is one that is certified by the state, and it must include the level of inflation protection coverage set by the state. Only if the policy is qualified as a partnership policy will an individual be eligible for certain asset protection if and when he or she applies for Medicaid.

♦ Policies issued prior to a state partnership program's effective date will not be considered partnership-qualified; however there are circumstances under which a policyholder may be able to exchange a policy he or she previously purchased for one that is partnership-qualified.

♦ It is important to buy the partnership-qualified policy from an agent who is specially trained to sell that type of coverage. States with partnership programs have additional educational requirements for agents who wish to sell partnership policies.

♦ It is important to note that eligibility for Medicaid is not automatic. An individual must still apply and meet the income, functional, and general eligibility requirements of the Medicaid program in his or her state. The long-term care services provided by Medicaid vary by state and may not be the same as the services an individual is eligible to receive under his or her private partnership long-term care insurance policy. For example, many state Medicaid programs do not pay for room and board costs in an assisted living facility even if a care recipient is also receiving personal care.

♦ States that have partnership programs are automatically considered to have reciprocity with each other and to honor the certain asset protection a policyholder earned under a partnership policy that he or she purchased in a different state. However, states can opt out of this requirement at any time.

The following map shows which states are not offering Long-Term Care Partnership Programs and are offering long-term care partnership policies as of April 7, 2011. To obtain more information on a particular state's program including which insurance agents are selling partnership policies, or to find out if a state is planning to offer a partnership program, contact the state's Department of Insurance.

**FIGURE 5-3**

**States without Long-Term Care Partnership Programs**

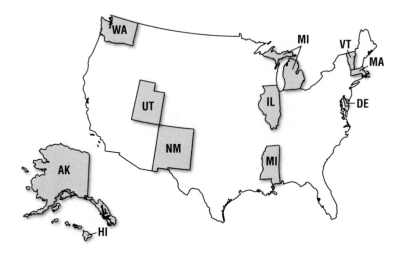

# Pension Protection Act of 2006 (PPA)

Under the Pension Protection Act of 2006 (PPA), as introduced in the *Linked Products* section of Chapter 4, favorable tax treatment provisions were implemented for long-term care insurance beginning January 1, 2010, which will be discussed in Chapter 6. These provisions are expected to have a substantial impact on consumer planning for long-term care events. The PPA not only provides tax clarification of linked long-term care insurance products, but also provides favorable tax treatment of the long-term care insurance premiums using life insurance or annuity cash values.

Before the PPA, the Internal Revenue Service (IRS) viewed a life insurance policy with a long-term care insurance component (a linked product) as two separate contracts; therefore linked product policyholders could receive an IRS Form 1099 for the long-term insurance care costs paid within the life insurance contract. Effective January 1, 2010, the PPA clarified that the long-term care insurance cost can be paid on a tax-free basis for linked benefit life and annuity policies purchased on or after January 1, 1997. In addition, the PPA states that long-term care insurance benefits paid from a linked annuity policy purchased on or after January 1, 1997 are tax-free, as long as the benefit does not exceed the greater of the actual cost of long-term care or that tax year's daily benefit cap prescribed in HIPAA for taxation purposes. Also, as with combination life and long-term care insurance policies, the internal transfer to pay the long-term care insurance cost in an annuity with long-term care insurance is tax-free.

The underlying message of these changes is that Congress realizes that there need to be stronger incentives for individuals to plan for their future long-term care expenses. The provisions of the Pension Protection Act of 2006 provide financial motivation for individuals to make use of additional financial tools to plan for long-term care.

## Conclusions

As the number of elderly Americans increases, long-term care needs and expenses are likely to escalate. Many believe that private long-term care insurance can and should play a more significant role in the financing of home care, community care, and facility services. Broader expenditure for long-term care insurance can remove the burden from individuals and the social insurance system. Without long-term care insurance, individuals most often are unprepared to pay for such care out of their own pocket and therefore are reliant on the social insurance system, which often serves as a default financier of long-term care services.

Like many financial experts, legislators are aware that the current system of paying long-term care services primarily with Medicaid, an underfunded entitlement program, is unsustainable. Along with government incentives for individuals, families, and employers to plan for long-term care expenses, the federal and state government's message is clearly stating that the responsibility and, to a large degree, the funding ultimately lie with individuals and their families.

# Taxation Issues Affecting Long-Term Care Insurance 6

Due to the same demographic changes that threaten the financial health of Social Security, Medicare, and Medicaid, the public funding of long-term care services will face increasing pressure in the years to come. Private long-term care insurance provides advance funding of long-term care expenses. This differs from the predominately pay-as-you-go approach underlying Medicaid and Medicare. The primary appeal to legislators of increased private long-term care insurance is the prospect of pre-funding a substantial part of the inevitable societal burden predicted for the baby boomer generation's need for long-term care. A secondary appeal is that a substantial share of the funding responsibility would shift from the government to the individual.

A tax policy that provides incentives for private long-term care insurance is one way to ease the financial pressure and increase the availability of long-term care coverage to those who need it. The legislation allowing for the favorable tax treatment of long-term care insurance products has been reviewed in previous chapters; this chapter will explain the tax allowances of such legislation.[1]

---

1. This chapter draws in part from Harley Gordon, Certification in Long-Term Care Course Handbook, Sections C, D (Release 8.0, Corporation for Long-Term Care Certification 2009), and from Harley Gordon, In Sickness & In Health: Your Sickness—Your Family's Health, chapter 6 (Financial Strategies Press 2007).

# Federal Tax Incentives

Federal tax policy is unavoidably intertwined with public policy considerations. The use of federal tax policy to create incentives for the purchase of private long-term care insurance is based on one or more of the following public policy objectives:

- The societal burden for long-term care as baby boomers age is great, and must be pre-funded now or paid as the costs are incurred later at a much higher price and spread over fewer available funding sources.
- Individuals need to plan for and pre-fund future long-term care expenses.
- Education, awareness, and understanding of long-term care needs and the potential role of private long-term care insurance are currently limited and need to be expanded for the public's benefit.
- Government expenditures and programs for long-term care should be based primarily on criteria of need, coverage, and cost, according to the American Academy of Actuaries.
- Pre-funding will minimize government risk for future unexpected and uncontrolled expenditures and maximize availability and quality of care for the truly disadvantaged.

Given the need to pre-fund future long-term care costs, the question is how to best accomplish this goal. Congress showed, through passage of the Health Insurance Portability and Accountability Act of 1996 (HIPAA), that private insurance is the suitable method of pre-funding long-term care expenses.

## *Health Insurance Portability and Accountability Act of 1996 (HIPAA)*

Under the Health Insurance Portability and Accountability Act of 1996 (HIPAA), premiums for tax-qualified long-term care insurance policies were given favorable tax treatment similar to that of accident and health insurance premiums.[2] Deductibility of the premium payment depends on which type of taxpayer (an individual or entity) is claiming the deduction. Furthermore, the taxpayer's method of accounting (cash or accrual) determines the timing of the deduction.[3] Limited premium deductions available for the following taxpayers are based on age:[4]

- non-self-employed individuals
- self-employed individuals
- partners in a partnership
- owners of more than 2 percent of the shares in S corporations

---

2. I.R.C. § 7702B(a)(1).
3. Treas. Reg. § 1.461-1(a)(1), (a)(2).
4. I.R.C. § 213(d)(10).

The deductible amount for these taxpayers is called the "eligible premium" and is included among eligible medical expenses for deduction.[5]

The following provisions are included in the HIPAA legislation:

♦ Employer premium contributions to qualified long-term care insurance policies are excludable from employee income,[6] even if the contributions exceed the age-based eligible premium limitations.[7] Employer contributions made under Internal Revenue Code (IRS) Section 125 plans, cafeteria plans, or flexible spending account (FSA) arrangements are not excludable. Employers may deduct their qualified premium contributions as trade or business expenses.

♦ Self-employed individuals may deduct qualified long-term care insurance premiums as health insurance expenses, under special rules with specified maximum limits.

♦ Tax-free distributions from health savings accounts may be used to pay qualified long-term care insurance premiums up to specified maximum limits.

♦ Qualified long-term care insurance premiums not covered by the first three provisions stated above are deductible from income as itemized medical expenses, to the extent that such expenses exceed 7.5 percent of adjusted gross income (AGI), with specified maximum limits. The aggregate of the eligible portion of all medical insurance premiums, including the eligible portion of the long-term care insurance premium, and unreimbursed medical expenses must exceed 7.5 percent of AGI. The amount in excess of 7.5 percent of AGI is deductible from gross income on Schedule A.[8]

The maximum limits for the annual amount of qualified long-term care insurance premium eligible for the tax-favored treatment in the provisions, as stated above, are indexed for inflation and increase with age. Because of the limit restrictions, only a limited percentage of taxpayers can utilize any of the tax incentives. Other tax incentives, including full deductibility by way of an above-the-line tax deduction mechanism, were not adopted in order to minimize lost tax revenue. Additionally, several bills were introduced in Congress from 2001 to 2004 to simplify the deductibility of premiums. The most popular would have permitted premiums to be deducted from adjusted gross income, similarly to IRA contributions, and not as part of the medical deduction; it would also not limit the deduction in accordance with age. Nevertheless, HIPAA clarified the tax-free receipt of qualified long-term care insurance proceeds and increased public awareness of private long-term care insurance. Refer to the Addendums in the back slot of the Guide for the most recent federal tax rules.

---

5. *Id.*
6. *Id.* § 152.
7. *Id.* § 106(a).
8. *Id.* § 213(d).

## Pension Protection Act of 2006 (PPA)

Chapter 4 discussed linked products and the Pension Protection Act of 2006 (PPA), which provides new tax benefits for certain long-term care insurance and long-term care insurance combination products, also known as linked products, asset based plans, or hybrid products. These new tax benefits apply to policies issued in 1997 or later, with the benefits starting in 2010 or later.

Although long-term care insurance riders have existed on life insurance and annuity riders for several years, the tax treatment has generally been significantly less favorable. Life insurance policies have generally provided for coverage by imputing income to the contract holder for long-term care insurance premiums that were deducted from the insurance cash value. Annuity contracts, on the other hand, have tended to simply credit any long-term care insurance benefits directly to the annuity cash value, forcing the beneficiary to still take an annuity withdrawal, with the associated ordinary income-gains-first treatment accorded under Internal Revenue Code (IRC) Section 72(e)(2)(B), and pay taxes accordingly.

For purposes of the new provisions, all riders to life insurance or annuity contracts must be tax-qualified to receive preferential tax treatment, and 1035 exchanges will only be allowed into tax-qualified long-term care policies. Under the new IRC Section 7702B (e)(4), the riders will not be available for qualified annuities purchased under an IRC Section 401(a) employer retirement trust, such as a 401(k) plan, a 403(a) or 403(b) annuity plan, or an Individual Retirement Account (IRA). Under the new Code Section 7702B(e)(2), any payments for long-term care insurance deducted under a life insurance or annuity contract will be denied an IRC Section 213(a) medical expense deduction for premiums paid.

Even with these stipulations, the new rules of the PPA seem to allow for the best of both worlds—tax-free use of cash value to cover long-term care insurance premiums under the new IRC Section 72(e)(11), and tax-free benefits under the new IRC Section 7702B(e)(1).

A long-term care insurance rider on a life insurance and annuity policy is treated as a qualified long-term care insurance contract. All insurance companies who offer this vehicle issue only tax-qualified long-term care insurance contracts. Therefore, the taxability of benefit payments received under these policies is similar to benefits received under other tax-qualified long-term care insurance contracts. There are three key components in the PPA that impact long-term care insurance policies:

1. *Non-tax-qualified annuities with a tax-qualified linked long-term care insurance (LTCI) rider*: Tax-qualified insurance riders under a non-tax-qualified linked benefit annuity contract will be treated as a separate account. As a result, tax-qualified long-term care benefits from these products are tax-free. Long-term care insurance rider charges taken from a linked benefit annuity account value are not taxable distributions. These charges do reduce investment in the contract, but not below zero. This

may have tax implications if the contract is surrendered, or at the death of the policyholder. Charges that reduce the basis in the annuity contract cannot be deducted as long-term care insurance premiums.

2. *Life insurance with a tax-qualified linked LTCI rider*: Charges for tax-qualified long-term care insurance riders that are part of, or attached as, riders to a contract of life insurance, if subtracted from the cash value of the base contract, are not includible as income. Under prior law, they were treated as taxable distributions. Charges that reduce the cost basis in the life insurance contract cannot be deducted as long-term care insurance premiums.

3. *Traditional long-term care insurance*: Exchanges of life insurance contracts, endowment contracts, and annuity contracts for qualified long-term care insurance contracts are eligible to be treated as tax-free exchanges under IRS Section 1035(a), and tax-qualified long-term care insurance and annuity contracts do not disqualify such life insurance and annuity contracts from eligibility for such tax-free exchanges.

After December 31, 2009, the tax-free exchange rules included long-term care insurance contracts.[9] For exchanges occurring after December 31, 2009, the paragraphs of IRC Section 1035(a) read as follows:

1. a contract of life insurance for another contract of life insurance or for an endowment or annuity contract or for a qualified long-term care insurance contract; or

2. a contract of endowment insurance (A) for another contract of endowment insurance which provides for regular payments beginning at a date not later than the date payments would have begun under the contract exchanged, or (B) for an annuity contract, or (C) for a qualified long-term care insurance contract;

3. an annuity contract for an annuity contract or for a qualified long-term care insurance contract; or

4. a qualified long-term care insurance contract for a qualified long-term care insurance contract.

Thus, in 2010 and thereafter, a life insurance contract, an endowment contract, a long-term care insurance contract, or an annuity may be exchanged for a long-term care insurance contract. The new IRC Section 1035(a)(4) also allows a tax-qualified long-term care insurance policy to be exchanged for another tax-qualified long-term care policy. However, a long-term care insurance contract may not be exchanged for anything other than another long-term care insurance contract. This will be true even where a life insurance policy has a long-term care insurance rider. Under the new IRC Section 1035(b)(2) and (3), an exchange to or

---

9. Pension Protection Act of 2006 § 844(b).

from a life insurance or annuity contract that has a long-term care insurance rider to a policy that does not have such a rider will still be treated as like-kind property for exchange purposes.

For tax purposes, a long-term care insurance rider on a life insurance policy or, beginning after 2009, on an annuity contract is treated like a tax-qualified long-term care insurance policy if its coverage conforms to the tax-qualified policy definition. However, only the amount of the deposit and premium that is considered payment for the long-term care benefits may be deducted as a medical expense.

## State Tax Incentives

Recognizing that federal and state governments cannot pay the bill for America's growing long-term care needs, an increasing number of states have implemented changes to their tax codes, now offering tax incentives to encourage Americans to take personal responsibility for their future long-term care expenses. Whereas HIPAA and PPA included provisions for favorable federal tax treatment of qualified long-term care insurance contracts, now more than two-thirds of states offer either a tax deduction or a tax credit on long-term care insurance premiums. These states offer tax deductions patterned after the federal tax deductions described previously in this chapter, IRC Section 213 (d)(1)(D), which addresses qualified medical expense deductions, or tax credits. The tax credits offered typically range from 10 to 25 percent on the long-term care insurance premium paid during a given tax year, usually with a maximum limit per policy or covered individual. Currently, all states except Maryland allow an ongoing deduction or credit as long as the policyholder owns the policy and pays the premium.[10] Some states provide the state tax incentive only if a policyholder does not apply the federal tax deduction on the policyholder's tax return.

A recent report found that most policyholders of long-term care insurance did not receive tax subsidies from the federal itemized medical deduction.[11] Policyholders who do benefit from the deduction tend to be older and more financially affluent. Moreover, the deduction favors higher income policyholders because of their higher tax brackets and older policyholders because deduction limits vary by age, with older age brackets able to deduct higher premium amounts.

Conversely, while many policyholders qualify for state tax incentives, the incentives are usually minimal because of low tax rates. A handful of states offer nonrefundable tax credits that could reduce long-term care insurance costs by as much as 25 percent. However, the value of these credits is generally limited by dollar

---

10. John Hancock Insurance Company, STATE TAX INCENTIVES FOR LONG-TERM CARE INSURANCE PREMIUMS (Jan. 2011).

11. Retirement Living News (Apr. 2010), http://www.retirementliving.com/RLletterarchive_410 .html.

limits. Also, insufficient taxpayer liability may prevent policyholders from receiving the maximum possible credit.[12] Taxpayers may need to meet state-specific requirements to qualify for deductions or credits. A very useful website containing state long-term care information is http://www.usa.gov/Agencies/State_and_Territories .shtml. Refer to the Addendums in the back slot of the Guide for the most recent state tax rules.

## Tax Status Overview

Current federal tax code provides individuals, employers, and employees favorable tax treatment of premiums and benefits for qualified long-term care insurance policies. The following is an overview of the current tax code benefits for individuals and corporations, which assist in the marketability of long-term care insurance.

### Individual Deductibility Considerations

As reviewed earlier in the chapter, tax-qualified long-term care insurance premiums are considered a medical expense. For an individual who itemizes tax deductions, medical expenses are deductible to the extent that they exceed 7.5 percent of the individual's adjusted gross income (AGI). The amount of the long-term care insurance premium treated as a medical expense is limited to the eligible long-term care insurance premiums, as defined by Internal Revenue Code 213(d), based on the age of the insured individual. The portion of the long-term care insurance premium that exceeds the eligible premium is not included as a medical expense. The yearly maximum deductible amount for each individual depends on the insured's attained age at the close of the taxable year. These deductible maximums are indexed and increase each year for inflation.

- ◆ Individual taxpayers can treat premiums paid for tax-qualified long-term care insurance for themselves, their spouses, or any tax dependents, such as parents, as a personal medical expense.
- ◆ A couple, married or not, who purchases a joint policy with only one owner and two insured persons is still allowed to claim an eligible premium deduction for each insured.
- ◆ The eligible premium may be reimbursed from an Archer Medical Savings Account (Archer MSA), health savings account (HSA), or health reimbursement account (HRA)[13] without the need to itemize and without being reduced by the 7.5 percent AGI exclusion.

---

12. David Baer & Ellen O'Brien, AARP Public Policy Institute, Federal and State Income Tax Incentives for Private Long-Term Care Insurance (Nov. 2010), http://assets.aarp.org/rgcenter/ppi/econ-sec/2009-19 -tax-incentives.pdf.

13. I.R.C. §§ 220(d)(2)(B), 223(d)(2); IRS Notices 2002-45, 2004-2, 2004-50.

♦ The eligible premium is not deductible from a flexible spending account (FSA).[14]

♦ Employer-paid premiums on a qualified long-term care insurance contract are excluded from an employee's income. However, such premium payments are not deductible by the employee. Furthermore, employees may not pay premiums on long-term care insurance contracts with pre-tax funds, as long-term care insurance is excluded from the list of qualified benefits that a cafeteria plan is allowed to provide.[15]

♦ Beginning after 2009, a premium payment made from the cash value of an annuity contract or the cash surrender value of a life insurance contract is not deductible as a medical expense.

♦ Currently, tax-qualified long-term care insurance premiums may not be paid with pre-tax funds in an employer-provided cafeteria plan.[16]

Generally, benefits received from a tax-qualified long-term care insurance policy that was purchased by an individual are non-taxable and therefore excluded from AGI. Benefits paid under an indemnity policy are not taxed unless they exceed the higher of the cost of qualified long-term care or a specified limit that is indexed for inflation. The 2011 limit is $300 per day.

Long-term care insurance policy premiums paid for a parent are deductible as qualifying medical expenses for income tax purposes if the parent is a dependent of the child by IRS definition.

Premiums of tax-qualified long-term care insurance policies represent qualifying medical expenses for the purposes of the annual gift tax exclusion if they are paid directly to the insurance company.[17]

## Current Taxation for Businesses and Owners

In general, substantial corporate tax deductions are available to employer-paid qualified long-term care insurance policies by deducting premiums as a usual business expense. Employers may deduct their qualified premium contributions as trade or business expenses.

Flexibility is one of the key advantages of a corporate-sponsored long-term care insurance program, allowing for customized plans designed for select groups of employees and permitting discrimination based on title, tenure, or income. Under HIPAA, an employer-sponsored qualified long-term care insurance program is treated as an accident and health plan not subject to ERISA anti-discrimination criteria, thus allowing companies to classify plans for one employee, plans for a select group of highly compensated employees, or different plans for different classes of employees.

---

14. I.R.C. § 125(f).
15. *Id.* § 106(c).
16. *Id.* § 7702B(b)(2)(A), (B).
17. *Id.* § 2503(e)(2)(B).

However, if a C corporation creates a long-term care insurance program designed to benefit only the owners, the IRS may treat the long-term care insurance premium as a dividend to the extent of profits and income thereafter. In this case, discrimination could be justified if the employer creates a benefit plan that includes some employees and excludes others for a reason other than the fact that the employees who benefit from the plan are owners. A plan where the intent is to reward a select group of employees based on their status as employees may be acceptable even if all members of that class are also owners. Using seniority to determine who will and will not be eligible to receive the benefit can be acceptable as long as seniority is not also a threshold qualification to become an owner in the business.

Regarding non-profit organizations, long-term care insurance premiums paid for by the organization for its employees receive similar tax treatment to those provided by a C corporation.

Professional corporations are generally taxed similarly to C corporations. It is recommended to contact the state in which the entity is domiciled for specific tax qualifications.

## Self-Employed Business Owners

The tax code treats self-employed individuals, or sole proprietors, more favorably than non-owner employees. Self-employed individuals

- ♦ Can treat their long-term care insurance premium as a self-employed health insurance premium.[18] Self-employed individuals can deduct 100 percent of their out-of-pocket long-term care insurance premiums, up to the eligible premium amounts.[19] The portion of long-term care insurance premiums that exceeds the eligible premium amount is not deductible as a medical expense. The deductible amount includes eligible premiums paid for spouses and dependents.[20] They need not consider the 7.5 percent AGI threshold for deductibility of medical expenses.[21]
- ♦ Can deduct their eligible premium from business income on Form 1040 as part of the deduction for self-employed health insurance premiums.[22] The deduction is allowed whether or not the taxpayer itemizes deductions. However, the deduction is limited to
  - ○ the eligible amount;
  - ○ the extent of the proprietor's business income from that activity; and
  - ○ the extent, determined on a monthly basis, that the taxpayer and taxpayer's spouse were eligible to participate in a similar plan offered by the spouse's employer during the year.[23]

---

18. *Id.* § 162(l)(2)(C).
19. *Id.* § 162(l).
20. *Id.*
21. *Id.*
22. *Id.* §§ 162(l), 162(l)(2)(C), 213(d).
23. *Id.* §§ 162(l)(2)(A), 162(l)(2)(B), 213(d)(10)(a).

In addition, because the deduction is taken on Form 1040 rather than on Schedule C, E, or F, the deduction does not reduce business income subject to self-employment tax (Schedule SE).[24]

♦ Can deduct the eligible premiums their business paid for their spouses and tax dependents, such as parents.[25]

♦ Can deduct the entire premiums paid for employees from business income on Schedule C, E, or F, as applicable.[26] These premiums are excluded from the employees' incomes, and benefits are tax-free.[27]

♦ Can discriminate by class, offering long-term care insurance to some employee classes but not others because, in general, group long-term care insurance plans are not subject to non-discrimination rules like other plans, because they are fully insured plans.[28]

## Partnership, Limited Liability Company (LLC), S Corporation, C Corporation

Partners in a partnership, members of a limited liability company (LLC) that is taxed as a partnership, and shareholders/employees of an S corporation who own more than 2 percent of the corporation are taxed as self-employed individuals. If the partnership, LLC, or S corporation pays the long-term care insurance premium, the partner, member, or shareholder/employee includes the long-term care insurance premium in the individual's AGI, but may deduct up to 100 percent of the age-based eligible premium. It is not necessary to meet a 7.5 percent AGI threshold.

If the sole shareholder/employee purchases long-term care insurance in the shareholder's own name instead of that of the S corporation, the S corporation is not treated as a partnership and the shareholder is not treated as a partner. As such, the shareholder is not treated as self-employed and can include only eligible long-term care insurance premiums in the shareholder's itemized deductions, which are subject to the 7.5 percent AGI threshold.

## Partnerships

Partnerships may treat the payment of long-term care insurance premiums made on behalf of their partners, their partners' spouses, and their partners' tax dependents in one of two ways:

1. As a guaranteed payment, or
2. As a distribution.

---

24. *Id.* § 162(l)(4).
25. *Id.* § 162(l).
26. *Id.* § 162(a)(1).
27. Treas. Reg. § 1.106-1.
28. *Id.* §§ 1.105-5, 1.106-1.

Normally, when payment of the premium is not dependent on partnership profits and is in exchange for services rendered, the payment will be treated as a guaranteed payment.[29] Partners may deduct eligible premiums as self-employed health insurance premiums on Form 1040 as follows:

- The premium, treated as a guaranteed payment on the partnership's tax return, is reported on the partner's Form K-1 and is subject to income and self-employment taxes.
- The premium, treated as a distribution on the partnership's tax return, is reported on the partner's Form K-1 and is not subject to income tax or self-employment tax. However, it may be subject to capital gains tax if the distribution is in excess of the partner's tax basis in the partnership.[30]
- Under either alternative, the partner deducts the amount of eligible premiums as self-employed health insurance premium on Form 1040.[31] The deduction is allowed whether or not the taxpayer itemizes deductions. However, the deduction is limited to the
  ○ eligible amount;
  ○ extent of the partner's business income from that activity; and
  ○ extent, determined on a monthly basis, that the taxpayer and taxpayer's spouse were eligible to participate in a similar plan offered by the spouse's employer during the year.[32]
- The partnership can deduct the entire premiums paid for other employees from business income.[33] The premium is excluded from employee income, and benefits are tax-free.[34]
- The partnership is not subject to anti-discrimination rules. It can discriminate by class, offering the insurance to some employee classes but not others.[35]
- If the partner's spouse is on the payroll and meets the criteria for a bona fide employee, the entire premium is deductible on the partnership's Form 1065.
- Most companies offer joint long-term care insurance policies covering domestic partners, if they share living expenses. A premium paid on a policy that also covers a dependent is deductible on the partnership's Form 1065. It appears that in a domestic partner relationship, the premium is deductible if the couple meets the following criteria:

---

29. I.R.C. § 61.
30. *Id.* § 731(a)(1).
31. *Id.* §§ 162(l), 213(d)(1)(D), 213(d)(10).
32. *Id.* §§ 162(l)(2)(A), 162(l)(2)(B), 213(d)(10)(a).
33. *Id.* § 162(a).
34. Treas. Reg. § 1.106-1.
35. *Id.* § 1.105-5.

- o The dependent received over half of his or her support from the tax-payer during the tax year.[36]
- o The dependent was a member of the taxpayer's household, which the taxpayer maintained by paying more than half of the household expenses, and the dependent lived with the taxpayer during the entire tax year, in a relationship recognized by state law.[37]
- o The domestic partner cannot have gross income greater than a specified amount determined annually and indexed for inflation.[38]

## Limited Liability Company (LLC)

A limited liability company (LLC) is a state business structure that protects owners from the liabilities of their companies.

- ◆ By default, an LLC with one owner is treated for tax purposes as a sole proprietorship.
- ◆ An LLC with more than one owner is treated as a partnership.
- ◆ An LLC may even elect another tax status, including that of a C corporation or an S corporation.

## S Corporation

With respect to fringe benefits, S corporations are treated like partnerships, and shareholders who own more than 2 percent of an S corporation are treated like partners, rather than employees.[39] Those greater-than-2-percent shareholders can deduct eligible premium payments as self-employed health insurance premium on Form 1040 as follows:[40]

- ◆ The corporation may pay the entire premium and deduct it.[41] Alternatively, if the long-term care insurance contract is in the name of the greater-than-2-percent shareholder and the shareholder pays the premium from personal funds, the corporation may reimburse the shareholder, if the shareholder provides the company with adequate proof of the premium payment.[42]
- ◆ The entire premium paid, whether paid by the corporation directly or through substantiated reimbursement, is treated similarly to the way in which a guaranteed payment is reported and taxed to a partner. It is considered part of the shareholder's salary and is reported on the sharehold-

---

36. I.R.C. § 152(d)(1)(C).
37. *Id.* § 152(d)(2)(H).
38. *Id.* § 151(d).
39. *Id.* § 1372(b).
40. Rev. Rul. 91-26.
41. I.R.C. § 162(a).
42. *Id.* §§ 162(l), 213(d)(1)(D), 213(d)(10).

er's Form W-2, as well as to the IRS on the S corporation's return, Form 1120S.[43] Generally, such income will be subject to income tax but excluded from employment taxes.[44]

♦ For the greater-than-2-percent shareholder to be allowed any deduction on the shareholder's Form 1040, all of the following must have occurred:

  ○ the premium must be paid directly by the company, or the shareholder must substantiate the premiums the shareholder paid to the company and be reimbursed by it;

  ○ the premium paid or reimbursed must be reported by the company on the shareholder's Form W-2 for that year; and

  ○ the shareholder must report the premium paid or reimbursed by the S corporation as gross income on the shareholder's Form 1040.

♦ If any of these three events has not occurred, the greater-than-2-percent shareholder is not allowed a deduction for any premiums paid or reimbursed on the shareholder's Form 1040.[45] If the above events have occurred, the greater-than-2-percent shareholder may deduct the eligible premium payments as self-employed health insurance premiums on Form 1040.[46] The deduction is allowed whether or not the taxpayer itemizes deductions. However, the deduction is limited to

  ○ the eligible amount;

  ○ the extent of the shareholder's business income from that activity; and

  ○ the extent, determined on a monthly basis, that the taxpayer and taxpayer's spouse were eligible to participate in a similar plan offered by the spouse's employer during the year.[47]

♦ The corporation can deduct the entire premium paid for other employees from business income.[48] The premium is excluded from employee income, and benefits are tax-free.[49]

♦ The corporation can deduct the eligible premiums it paid for a shareholder's spouse and tax dependents, such as parents.[50]

♦ The corporation is not subject to anti-discrimination rules. It can discriminate by class, offering the insurance to some employee classes but not others.[51]

---

43. Rev. Rul. 91-26.
44. I.R.S. Notice 2008-1, 2008-2 I.R.B. 251.
45. I.R.S. Notice 2008-1, 2008-2 IRB 251.
46. I.R.C. §§ 162(l), 213(d)(1)(D), 213(d)(10).
47. *Id.* §§ 162(l)(2)(A), 162(l)(2)(B), 213(d)(10)(a).
48. *Id.* § 162(a).
49. Treas. Reg. § 1.106-1.
50. I.R.C. §§ 162(l), 162(l)(2)(C), 213(d).
51. Treas. Reg. § 1.105-5.

- Employment of a spouse or dependent parent yields no additional tax benefit because of the rule of attribution; the spouse's premium deduction is still limited to the eligible premium.[52] Premiums paid by the company for such family members must be included as wages on their Forms W-2, and the family members can deduct the amount, if they meet the other requirements of Internal Revenue Code § 162(l).

- If a shareholder's domestic partner is a bona fide employee, the shareholder can purchase a joint policy, with the domestic partner as the owner and the domestic partner and the shareholder as the insureds, and deduct the entire premium.[53]

## C Corporation

A C corporation can deduct the entire premium paid for an employee, regardless of whether the employee is a greater-than-2-percent shareholder in the corporation and regardless of the eligible premium limits.[54] The employer's method of accounting (cash or accrual) determines the timing of the deduction.

- When the employer pays the premium on a tax-qualified long-term care insurance contract covering an employee, the premium is excluded from the employee's income and, therefore, is also not subject to federal income tax withholding, Social Security, Medicare, and federal unemployment taxes.[55] However, if the employee pays for such coverage through an after-tax payroll deduction, all such taxes do apply, as tax-qualified long-term care insurance contracts are not eligible for payment from cafeteria plans.[56]

- If the employer pays a portion of the premium, the employee is able to include the balance of the premium for which he or she is responsible as a medical expense, up to the age-based eligible premium limit, and accordingly will be entitled to an itemized deduction for medical expenses that exceed 7.5 percent of AGI.

- A C corporation may deduct the long-term care insurance premiums whether the coverage is provided under a group contract or under an individual contract.

- The corporation can also deduct the entire premium paid for an employee's spouse or tax dependents, such as parents.[57]

- The corporation is not subject to anti-discrimination rules. It can discriminate by class, offering the insurance to some employee classes but

---

52. I.R.C. §§ 318, 1372.
53. *Id.* § 152(d)(1)(C).
54. *Id.* § 162(a).
55. *Id.* §§ 106, 3121(a)(2)(B), 3306(b)(2)(B); Treas. Reg. § 1.106-1.
56. I.R.C. § 125(f).
57. *Id.* §§ 162(l), 162(l)(2)(C), 213(d).

not others, or offering different benefit designs for different classes.[58] Tax rulings have stipulated that the class cannot, however, be based on stock ownership.

♦ A premium paid for a shareholder who is not an employee, other than an employee's shareholder spouse or dependent, is not tax-deductible to the corporation.

♦ The use of limited premium payments, also called accelerated premiums, can provide higher tax deductions for the corporation and enables the long-term care insurance premium to be fully paid up by the time the owner retires or sells his or her ownership in the company, with no ongoing premiums.

♦ Board resolution minutes must be drafted to adopt the long-term care insurance plan and describe who is covered for tax deductibility. To review a sample document of a corporate resolution to establish a long-term care insurance plan, please see Appendix 3.

Table 6-1 provides a summary of the tax deductibility of long-term care insurance.

### Employer Contribution Arrangement

Employer contribution arrangements are defined as the employer paying part of the premium, and the employee paying the remaining premium.

The employer receives the same federal income tax treatment on the portion of long-term care insurance premium it pays that it receives when paying the entire premium.[59] If an employer pays all or a portion of the tax-qualified long-term care premiums on behalf of an employee, the amount paid is deductible by the employer as a business expense. The deduction is not limited by the age-based limits. The entire employer contribution will also be excluded from the employee's AGI.

All employers, whether self-employed, C corporations, partnerships, LLCs, or S corporations, may deduct tax-qualified long-term care insurance premiums paid for policies owned by their employees. In the case of an S corporation, this includes employees who are also 2-percent-or-less shareholders and employees' spouses and eligible dependents without regard to the age-based eligible premium limits.[60]

In addition, partnerships, LLCs, and S corporations may deduct long-term care insurance premiums paid for policies owned, respectively, by those entities' partners, members, and greater-than-2-percent shareholders, and their spouses and eligible dependents. The entity then reports the premium as income to the owner.

---

58. Treas. Reg. § 1.105-5.
59. I.R.C. § 162.
60. *Id.* § 152.

**TABLE 6-1**
**The Tax Deductibility of Long-Term Care Insurance**

| Entity | Deductibility | Income Reporting | Discrimination Rules | Tax Treatment of Benefits |
|---|---|---|---|---|
| Individual | The lesser of the premium or the eligible premium. Medical expenses are deductible to the extent they exceed 7.5 percent of Adjusted Gross Income. | Not applicable (N/A) | N/A | Tax-Free |
| Self-Employed | The percentage of the lesser of the premium or the eligible premium is deductible as a business expense. The remaining percentage is included as a medical expense under the 7.5 percent rule. | No | None | Tax-Free |
| S Corporations Partnerships LLCs | Same as self-employed. | The portion of the premium paid by the entity on behalf of a partner is included in the partner's income. | None | Tax-Free |
| C Corporations | The entire premium is fully deductible by the corporation. | No | None | Tax-Free |

Source: All Insurance Matters, Inc. (2011).

If the employer only pays a portion of the premium, the employee can apply the balance to the employee's medical expenses, up to the age-based eligible premium limit, and will then be entitled to a deduction for medical expenses that exceed 7.5 percent of AGI.

## Health Savings Accounts (HSA)

The Medicare Act of 2003 allows individuals to create Health Savings Accounts (HSAs). Contributions to HSAs are deposited on a pre-tax basis, while withdrawals for qualified medical expenses are considered tax-free. Any growth inside an HSA is tax-free if withdrawals are made for qualified medical expenses, or tax-deferred if withdrawals are made for other purposes.

Qualified long-term care insurance premiums are a qualified medical expense.[61] As a result, an individual may use his or her HSA to pay qualified long-term care insurance premiums. Qualified long-term care insurance premiums are the eligible premiums, less the actual premiums paid and the eligible age-based premiums. Therefore, only eligible long-term care insurance premiums may be withdrawn tax-free from an HSA.

Specifications for owning an HSA include the following:

- The individual must be covered by a high-deductible health plan (HDHP), defined as having an[62]
  - annual deductible that must be a minimum dollar amount, specified for an individual and for a family, indexed annually and adjusted for inflation;
  - annual out-of-pocket limit that cannot exceed a specific threshold, specified for an individual and for a family, indexed annually and adjusted for inflation.
- The individual may not be covered under a non-high-deductible health plan (HDHP) or a plan that duplicates benefits of the individual's own plan, such as a spouse's plan through the spouse's employer.[63] However, an individual may be covered under some types of insurance that do not require high deductibles, such as a qualified long-term care insurance policy, and still own an HSA.[64]
- Deductibility for contributions to an HSA is denied when
  - the individual is claimed as a dependent on another's income tax return;[65] or
  - the individual becomes covered by Medicare.[66]
- The maximum monthly contribution amount is one-twelfth of the statutory annual maximum, specified for individuals and for families, indexed annually and adjusted for inflation.[67] These limits are decreased by aggregate contributions made to an Archer Medical Savings Accounts (Archer MSA).[68]

---

61. I.R.S. Notice 2004-50, Q & A 41.
62. I.R.C. § 223(c)(1)(A)(i).
63. *Id.* § 223(c)(1)(A)(ii).
64. *Id.* § 223(c)(1)(B)(ii).
65. *Id.* Internal Revenue Code § 223(b)(6).
66. *Id.* § 223(b)(7).
67. *Id.* § 223(a)(2).
68. *Id.* § 223(a)(4).

- Individuals who first become eligible on or before December 1 of a tax year are treated as though they had been eligible for that entire year. The individual, though, must continue to be eligible for a 12-month period beginning in December of the enrollment year; otherwise, contributions attributed to months prior to the month of enrollment will be included in taxable income and subject to a 10 percent penalty tax.
- Any other type of distribution is included in taxable income and subject to a 10 percent penalty tax.
- Individuals between ages 55 and 65 may make additional catch-up contributions.
- Unlike with flexible spending accounts, HSA balances do not have to be entirely withdrawn by the end of the year or forfeited.

## Health Reimbursement Accounts (HRA)

Reimbursements for insurance-covering medical care expenses, as defined in IRC Section 213(d), which includes qualified long-term care services and qualified long-term care insurance premiums, are allowable under a Health Reimbursement Accounts (HRA) arrangement. Although employers pay for HRAs, an HRA cannot be provided by salary reduction or IRC Section 125 plans. As such, the long-term care insurance premiums cannot be paid on a pre-tax basis through an HRA.

## Internal Revenue Code Section 125 Plans—Cafeteria Plans and Flexible Spending Accounts

Tax-qualified long-term care insurance premiums cannot be purchased with pre-tax dollars under an employer-provided cafeteria plan.[69] Nor can premium payments for tax-qualified long-term care insurance premiums be reimbursed tax-free through a flexible spending account (FSA).[70] However, long-term care insurance premiums may be paid through an HSA that is offered under an employer-provided cafeteria plan.

## Grandfathered Tax-Qualified Status

Final IRS regulations apply to "grandfathered" long-term care insurance policies issued before January 1, 1997. Certain provision changes to grandfathered long-term care insurance policies will be considered disqualifying for favorable tax status, while others will not (Table 6-2).[71]

---

69. *Id.* § 125(f).
70. *Id.* § 106(c).
71. Treas. Reg. § 1.7702B-2.

**TABLE 6-2**

| Changes Not Considered Disqualifying | Changes Considered Disqualifying |
| --- | --- |
| (WILL NOT affect tax-qualified status) | (WILL affect tax-qualified status) |
| • Reductions in Coverage (at lower premiums) | • Increase in Daily Benefit Amount |
| • Decrease in Daily Benefit Amount | • Decrease in the Length of the Elimination Period |
| • Increase in the Length of the Elimination Period | • Increase in Benefit Period/Policy Maximum Benefit Amount |
| • Decrease in Benefit Period or Policy Maximum Benefit Amount | • Addition of Currently Available Inflation or Benefit Increase Riders |
| • Deletion of Inflation or Benefit Increase Rider | |
| • Changes in Premium Mode | |
| • Addition of a Couples Discount | |

Source: Genworth Life Insurance Company.

# Conclusions

The current blend of private long-term care insurance and public long-term care systems can become more effective with additional tax incentives. Such tax incentives for private long-term care insurance can be provided to individuals and employers with the expectation that the cost to the federal and state governments will be better managed. Participation in the private system will be more likely for those who can afford it. Although tax incentives have been implemented with the expectation to increase the ownership of private long-term care insurance, there still continues to be a very large segment of the population that is not adequately insured through either the private or public system due to personal choice or lack of education about long-term care needs and costs. For these individuals, commitment to education and dedication to the long-term care insurance industry by insurance advisors is necessary.

# *Selecting a Long-Term Care Insurance Company* 7

COMPARED TO OTHER INSURANCE products, at just over three decades old, long-term care insurance is a relatively young product in the insurance industry. Many insurance companies are finding it a challenging market in which to operate because there is less data available to effectively price products and manage profits.

Choosing a company from which to purchase long-term care insurance is one of the most important decisions in the analysis, as this is a product that potentially has a very long time period before it will be utilized. To be able to pay benefits 20 to 30 years from the purchase of the policy, insurance companies must build reserves that appreciate adequately. They need to effectively price and manage risk, collect sufficient premiums, and invest the premiums wisely if they are to meet the needs of their policyholders when the policyholders need benefits, many years later.

All the provisions decided upon prior to the purchase of the long-term care insurance policy—the benefit design, premium, and tax advantages—are irrelevant if the insurance company is unable to deliver when a claim is submitted. At the time of a claim, the depth of commitment, integrity, and financial strength of the insurance company are what matter most.

## Long-Term Care Insurance Company Landscape

Respectable insurance companies draw on extensive experience to make informed business decisions. Maintaining a comprehensive risk management strategy built on targeted underwriting principles, a deep understanding of morbidity and mortality trends, and a disciplined approach to overall pricing is foundational to the success of an insurance company and its products. The long-term care insurance industry is no different. Some insurance companies have been devoted to the long-term care industry for more than 30 years, while other insurance companies are much newer to the industry. It is important to select a company that has demonstrated a strong commitment, with continued investment in the business.

## Industry Overview

Since its inception, the long-term care insurance industry has evolved in terms of product design, risk management, and how and where care is received. Recently, there has been significant action taken by long-term care insurance companies that should be carefully considered by advisors and consumers alike.

Recent studies by insurance companies, using their in-force policyholders as criteria for the studies, have provided substantially more insight than past studies. Providing over twice the amount of claims data as previous studies, with over four times the amount of data in older age groups, the studies found that as the block had matured, companies had implemented rate increases on existing blocks of business. One specific study confirmed that, with respect to morbidity, the incidence and severity of claims were significantly higher, the duration of claims was longer, and claims terminations were lower than expected. Mortality improvements observed throughout the long-term care and life insurance industry have also led to more people reaching the age where claims are more likely to occur. The conclusion is that more people used the insurance than anticipated, reinforcing the value of the product to policyholders, but at the same time creating a pricing issue.[1]

Other insurance companies have suspended sales of specific long-term care insurance products, or have decided to withdraw from participating in future long-term care insurance sales. It is clear from these actions that the long-term care insurance industry is not shielded from significant and sudden change, including pricing pressures on in-force blocks of business. While as a whole, long-term care insurance companies remain resilient and financially strong within the insurance industry, even large, diverse insurance companies are no longer immune to widespread pricing challenges that previously only affected smaller insurance companies. More than ever, the due care process of evaluating an insurance company is requisite in an advisor's insurance analysis for a client.

Many insurance companies entered the long-term care insurance market expecting quick success. However, long-term care insurance products have proven to be more difficult to market successfully to consumers than originally expected, despite an aging population and a government increasingly more reluctant and truly unable to pay for long-term care. Even with compelling data,

---

1. John Hancock Insurance Company, 2010–2011 LTC Individual Policy Rate Action Information Guide (3d ed. Mar. 2011).

long-term care insurance has not been purchased by consumers as quickly as the insurance industry anticipated. Not nearly enough individuals purchase and maintain private long-term care insurance to cover the costs associated with the product.

There are approximately eight million policyholders.[2] Given that costs for long-term care could easily reach seven figures per individual 20 or 30 years from now, that is a negligible amount of policyholders.[3] The nation's ten leading long-term care insurance companies paid over $10.8 million in daily claims benefits in 2010 according to a study conducted by the American Association for Long-Term Care Insurance (AALTCI).[4] Approximately 70 percent of Americans over age 65 are expected to require some type of long-term care services in their lifetime.[5] An increase in long-term care insurance sales will create economies of scale, allowing insurance premiums to be more affordable, as well as creating an opportunity for continued growth in the long-term care insurance industry.

## FIGURE 7-1

### Individual Long-Term Care Insurance Trends*

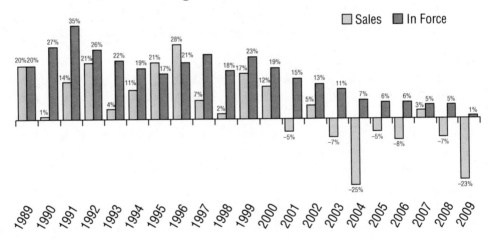

*Percent change in premium

Source: LIMRA, Individual Long-Term Care Insurance Annual Review, ongoing.

2. Jesse Slome, AMERICAN ASSOCIATION FOR LONG-TERM CARE INSURANCE, EMPLOYEE BENEFIT NEWS (Feb. 4, 2011).

3. Ron Lieber, *Your Money: Ignore Long-Term Care Planning at Your Peril*, THE NEW YORK TIMES (Nov. 4, 2010).

4. American Association for Long-Term Care Insurance, 2011 LONG-TERM CARE INSURANCE CLAIMS PAID REPORT, www.aaltci.org/news/long-term-care-insurance-association-news/long-term-care-insurance-claims-report.

5. Agencies on Aging, National Clearinghouse for Long-Term Care (Jan. 31, 2011).

## *Due Care Analysis*

The economic downturn that began in 2008 is of such proportion that everyone has been affected and has faced a level of volatility and significant change. Included in the instability is an unprecedented level of concern over insurance solvency. Interest rate risk, caused by the challenging economic environment, is of critical concern for insurance companies,[6] and long-term care insurance companies in particular. Evaluating an insurance company through a comprehensive due care analysis allows an advisor to provide clients with a suitable recommendation of an insurance company.

In the due care analysis process, it is essential to understand the insurance company's business philosophy, product strategy, and commitment to advisors, employers, and policyholders. It is important to evaluate whether the insurance company providing coverage will be able to responsibly manage its long-term care insurance business to ensure it will be able to pay claims many years into the future. The insurance company should have established, sound, and effective risk-management systems in place for monitoring the performance of its long-term care insurance portfolio. Procedures need to be in place that effectively monitor and respond to deviations in key profitability drivers, claims experience, underwriting, demographic diversity, distribution, persistency, and investment income.

### Company Size/Financial Strength

A strong financial rating is a vital part of the evaluation of the insurance company's financial stability. Financial rating service companies analyze the risks that could affect an insurance company's long-term survival in the industry. Before a decision is made about which policy to purchase, the financial ratings of the insurance company need to be considered. When considering long-term care insurance protection, the rating of the insurance company is an important piece of information to request. While these ratings do not offer a crystal ball's look into the future, they can provide valuable current and historical information.[7] As stated earlier in the chapter, if and when it is time to file a claim, possibly many years in the future, it is important to consider whether the long-term care insurance company will be able to pay the claim.

There are several large independent rating services that analyze insurance companies' financial strength. The oldest of these is A.M. Best, established in 1899. Other rating services include Standard and Poor's, Fitch Ratings, Moody's, and Weiss Ratings. The financial rating services all use various letter grades for their ratings. In addition, the state insurance departments are able to provide financial information on the insurance companies licensed to conduct business in a particular state.

---

6. John Fenton et al., Interesting Challenges for Insurers (Mar. 2011).

7. American Association for Long-Term Care Insurance, The 2011 Sourcebook for Long-Term Care Insurance Information (2011), www.AALTCI.org/ratings.

### A.M. Best

*An A.M. Best Financial Ratings Strength is an independent opinion, based on a comprehensive quantitative and qualitative evaluation, of a company's balance sheet strength, operating performance, and business profile. The rating process uses specific methodologies designed to address the life and health insurance industry. The top four ratings are A++ (Superior), A+ (Superior), A (Excellent), and A- (Excellent).*

### Standard and Poor's

*A Standard and Poor's Insurer Financial Ratings Strength is a current opinion of the financial security characteristics of an insurance organization with respect to its ability to pay under its insurance policies and contracts in accordance with their terms. This opinion does not take into account deductibles, surrender or cancellation penalties, timeliness of payment, or the likelihood of the use of a defense such as fraud to deny claims. The top four ratings are AAA (Extremely Strong), AA (Very Strong), A (Strong), and BBB (Good).*

### Fitch Ratings

*A Fitch Ratings Insurer Financial Ratings Strength (IFS Rating) provides an opinion as to the financial strength of an insurance organization and its financial capacity to meet obligations to policyholders and contract holders on a timely basis. The IFS Rating does not address the willingness of an insurance organization's management to honor its company's obligations, nor does the IFS Rating address the quality of an insurer's claims handling services. The top four ratings are AAA (Exceptionally Strong), AA+ (Very Strong), AA (Very Strong), and AA- (Very Strong).*

A.M. Best is one of the better-known insurance rating companies. Here is an overview of what the A.M. Best rating system means:

A++ and A+ (Superior): The company has demonstrated superior overall performance and has a very strong ability to meet its obligations to policyholders over a long period of time.

A and A- (Excellent): The company has demonstrated excellent overall performance and has a strong ability to meet its obligations to policyholders over a long period of time.

B++ and B+ (Very Good): The company has demonstrated very good overall performance and has a good ability to meet its obligations to policyholders over a long period of time.

B and B- (Adequate): The company has an adequate overall performance and can meet its obligations to policyholders but may be vulnerable to unfavorable changes in underwriting or economic conditions.

C++ and C+ (Fair): The company has demonstrated fair overall performance and can meet its current obligations to policyholders but is vulnerable to unfavorable changes in underwriting or economic conditions.

BC and C- (Marginal): The company has demonstrated marginal overall performance. It can meet its current obligations to policyholders but is very vulnerable to unfavorable changes in underwriting or economic conditions.

D (Very Vulnerable): The company has demonstrated poor overall performance. The company can meet its obligations to policyholders but is extremely vulnerable to unfavorable changes in underwriting or economic conditions.

E (Under State Supervision): The company is under state insurance regulatory authority supervision, control, or restraint, such as conservatorship or rehabilitation, but not including liquidation.

F (In Liquidation): The company has been placed under an order of liquidation by a court of law, or its owners have voluntarily agreed to liquidate. Companies that voluntarily liquidate or dissolve their charters are generally not insolvent.

It is important to select a long-term care insurance company with a grade of "A" or higher from A.M. Best Financial Rating Service. If a client is in excellent health, he or she can expect to qualify for insurance coverage from a highly rated insurance company. Those clients with higher-risk health conditions may not be able to obtain insurance coverage with such a company, and may be willing to consider coverage with a lower-rated company, but it is not recommended. It exposes the advisor, the client, and the family to unnecessary future risk. Smaller, poorly rated insurance companies in the long-term care insurance market that generally sell only a few lines of insurance products, including long-term care insurance, are particularly vulnerable over a long period of time. Such smaller insurance companies have been known to charge relatively low premiums to attract more business and therefore have found themselves required to increase premiums to avoid bankruptcy. If claims experience deteriorates, a larger insurance company with extensive financial wealth or resources is in a better position to continue to service its policyholders, whereas a small, poorly rated insurance company will have little chance of surviving the substantial losses incurred with adverse claim experience.

Other factors an advisor can use to evaluate the insurance company's stability, in addition to the rating service grade it receives, are

- ◆ history with the product, and
- ◆ size of long-term care insurance block of business, to include

- number of in-force policies;
- number of policyholders;
- premium received; and
- size and experience of the support staff.

### Company Commitment to Long-Term Care Insurance

It is important that the insurance company is committed to the long-term care insurance industry for the very reason of the long-term nature of the insurance product. An insurance company should be dedicated to maintaining the strength and innovation of long-term care insurance products for the future. However, even market leaders have been rethinking participation in the long-term care insurance market. Some insurance companies may enter the long-term care insurance market as a defensive move. Without a firm commitment, the insurance company will not stay in the market if it becomes volatile. History suggests that most insurance companies that enter the long-term care insurance market may not remain in the market for an extended period of time.[8]

It is wise to evaluate insurance companies based on

- being highly committed to the industry;
- having a strong history of overall rate stability; and
- having published claims history.

One way of gauging the insurance company's commitment is to ask about its market share and percent of resources devoted to this line of its business. In general, major insurance companies have the largest share of long-term care insurance policies, but this should not stop the advisor from also looking at smaller insurance companies with a proven commitment to long-term care insurance.

Conventional wisdom suggests that the longer an insurance company has been in the long-term care insurance business, the more likely it is to remain in the business. As a general rule, it is best to select an insurance company that has been in the market for ten years or longer.[9] Additionally, it is wise to avoid insurance companies whose pattern is to enter the market, exit the market, and re-enter the market. These actions clearly indicate a lack of commitment to the long-term care insurance industry. Unlike most other insurance products buyers, purchasers of long-term care insurance buy coverage years before they may actually file a claim. According to the American Association for Long-Term Care Insurance, 67.4 percent of new claims that began in 2010 were from policyholders age 80 and older.[10] Yet, 56 percent of those purchasing individual policies were between ages 55 and 64, whereas 35 percent of individuals purchasing group polices were under

---

8. Long-Term Care Insurance, *Choosing the Right Insurance Carrier* (2007), http://www.long-term -care-insurance-advice.com/long-term-care-insurance-choosing-the-right-carrier.html.

9. *Id.*

10. American Association for Long-Term Care Insurance Claimant Study, The 2011 Sourcebook for Long-Term Care Insurance Information (2011).

age 35.[11] These figures suggest that it could be upward of 30 to 40 years before an insurance claim is filed. Unlike with other group insurance products, employees will likely keep their group long-term care insurance policy for their remaining years. Group long-term care insurance products are portable, meaning employees can take their policies with them when they depart employment. Group policies may be offered by an employer with provisions very similar to individual policy provisions, so the need to cancel the policy and purchase an individual policy may be unnecessary. Because policies are issued on an attained-age basis, cancelling and repurchasing at an older age is not prudent. From these factors and averages alone, it is obvious how extremely important it is to choose a financially stable insurance company that is committed to longevity in the industry.

Historically, name recognition of the insurance company has been another indicator that the company will more likely remain committed to the market. Companies that have built name recognition and have protected their brands over the decades are more likely to continue protecting the reputations of their names. In addition, large-name companies rarely make short-term decisions, such as entering a market without thoroughly researching their options. However, recent changes in the long-term care insurance industry prove this is not as effective an indicator as it was in the past.

An additional indicator that the insurance company is committed to the market is the level of resources devoted to this line of business. For instance, the use of a third-party administrator for service and claims, as opposed to an established, dedicated long-term care insurance administration department within the home office, may be a relevant indicator of commitment. Some large insurance companies may form a separate entity that sells only long-term care insurance and a separate administration entity.

## Rate Stability and Pricing

In-force rate increases are never well-received or wanted by policyholders, advisors, or insurance companies; therefore it is important to understand the main contributors to such actions. As previously discussed, the justification for broad rate increases is that they are largely due to morbidity, where the incidence and severity of claims is significantly higher than expected and the duration of claims is longer than expected. Some actuaries have noted that the justification for rate increases attributed to persistency assumptions came from blocks of business that were more than ten years old. Mortality experience in both the life and long-term care insurance industries has caused more people to reach ages where long-term care services will likely be needed, and therefore claims are more likely to occur. Due to these factors, more policyholders have used their insurance benefits than originally anticipated.

This reinforces the value of the long-term care insurance product but creates significant pricing challenges for insurance companies. It is difficult to predict

---

11. *Id.*

what long-term care insurance companies will do with their future pricing, but it seems safe to assume they will experience generally similar results and pressure due to policy pricing consistency in the early years of the industry.

Long-term care insurance companies do not sell "non-cancellable" long-term care insurance policies, common in the disability income market. Non-cancellable is defined as level premiums and provisions guaranteed up to a specified age or for the life of the policy. Long-term care insurance is offered on a *"guaranteed renewable"* basis, meaning that although the insurance company must guarantee that it will renew the policy as long as premiums are paid every year, it does not guarantee the premium rate. In a guaranteed renewable insurance policy, the premium rate cannot be increased due to an individual's health or age change. The insurance company may file with the state insurance department for a premium rate increase for a class of policyholders or for all policyholders with a specific policy form within that state. It is important to understand that it is illegal for an advisor to give an impression that guaranteed renewable policies will remain level for the life of the policies. They may ultimately remain level; however, the possibility may not be stated as fact.

In a relatively young industry with relatively limited claims history and product experience, it is not possible to offer guaranteed level premium rates to policyholders who may not use the benefits for possibly 20 or more years. Insurance companies that may have to file for premium increases sometime in the future are not always easy to identify, as those with the lowest premiums may not always be the ones having premium solvency issues.

Some insurance companies may offer short-term, initial rate guarantees, but such offerings are limited, often found in group policy offerings or individual limited pay period policies. As the industry develops new products, the products should be priced to reflect growing experience. As well, the insurance companies should constantly monitor a number of factors that impact pricing, such as demographics, claims, interest rates, and annual lapse rates. This approach enables insurance companies to respond to changes in the financial environment that affect new product development and pricing, and more effectively implement in-force policyholder pricing adjustments in the future.

The intent of insurance regulators is to promote rate stability in the long-term care insurance industry, similar to that of the life insurance industry. The objective is to protect older policyholders on fixed incomes from having to give up coverage due to non-payment of premium caused by rate increases. Premium rates throughout the industry have been reasonably stable over the past ten years. Occasionally there will be a shock in the industry due to a large rate increase, with resulting media attention referencing ensuing litigation threats, but fortunately this is the exception rather than the rule.[12] Choosing a product that has

---

12. Thomas Day, *Guide to Long Term Care Planning: Long Term Care Insurance* (2011), http://www.longtermcarelink.net/eldercare/long_term_care_insurance.htm.

lower-than-average premium rates may foretell a rate increase sometime in the future; however, choosing to purchase a product from an insurance company with substantially higher-than-average premium rates does not mean such a product will not increase in the future. Rational premium rates are the important consideration when selecting an insurance company. A tool that can provide assistance as to which insurance companies have adequate premiums and which do not is the *Long-Term Care Experience Report*, published annually by the National Association of Insurance Commissioners (NAIC) (**cf. Chapter 4**).

Insurance companies with high loss ratios may be more likely to need future rate increases, but this is not always an accurate indicator. As stated previously, the insurance companies should conduct regular experience studies, to include the following:

- claim incidence
- claim severity
- morbidity experience
- expenses
- policy lapse rates
- financial results
- appropriateness of premiums

It should be noted that insurance companies conduct internal morbidity studies, but they are not publicly shared with advisors. Insurance companies review their experience and make adjustments accordingly.

Additionally, statutory active life reserves, Generally Accepted Accounting Principles (GAAP) reserves, and claim reserves need to be evaluated to determine if solvency and adequacy requirements are met. Active life reserves are defined as those reserves that are not claim reserves but that include premium reserves. Due to a presence of international insurance companies represented in the insurance industry, not all insurance company pricing pressures are the same. One such example is the use of the more conservative accounting practices of the Canadian GAAP for Canadian insurance companies. Canadian GAAP recognizes the need for reserving sooner than U.S. GAAP, due to the higher, more conservative reserving required. John Hancock is an example of a Canadian-based long-term care insurance company. Synchronizing accounting standards across the globe is an ongoing process in the international accounting community. For fiscal years beginning January 1, 2011, publicly traded companies based outside the United States began using International Financial Reporting Standards (IFRS).

The U.S. Financial Accounting Standards Board (FASB) is to continue moving forward as the U.S. standard setter for public companies and is expected to incorporate IFRS into U.S. GAAP over a defined period of time. The Securities and Exchange Commission (SEC) suggests that this period is to be five to seven years. FASB will incorporate new and amended IFRS into U.S. GAAP through an endorsement protocol. The protocol will give FASB the authority to modify IFRS before incorporating the standards into U.S. GAAP. There are fundamental, technical, and philosophical differences between IFRS and U.S. GAAP. However, the SEC stated that the preferred approach would be for FASB to work with the International Accounting Standards Board (IASB) to prevent the need for modifications, and U.S.-specific modifications should be rare. Where other countries initially aligned their standards through a first-time adoption on a specific date, the SEC plan includes a transitional element. During a period of five to seven years, FASB is to amend U.S. GAAP to align with IFRS.[13]

In addition, insurance companies may show mark-to-market accounting where the value of a corporate liability should be accounted for near term. This accounting philosophy promotes full accounting for liabilities when recognized rather than deferring or marginally accounting for liabilities. As well, U.S. GAAP does not require annual review or review by policy series. GAAP is imposed on companies so that investors have a minimum level of consistency in the financial statements they use when analyzing companies for investment purposes. GAAP covers such things as revenue recognition, balance sheet item classification, and outstanding share measurements. Companies are expected to follow GAAP rules when reporting their financial data by way of financial statements. If a financial statement is not prepared using GAAP or IFRS principles, it is wise to be very cautious. GAAP is a set of standards; however, even when an insurance company uses GAAP, financial statements still need to be scrutinized.

While pricing adjustments for in-force insurance policies are becoming more common throughout the industry, some of the increases are perceived by advisors as excessive.[14] It is generally not an insurance company's intention to purposely lapse business through dramatic increases. The insurance companies work with the state insurance departments to approve rate increases, while also providing policyholder options for alternative plan designs and pricing offers. This allows the most severely impacted policyholders, such as those with rich benefit designs, to potentially avoid an increase if they amend their policy. With the assistance of an astute advisor, a policyholder may be able to redesign the policy to be more consistent with the policyholder's current objectives, which may have changed since originally purchasing the policy.

As mentioned earlier in the chapter, rate increase history needs to be part of the due care analysis. It is prudent to only consider insurance companies that have demonstrated reasonableness in their rate increases. The in-force premium rate increase announcements are received by a market made up of largely skeptical consumers. When dealing with the cautious, price-conscious client, advisors need to assure the client that they are committed to the industry and that the insurance company they are recommending is committed to the industry.

---

13. American Institute of Certified Public Accountants (AICPA) (2011).
14. Darla Mercado, *Hancock's LTC Rate Hike Puts Advisers in Tough Spot*, Investment News (Sept. 22, 2010).

## Underwriting

Another important due care consideration is the insurance company's underwriting philosophy. The insurance company's focus and emphasis placed on the potential policyholder's health history and health risk, which are predictive of morbidity, determine the underwriting philosophy. Today's decisions related to this philosophy will, in the future, make a significant difference in how the business performs. For individually underwritten insurance policies, a recent study by the consulting actuary firm of Millman & Robertson, Inc., reports that companies with liberal underwriting procedures have about three times higher claims loss ratios in the first three years than those insurance companies with conservative underwriting procedures.[15] For policies in force five to nine years, the average loss ratio for liberal underwriting was about 45 percent higher than conservative underwriting.[16] So it is clear that underwriting will have the greatest effect on rate stability. As a rule, underwriting philosophy combined with loss ratio is an accurate predictor of rate increases. Carriers are concerned with both loss ratios and expense ratios as they seek to profitably write LTC coverage.

> *Loss Ratio = Incurred Losses + Loss Adjustment Expense / Earned Premiums*
>
> *Expense Ratio = Incurred Expenses / Written Premiums*

A loss adjustment expense is defined as a specific cost associated with investigating, administering, defending, or paying an insurance claim. The loss adjustment expense can vary greatly depending on the complexity of a claim. It can also depend upon the capacity of the insurance company's personnel to perform all the necessary tasks related to a claim. Because claims reflect an insurance company's underwriting philosophy, for clients in relatively excellent health, it is recommended to select an insurance company with a rigorous underwriting process. Choosing to conduct business with an insurance company with a conservative underwriting philosophy is the best strategy for achieving stable premiums in the future. A stringent underwriting process is also a strong indication that the insurance company is committed long-term to the industry. Unfortunately, a rigorous underwriting process is not feasible for clients with adverse health conditions. It is important as an advisor to establish a relationship with a brokerage agency that specializes in placing business with insurance companies that have proven records of stability yet are also willing to underwrite a higher health risk. There is the possibility that a client may exceed even the high health risk insurance market and will need to seek alternative funding for long-term care planning (**cf. Chapter 3, p. 55**).

---

15. Christine Walker, *Choosing the Right Long-Term Care Insurance Provider* (2011).
16. Day, *supra* note 12.

Many group long-term care insurance programs are not medically underwritten, which can pose a challenge for insurance companies to properly price a product for the long term. The use of "bid information," benefit design, and participation levels as a way to spread risk can provide meaningful pricing criteria. Due to adverse selection in the past, the underwriting trend for group long-term care insurance is to increase premium rates more frequently than premiums for individually issued policies.[17] Companies that offer policies at rates that are too high will find that they cannot write policies, or that only the higher health risk employees purchase policies because they only qualify for coverage in a group insurance setting. This results in adverse selection; the insurance company only attracts those who will most likely file a claim due to their health history. Older group insurance policies are already experiencing raised premium rates to the point that some employees are cancelling their insurance coverage. The consequence of adverse selection occurs in this scenario as well, due to the remaining policyholders having adverse health conditions. The healthy policyholders who remain in the program subsidize the current premiums as well as the more frequent premium increases caused by the claims of the unhealthy policyholders.

Additionally, price strains are created for older group policies when new entrants are added to a group long-term care insurance plan. New entrants receive the rates set for the group, even if rates have changed since the group plan was established. In contrast, purchasers of individual long-term care insurance policies are obtaining the most current product offered in the market, which will have the most current rating structure.

## Care Management/Claim Practices

It is important that the insurance company is consistently managing a block of claims that has been providing significant benefits to its policyholders. Because few companies have more than ten years of claims experience, most companies do not have definitive actuarial guidelines for the premium reserving required for claims that will be incurred 20 to 30 years from now. As the long-term care insurance industry matures, insurance companies gain claims administration knowledge on how to best adjudicate a claim, the types of people who need care, and how and where such people should receive care. Such knowledge is critical in assessing potential underwriting risks and pricing models, and developing appropriate claims administration.

As an advisor, it is important to understand the general claims procedures implemented by insurance companies, such as

- ♦ average claim processing time;
- ♦ specific case management practices;
- ♦ available long-term care provider discounts;

---

17. Long-Term Care Associates, Inc. (2011).

- coordination of benefits with other applicable insurance or government programs;
- care advocacy; and
- alternate plans of care.

Additional criteria an advisor should evaluate when choosing an insurance company for recommendation to a client are in the area of claim and care management:

- The insurance company should make an investment in training claims associates. During the emotionally difficult time of claim application, the insurance company should strive to provide exceptional claims support with sensitivity and respect to policyholders and their families.
- Initial claim contact should be handled by trained representatives. Professional nurses, at the onset of the claim, will provide expertise and efficiency. It also is a good indicator of claims sophistication.
- Policyholders should be the central focus of the claims team. A care coordination team should include registered nurses and licensed social workers, having a common goal to make the long-term care claims process as streamlined as possible, every step of the way.

## Company Sales Suspension and Insolvency

The long-term care insurance industry appears to be in synchronization with the cyclical nature of the economy. Since 2006, three significant factors have impacted insurance companies and regulators:

1. Signing of the CLASS Act (which was subsequently tabled), the government's failed voluntary long-term care program, as part of the health care reform package.
2. Long-term care insurance companies suspending new business sales or increasing premiums for existing policies.
3. Pension Protection Act of 2006 (PPA) rules becoming effective on January 1, 2010, which increased the attractiveness of linked product offerings.

Suspension and insolvency are to be expected—although certainly not welcomed—in an immature industry. Mergers and acquisitions are a part of the business. It is important to realize that the insurance company chosen to provide long-term care benefits may not be the same insurance company 20 to 30 years from now. This reaffirms the importance of completing a thorough due care analysis, so that even if the insurance company is acquired, the insurance protection the client purchases remains intact.

If an insurance company chooses to exit the long-term care insurance industry, the acquiring insurance company typically respects the premium rate structure, and rate increases do not occur immediately. Premium increases should be expected at some point, as the acquiring company may apply new financial standards and find it necessary at some future date to increase the premiums on the acquired block of business.

The strength and size of an insurance company is a key component, as the long-term care insurance industry is not large enough to accommodate all the insurance companies presently involved in the market. It takes an extraordinary amount of capital to introduce a new product, build market share, and achieve sufficient premium income to eventually be profitable. Generally, only large, successful companies have the resources to stay the course and build market share. Companies not large enough to have capital to fund growing sales may have to rely heavily on new equity issued to fund growth. If equities underperform and the company is unable fulfill its financial obligations by finding additional capital, it must either find a viable buyer or seek remedy through the state insurance regulators. If the company finds a viable buyer, it is likely that both the buyer and seller of the business will be set on purging the unprofitable lines of business.

If an unstable insurance company is chosen, there is greater risk of the company failing to meet its financial obligations. Fortunately, in the event of insurance company failure, policyholders will not lose their policies. The insurance commissioner for the state in which the insurance company is conducting business typically finds a buyer for the block of business. Even if no buyer is found, the state exercises protection through the state guaranty association. While technically there is still a policy in force, claiming benefits may prove to be a challenging process. More information on state guaranty associations will follow in the next section of this chapter.

To provide a practical example of how an insurance company's stability affects its insurance policies, when offering a long-term care insurance policy, certificate, or rider, there is a state requirement that the insurance company must offer a non-forfeiture protection provision within the contract. This provision offers reduced, paid-up insurance, an extended term, a shortened benefit period, or another benefit approved by the state insurance department to provide insurance coverage in the event all or part of the premium is not paid by the policyholder. Non-forfeiture benefits and any additional premium for such benefits must be computed in an actuarially sound manner, using a methodology that has been filed with and approved by the state insurance department. This provision, along with the insurance contract being guaranteed renewable, provides protection for clients to continue their policies, even when the insurance company they purchased their policies from is no longer administering the policies. Therefore, the stability of the insurance company is of critical importance so that actuarially sound premiums can be determined.

## Other Considerations

### Guaranty Associations

One may question why the initial insurance company selection is so important, given the amount of default protection available. The answer is that if the underperforming block of business led to the defaulted insurance company's failure, it will not be an asset to an acquiring company either. Inevitably, it is not just the block of business that leads to the liquidation of an insurance company.

Where no buyers are found, the state guaranty association is triggered to provide continuing coverage and benefits to the insurance company's policyholders in the related state. Each state, as well as the District of Columbia and Puerto Rico, has a life and health insurance guaranty association to protect its residents if an insurance company is liquidated—the equivalent of the banking industry's Federal Deposit Insurance Corporation (FDIC). All companies licensed to conduct business in the state are required to be members of the guaranty association. If a company is licensed to conduct business in 25 states, they are required to belong to those 25 states' guaranty associations. Actually, each state has two associations, one for life and health insurance and another for property and casualty insurance. Should an insurance company fail, policyholders are protected up to certain limits. Every insurance company that sells policies in the state is assessed a fee to cover any costs. This is not an optional fee; it is part of the cost of conducting business in a particular state.

Few people are aware that these guarantees apply to long-term care insurance. Long-term care insurance is typically considered health insurance for guaranty coverage purposes. Guaranty associations provide continuing coverage, as it may prove difficult for a policyholder to find comparable coverage, either placing the insurance policies of the insolvent insurance company with a healthy insurance company or taking over the insurance policies themselves and fulfilling the terms and obligations of the contract.

Like the FDIC, state guaranty associations have maximum benefit limits. These limits are established by state law and can vary from state to state, but virtually all states offer at least the following limits. It's important to check the state guaranty association's website, as many states offer higher limits for certain products:

- ♦ $300,000 in life insurance death benefits
- ♦ $100,000 in cash surrender or withdrawal values for life insurance
- ♦ $100,000 in withdrawal and cash values for annuities
- ♦ $100,000 in health insurance policy benefits

The overall benefit limit in most states is $300,000, although some states have maximums that are much higher. The above coverage limits apply separately for each insolvent insurer.

All 52 insurance guaranty associations are members of the National Organization of Life and Health Insurance Guaranty Associations (NOLHGA). Through NOLHGA, the associations work together to provide continued protection for policyholders in the event of a multi-state insurance insolvency. NOLHGA established a task force of representative guaranty associations to work with the insurance commissioner to develop a plan to protect policyholders.[18] This is valuable added protection that provides the client and the client's family with some additional peace of mind.

### Dividends

Dividends are a non-guaranteed policy element within an insurance policy. Non-guaranteed policy elements are those components in an insurance policy that the insurance company is able to change unilaterally. Another example of a non-guaranteed policy element is the interest rate credited on a linked long-term care insurance product.

Under participating insurance policies, dividends are intended to represent an equitable distribution of the surplus that an insurance company accumulated on behalf of the policies. Participating insurance policies are those policies in which the policyholder has a contractual right to participate in the insurance company's favorable, and unfavorable, operational experience.

Neither the existence nor the amount of a dividend is guaranteed in any given year. Decisions with respect to the determination and allocation of divisible surplus are left to the discretion and business judgment of the board of directors of the insurance company. There is no guaranteed specific method or formula for the determination and allocation of divisible surplus. Every insurance company that offers dividends in its policies states that its approach is subject to change.

The ability to pay a dividend in a volatile economy, when other insurance companies are exiting the market or increasing rates, sends a strong message from the insurance company paying the dividend that its goal is to stay uniquely aligned with its policyholders, and focus on long-term value and stability for its policyholders.

## Conclusions

Each state has its own laws and regulations governing all types of insurance. The insurance departments are responsible for enforcing these laws, as well as providing the public with information about insurance. Each state's Agencies on Aging are responsible for coordinating services for older Americans. Each state provides insurance counseling programs, toll-free telephone numbers and internet tools for ease in comparing insurance companies and insurance policies, and general education on long-term care insurance among all other types of insurance.

It is the responsibility and the duty of every long-term care insurance advisor to be intimately familiar with the policy he or she is marketing. Some advisors may contract on a single-case basis if the insurance company does not meet the

---

18. National Organization of Life and Health Insurance Guaranty Associations, *Frequently Asked Questions* (2011), http://www.nolhga.com/policyholderinfo/main.cfm/location/questions#thirteen.

client's objectives, or if the client is uninsurable with the insurance company that the advisor typically markets. There is nothing wrong with exploring alternative markets; the concern comes when the advisor chooses not to read the specimen policy in its entirety. Often, all that is studied are the sections of the contract that either the client or advisor is interested in, or sections that do not appear in the policy that the advisor regularly markets. With the NAIC LTCI Model Act and Regulation, plus new regulations that hold the advisor accountable, it is neither an option nor an excuse to not conduct due care analysis on the insurance companies included in the advisor's portfolio of products. Careful attention must be paid to the coverage triggers, whether the plan is reimbursement or indemnity, and all other policy features. A recommendation is to place a familiar policy, one in which all the details are known to the advisor, alongside the unfamiliar policy and compare them provision by provision. More often than not, there are some surprises. This is particularly important if another policy is being sought because the client is not medically qualified for one policy but may qualify for an alternative policy.

Advisors are encouraged to build and maintain strong relationships with distribution partners so that they may offer long-term care planning solutions that help families find the right options for their needs and objectives.

As an industry, long-term care insurance companies are responding diligently to pay claims. Americans as a whole are still in denial of needing care some day, and therefore they procrastinate in planning and purchasing coverage for such care. Like life insurance planning, long-term care insurance planning involves the benefit possibly not being needed for many years; therefore it may seem like an unreasonable concept. It is more a matter of getting people to think about designing the quality-of-life environment they want as they move through the different ages and stages of their lives.

# *Long-Term Care Insurance Applications for Individuals— Estate Planning and Wealth Preservation*

# 8

THE SEVERE CONSEQUENCES OF providing care to family members over an extended period of time have been addressed in earlier chapters. How to mitigate those consequences through the creation of a long-term care plan, and how to fund such a plan through long-term care insurance, will now be examined.[1]

Of particular focus are those individuals ages 50 to 70, as those in this demographic are beginning to see family and friends becoming frail or deceasing, or are becoming the caregivers for their parents. For this demographic, retirement is quickly approaching, and their earned income stream will be ending in the near future, resulting in their taking what they have earned into retirement. Many in this stage of life begin to recognize that they are taking great financial responsibilities into retirement, highlighting the need for a plan for extended health care as an essential element in their retirement portfolio. Assuming that their income increases as they progress through their income-earning years, so does their responsibility increase to plan for long-term care, or face the consequences of failing to plan for care.

---

1. This chapter draws in part from HARLEY GORDON, CERTIFICATION IN LONG-TERM CARE COURSE HANDBOOK, Sections A, C, D, E, F (Releases 5.0, 8.0, 9.0, Corporation for Long-Term Care Certification 2003, 2009, 2011), and from HARLEY GORDON, IN SICKNESS & IN HEALTH: YOUR SICKNESS—YOUR FAMILY'S HEALTH, Chapter 6 (Financial Strategies Press 2007), and from HARLEY GORDON, WHY PLANNING WITH LIFE STAGE, PowerPoint presentation (2011).

Poverty is increasing with age, due to more Americans becoming increasingly responsible for their own financial security in retirement, which is becoming increasingly expensive.[2] Expectations and reality for the retirement years often are in contrast, as the following chart illustrates:

**FIGURE 8-1**

**The Benefits of Growing Older**

Reality doesn't measure up to expectations

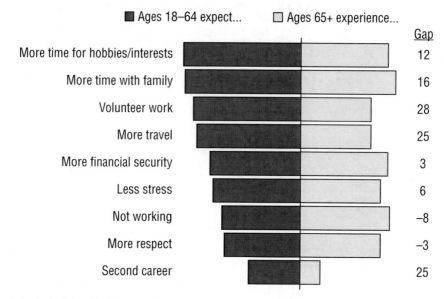

Note: Asked of adults 18–64, n=1, 631; and adults 65+, n=1, 332.

Source: Pew Research Center (June 29, 2009).

One of the main objectives of estate planning is achieving the client's goals, which typically center on preserving and protecting assets for the client and the client's spouse and children. Discussion of the threat that long-term care can be to achieving those goals is imperative. Therefore, in the financial and estate planning process, the advisor needs to always ask the client whether he or she has long-term care insurance. It is human nature to put up barriers when someone is trying to discuss a product that the seller will financially benefit from; therefore it behooves the attorney, the accountant, and the insurance advisor to work together as a team to counsel the client with the client's best interests in mind.

The need for care manifests from a chronic medical condition or catastrophic injury that compromises one's ability to perform the most basic daily routines or from a cognitive impairment that compromises one's ability to safely interact with one's environment. By definition, long-term care is all-consuming. Therefore, the first consequence, as stated in Chapter 1, is what long-term care does to the

---

2. Alliance for Retired Americans (2010).

emotional and physical well-being of one's caregiver due to the nature of long-term care.

The continuum of care required as people age typically follows a linear path as illustrated below:

### FIGURE 8-2

### The Progression of Care Commitment

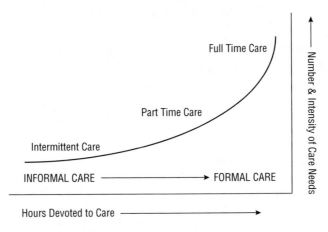

Source: National Care Planning Council (2011).

The second consequence is what long-term care does to one's retirement portfolio. Without a pre-funded plan, usually two categories of assets will be compromised:

1. Financial resources, creating fixed income
2. Investment principal

Paying for care requires a reallocation of these assets, which creates significant financial consequences, such as

♦ unnecessary taxes;
♦ investment opportunity costs; and
♦ undermining the financial well-being of the spouse or children for whom an inheritance is planned.

The ultimate goal of the long-term care plan, as stated earlier in Chapter 3, is to place the family back to where they were emotionally, physically, and financially, as best as possible prior to a long-term care event occurring.

## Safeguarding Retirement Strategies

At retirement, individuals shift from asset accumulation to asset conservation. As such, risk management becomes a top priority. The following are some risks that expose a seemingly well-conceived retirement plan to failure:

- Longevity risks
  - Outliving retirement resources
  - The death of a spouse
  - A change in marital status[3]
  - Unforeseen needs of family members
- Health risks
  - Unexpected health care needs and expenses
  - Loss of the ability to live independently
  - Lack of available facilities
  - Cost of caregivers and the health risk cost to caregivers
  - Change in residential setting needs
- Financial and economic risks
  - Inflation
  - Interest rate fluctuation
  - Stock market performance
  - Investment risk and returns
- Business risks
  - Employment risk due to economic changes
- Public policy risks
  - Regulatory and legislative changes
  - Cost of medical technology and pharmacology

As mentioned in Chapter 3, the Employee Benefits Research Institute's research shows that a couple today needs $295,000 for retiree health care expenses, assuming average life expectancy, without including long-term health care expenses. To confirm this figure, according to an MSNMoney.com Market Watch report, published on March 28, 2008, a 65-year-old couple currently retiring will need more than $300,000 set aside just to pay for health care costs over 20 years and will need $550,000 if they live into their early 90s. Particularly alarming, according to the report, is the fact that these numbers have not factored in the costs of nursing homes, assisted living facilities, or home health aides. The reality is that very few people will have half a million dollars to cover health care costs, without even accounting for the costs associated with long-term care and retirement living.

A truly comprehensive financial plan should take into account all aspects of an individual's life, including health care. However, many advisors and clients focus only on lifestyle issues and financial growth strategies. A long-term care plan is an umbrella over the retirement plan. As the following chart illustrates, long-term care insurance planning, in particular, warrants considerable attention:

---

3. U.S. DEPARTMENT OF HEALTH AND HUMAN SERVICES, THE EFFECTS OF MARRIAGE ON HEALTH: A SYNTHESIS OF RECENT RESEARCH EVIDENCE (June 2007), http://aspe.hhs.gov/hsp/07/marriageonhealth/rb.htm.

**FIGURE 8-3**

**A Long-Term Care Decision Tree**

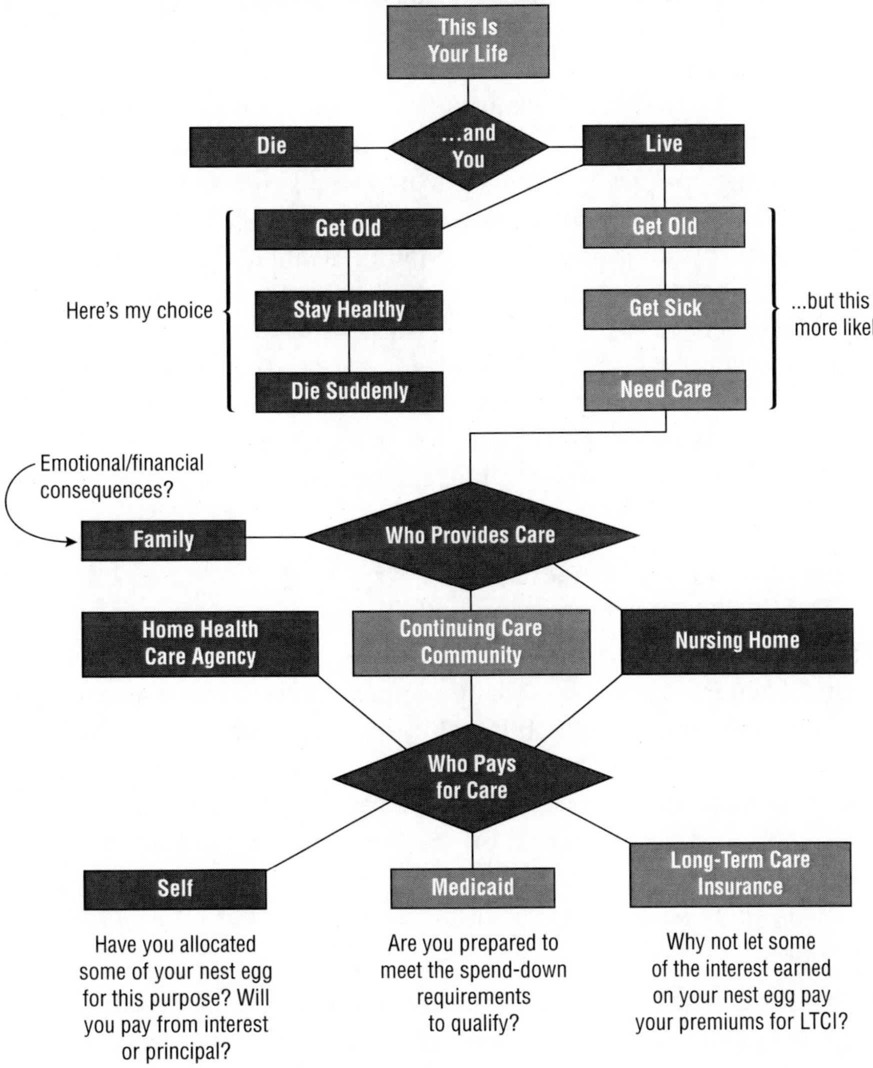

Source: The Thompson Agency, Inc. of New England (2011).

## Suitability Solution

Creating and implementing a suitable solution is a planning process that incorporates "social factors" such as personal and family values, concerns, and goals with "financial factors" such as current and expected income, expenses, assets, and obligations. These factors are then applied to the long-term care insurance product features to tailor a policy that is appropriate for the client's specific objectives. There are three main stages in the suitability solution planning process: the initial client interview, the analysis and plan design, and the presentation and client agreement.

## The Initial Client Interview

During the initial client interview stage, the objective is two-fold: to identify the client's social factors and to identify the client's financial factors. First, set the stage by identifying the client's values, concerns, and goals as they relate to retirement planning by including questions on family relations, heirs, income expectations, health care, and taxes. With the knowledge gained from the answers, then focus on questions that measure the client's finances to assist in developing a financial strategy for long-term care planning. Clients should consider how their lives and their family's lives would change if they were to need care today. It is beneficial to have them identify what is important in their present lifestyle and what it will take to preserve those values. Asking the right questions should lead to a discussion of the consequences of not having a plan, rather than focusing on a product. This discussion should then lead to the establishment of a plan for providing care over an extended period of time. The risk of diverting income and invading principal otherwise allocated for retirement is near certain should a person need long-term care. The only logical conclusion is that the retirement plan should be protected by insurance.

## The Analysis and Plan Design

The goal of the analysis and plan design step is to develop an asset preservation strategy and optimum long-term care plan design, based on the client's social and financial factors, by first establishing a maximum insurance premium amount that is comfortable for the client. Develop several feasible long-term care insurance configurations and test those configurations against client values, concerns, and goals. Compare the impact to the financial plan if a long-term care situation occurs. The optimal design, based on risk tolerance and premium, will produce the lowest economic impact to the overall financial plan, due to a long-term care event, for the client who owns long-term care insurance. Factors to be evaluated should include

- ♦ lost investment opportunity of current assets and investment returns;
- ♦ asset liquidation charges—liquidation taxes, cost basis, and market timing;
- ♦ long-term care insurance plan design and premium payments; and
- ♦ long-term care event assumptions including
  - ○ cost of care at local and preferred locations;
  - ○ cost of care increases; and
  - ○ timing of care events—rapidly escalating long-term care costs that outpace investment returns.

During the plan design and analysis stage, it is helpful to use long-term care financial analyzing tools to develop several feasible configurations and test those configurations against client values, finances, and concerns in order to create a tailored plan suitable for clients. This will assist in describing policy provisions and their practical significance in the presentation stage. Accordingly, clients will understand the economic value of long-term care insurance as an asset-protection and risk-transfer vehicle, which will reinforce long-term care insurance as a sound investment decision.

## The Presentation and Agreement

During the presentation and agreement stage, it is important to review the policy designs with the client to illustrate how each policy design protects the client's values, concerns, goals, and financial strategies:

- Describe policy provisions and their practical significance.
- Demonstrate the reality of long-term care as an end-of-life issue for most families.
- Stress the psychological value of creating a firewall as a buffer against the vast cost of facility confinement or home care expenses.
- Use key agreements and transitions.

Discussing long-term care is more emotional than discussing life insurance or disability income insurance, which tends to be a more straightforward insurance to discuss with a client. Drawing out clients' personal experiences with long-term care, whether they were directly or indirectly involved, is one of the most critical aspects of the meeting. After the clients share their experiences with long-term care, to validate the need to plan, the advisor may want to share his or her own personal experiences with long-term care. It lets the clients know they are not alone. If statistics are used, relate them to the clients' personal experiences.

The following are the six most common concerns about long-term care and the reasons people buy long-term care insurance:

1. Burden—not wanting to be a financial or emotional burden on others.
2. Access to quality care—being able to select a quality facility in a location of their own choosing.
3. Aversion to welfare (Medicaid)—not wanting to be dependent on the government for care.
4. Control and independence—wanting to maintain personal control in the choices they make.
5. Peace of mind—knowing they are protected instead of worrying about what could happen.
6. Asset protection—preserving assets for a healthy spouse, inheritance for children, or donation to charity.[4]

---

4. Guide to Long Term Care, *Privacy & Usage Policy* (2011), http://www.guidetolongtermcare .com/privacy.html.

Acknowledge and respond to the first five listed priorities in the process of opening up the discussions with clients, but focus on the sixth priority during the sales process.

Clients may insist that they will never go into a nursing home because their spouse, children, or siblings will take care of them. However, as stated previously, purchasing a long-term care insurance policy does not prevent family members or friends from providing care. Rather, one is simply removing some of the financial and emotional burden from family members or friends, and instead providing them with caregiving options to provide supervision of care. A comprehensive long-term care insurance policy will pay for care where one desires—home, a loved one's home, an adult day care center, or a facility.

## Funding Analysis: Self-Insuring versus Insuring the Risk

Those with substantial assets often consider investing the cost of the premium rather than buying insurance. However, the invested amount of premiums over 20 years may be only 5 to 12 percent of the potential insurance benefit. A six-year insurance benefit may only yield a half-year of long-term care if the premiums are invested instead rather than used to pay an insurance premium to an insurance company. In addition, if someone invests the premium amount, where will the money come from if the person needs long-term care next year, or even five to ten years from now? The "saved premium" account would not have time to grow. The following graph illustrates the potential funds available to pay for long-term care expenses. The conclusion can be drawn that it is not prudent to self-insure.

The same question could be asked of automobile, homeowners, or medical insurance. Why not self-insure these types of coverage as well? Couldn't individuals just as easily pay medical bills from their own pocket, or pay for damage to their cars or loss of their homes out of pocket, and possibly save a lot of money over time? The purpose of insurance is to transfer risk to preserve assets, which is accomplished by leveraging premiums to buy a benefit at pennies on the dollar instead of paying dollar-for-dollar out of pocket for a loss. No matter what the risk, the total cost of premiums over a long period is usually a fraction of the cost of paying a claim from one's own pocket.

Most retirees are not concerned about just investment returns, but also the stability of their investments. Choosing to self-insure long-term care has a tremendous impact on portfolio risk and volatility. Modern portfolio philosophy is not as concerned about investment upside, but rather seeks to protect the downside based on one's level of risk tolerance. Investments with a large upside potential typically have a large downside risk. Conversely, most insurance products are designed to protect the downside and have little impact on upside investment potential. Consideration must be given to protect the downside against the most volatile risks one may encounter.

## FIGURE 8-4

### Can a Client Afford to Self-Insure?

Amounts Available at age 78:
Self-Insure        $237,960.00
LTC Benefit*    $1,277,591.25

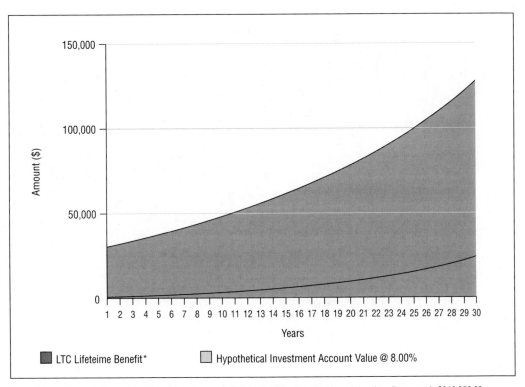

Assumptions: 48 year-old insured $170 daily benefit amount, 5-year benefit period. Year 1 maximum benefit amount is $310,250.00.

The above chart is hypothetical and for illustrative purposes only. The investment performance shown is not intended to refer to any specific policy, contract, or other investment.

*Benefits under the Long-Term Care Insurance policy are available only if you are chronically ill and otherwise qualify for benefits puruant to the terms of the policy.

Source: The Metropolitan Life Insurance Company (2007) (annual long-term care insurance premium = $2,049.86).

## FIGURE 8-5

### Self-Funding of Long-Term Care Expenses

While self-funding is an option, drawing income for everyday living and to cover long-term care expenses can quickly deplete client savings. The chart below shows how $500,000 in retirement plan assets can be depleted when long-term care expenses are self-funded.

| | Assets at Beginning of Year | Net Interest Earnings | Income Needs | LTC Expenses | Assets at End of Year |
|---|---|---|---|---|---|
| Year 1 | $500,000 | $28,618 | -$30,000 | -$75,000 | $421,618 |
| Year 2 | $421,618 | $21,765 | -$30,900 | -$78,750 | $333,733 |
| Year 3 | $333,733 | $16,335 | -$31,827 | -$82,688 | $235,554 |
| Year 4 | $235,554 | $10,281 | -$32,782 | -$86,822 | $126,231 |
| Year 5 | $126,231 | $3,550 | -$33,765 | -$91,163 | $4,853 |
| Year 6 | $4,853 | Depleted | Depleted | Depleted | Depleted |

This is a hypothetical example used for illustration purposes only. It assumes net interest earnings after tax of 6%, inflation of 3% per year, and increase of LTC expenses of 5% per year. These hypothetical expenses may not be representative of the costs you may incur.

Source: ProducersWEB, Summit Business Media (2011).

Clients may consider self-insuring for custodial care only, thinking such care will be less expensive than the self-insuring skilled nursing expenses. The majority of care in all types of care settings is custodial care, and the cost can add up significantly. This graph represents a sample cost of custodial care:[5]

---

5. Cost of 365 days of in-home care, 4.5 hours per day, by a home health aide at the average 2008 hourly cost of $19.00 is $31,207.50. The average 2008 cost of care in an assisted living facility is $35,544. The average 2008 cost of care in a private room at a skilled nursing facility is $74,460. All costs are national averages. Costs depend on duration of care, provider, and location. Source: CareScout, John Hancock 2008 Cost of Care Survey (Nov. 2008). The average premium is based on policies sold January 1, 2009 through March 31, 2009. The actual premium may vary based on age, health, amount of coverage selected, and other factors. This average policy premium closely represents the $1,961.03 annual premium for a 57-year-old married person with preferred rates with $200 daily benefit, four-year benefit period, 90-day elimination period, and 5% compound inflation option. John Hancock Custom Care II Enhanced Policy Form LTC-03 TX. This is a general description of coverage and is not an insurance contract. Refer to the Outline of Coverage provided by a licensed agent for an explanation of features and options. Only the individual long-term care insurance policy contains governing contractual provisions. Source: USAA Life General Agency (2011).

**FIGURE 8-6**

**Average Annual Cost of Care**

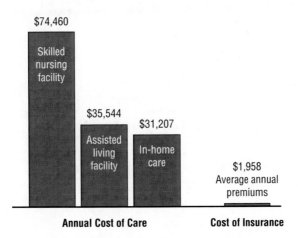

Annual Cost of Care        Cost of Insurance

Understanding that the average cost for custodial care is substantial and will continue to escalate, Table 8-1 summarizes what funding options are available for payment of custodial long-term care. It is important to understand the resources required to provide formal care in or out of a client's home with the type of funding that will pay for it (**cf. Chapter 3**). An advisor's ability to quickly reference this type of information is critical in establishing the advisor as the expert who understands what information is needed to implement a solution.

**TABLE 8-1**
**Payment Sources for Custodial Care**

| | Home care |
|---|---|
| PAYMENT | |
| Veterans Administration (VA): | Very Limited[6] |
| Medicare: | No |
| Medicaid: | Very Limited[7] |
| Private funds: | Yes |
| Long-term care insurance: | Yes |

continued

---

6. Under the Aid & Attendance Special Pension or Domiciliary Care Benefit.
7. VA hospitals will contract with the facility for a limited amount of funds.

## Adult day care centers

PAYMENT

| | |
|---|---|
| Veterans Administration (VA): | Very Limited[8] |
| Medicare: | No |
| Medicaid: | Very Limited[9] |
| Private funds: | Yes |
| Long-term care insurance: | Yes |

## Assisted-living facilities

PAYMENT

| | |
|---|---|
| Veterans Administration (VA): | Very Limited[10] |
| Medicare: | No |
| Medicaid: | Very Limited |
| Private funds: | Yes |
| Long-term care insurance: | Yes |

## Continuing care retirement communities (CCRCs)

PAYMENT

| | |
|---|---|
| Veterans Administration (VA): | No |
| Medicare: | No |
| Medicaid: | No for independent living; Very Limited for assisted-living facilities; Yes for skilled nursing facility |
| Private funds: | Yes |
| Long-term care insurance: | No for independent living; Yes for all other care |

## Institutional care

Institutional care is defined as skilled or rehabilitative services provided in settings that are licensed to provide them. These services are covered by health insurance plans. The exception is skilled nursing facilities, which, although they provide skilled or rehabilitative services, also provide custodial care.

---

8. Under the Aid & Attendance Special Pension or Domiciliary Care Benefit.
9. Under HCBS and PACE programs.
10. Under the Aid & Attendance Special Pension or Domiciliary Care Benefit.

| Hospitals | |
|---|---|
| PAYMENT | |
| VA: | Yes |
| Medicare: | Yes |
| Medicaid: | Yes |
| Private funds: | Yes |
| Long-term care insurance: | No |

| Custodial care in skilled nursing facilities | |
|---|---|
| PAYMENT | |
| VA: | Very Limited[11] |
| Medicare: | No |
| Medicaid: | Yes |
| Private funds: | Yes |
| Long-term care insurance: | Yes |

One of the useful benefits of life insurance is to provide liquidity. Long-term care insurance is no less important for the same reason. Does the client have investments in illiquid assets such as real estate or small businesses? Paying for care may force their sale, if it is possible to sell at all, at reduced prices. Paying for care may mean liquidating assets with a low cost basis or tax-deferred (qualified) funds. The former creates a capital gains tax, and the latter creates an ordinary income tax plus additional state taxes. It is helpful to compare the cost in taxes with the premium for long-term care insurance.

The issue of lifestyle should never be underestimated. The income generated from a couple's portfolio may be able to support a certain lifestyle, but can it support that lifestyle and pay for care at the same time? The key considerations for wealthier individuals are the same:

♦ liquidity
♦ market conditions if assets have to be sold
♦ taxes on sale of assets
♦ legacy assets

Another approach is based on reasons why wealthy clients purchase life and disability income insurance. They never look at the risk of dying or becoming disabled during working years; they look at the consequences of these things happening and what impact they will have on those they love. There is no reason not to employ the same strategy in creating the need and urgency for long-term care insurance. Consider the two sets of consequences: the emotional and physical well-being of caregivers, and their financial viability.

---

11. VA hospitals will contract with the facility for a limited amount of funds.

## Cost of Waiting to Purchase Long-Term Care Insurance

Long-term care insurance premiums are based on the insurability of the applicant, his or her age at time of application, and the plan design. Each year someone delays purchasing a policy, the more expensive it becomes. As well, with age the risk of needing care increases and the chance of being accepted for insurance decreases.

The value in long-term care insurance is in spreading out possible costs over many years instead of having potentially unmanageable expenses occur over a short period. There is a strong possibility that care will be needed prior to the elder years, as 43 percent of those needing long-term care are under age 65.[12] There are compelling reasons not to delay purchasing long-term care insurance:

- ◆ Upon policy approval, the policyholder has insurance coverage as of the effective date of the policy.
- ◆ Unlike health insurance premiums that increase annually along with a person's age, long-term care premiums are determined by the age when coverage is first obtained and then can only be increased if all policyholders within a class or a specific product receive increases as well.
- ◆ Rates typically begin rising after the age of 30 (from age 18 to age 30 premium rates are usually age-banded with an insurance company), so the premium will never be less expensive than when one is 30 years old.
- ◆ The cost of waiting exceeds the money saved by delaying the purchase, assuming that long-term care insurance is eventually purchased.
- ◆ Regarding eligibility, there is no guarantee an applicant will be accepted. The requirements vary based on an applicant's age, medical history, medical follow-up, functionality, and cognitive awareness. Any change in health status increases the risk of being uninsurable.
- ◆ To qualify for long-term care insurance, applicants must answer questions relating to their health. If they wait, they may develop a condition that would prevent them from obtaining coverage.

Insurance companies have historically come out with new policies roughly every two to three years. Although these policies contain many new benefits and features, they are also more expensive for new purchasers than the previous policy. Because of this rate creep, new applicants for long-term care insurance are expected to pay about 5 percent more each year than applicants at the same age would be paying with older policies. At this rate, ten years from now, a policy for a 50-year-old applicant will likely cost 50 percent more than an equivalent policy for a 50-year-old applicant costs today.[13] In summary, younger applicants are able to obtain a premium rate that is relatively inexpensive, while older applicants face much more expensive rates, as illustrated in the following chart:

---

12. National Care Planning Council (2011).
13. *Id.*

## FIGURE 8-7

### Total Premiums Paid from Issue Age to Age 85

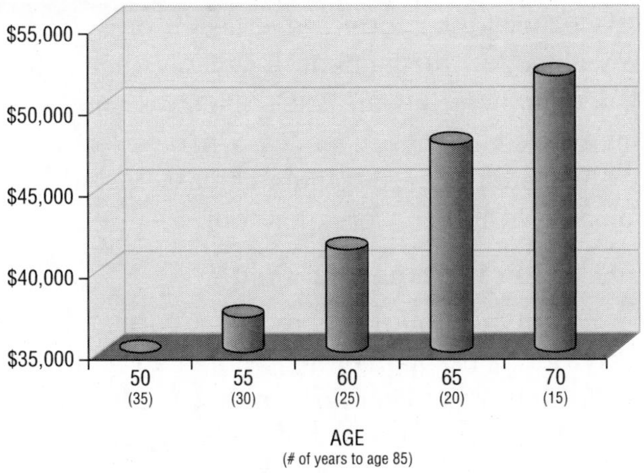

Source: David Backus, MBA, CLTC, Long Term Care Resources.

## Funding the Purchase of Long-Term Care Insurance

Funding the long-term care plan was discussed quite extensively in Chapter 3. This section will review the possible funding methods within a client's financial plan that will pay the long-term care insurance premium.

People purchase long-term care insurance for a variety of reasons, including

♦ access to care;
♦ asset and income protection;
♦ quality of care; and
♦ wealth transfer.

Motivations change with wealth levels. For example, access to care is a concern that is closely aligned with lower levels of wealth. Affordability is the goal, and annual income is the key. As a guideline, the National Association of Insurance Commissioners recommends that a long-term care insurance premium should not exceed 7 percent of annual income.[14]

Long-term care insurance has more than a 99 percent persistency rate.[15] As people age, long-term care insurance becomes more important. Clients need to be able to afford premiums now and 20 years in the future with the potential of rate increases.

At higher levels of wealth, quality of care and wealth transfer issues become the key motivators. Levels of coverage may vary from more coverage when

---

14. Nicole Gurley, *Long-Term Care Expense Planning for Financial Advisors: Four Factors to Consider* (2011).

15. Nicole Gurley, GᴜʀʟᴇʏLTCI.ᴄᴏᴍ (2011).

the goal is to maintain an affluent lifestyle to less coverage as insuring against catastrophic loss becomes the objective. What clients want to achieve with their wealth also plays a part in recommending a prudent long-term care insurance funding solution. Financial goals drive coverage. If preserving assets for wealth transfer is the key objective, the amount of coverage needs to be appropriate to protect assets. If not, outliving income is the objective, and coverage that protects income-producing assets becomes the focus. When part of a strategy is to reduce estate taxes and eliminate the need to liquidate assets, long-term care insurance can become a valuable wealth conservation tool.

### Funding Vehicles within the Financial Plan[16]

Even though the majority of Americans receiving formal care depend on public funds for their care, the baby boomer generation is rapidly expanding the number of those ages 65 and over. Therefore, public funds will become harder and harder to access. Additionally, with volatile economies, many people who thought they could rely on equity built up in their homes or stocks are finding out just how uncertain that proposition can be. When a client recognizes the need for long-term care insurance, the client is likely willing to forfeit some discretionary income to pay the premium. Frequently, the advisor can identify expenses that can be adjusted or eliminated, and even small expenses can add up to a savings.

Reviewing a client's medical insurance policies can possibly identify ways to help free up cash flow. Changing the medical insurance plan to a more affordable company, or if the client is under age 65, considering a high-deductible health plan with a health savings account, may be a viable alternative. If the client has a health savings account (HSA), he or she can pay long-term care insurance premiums from the account up to the eligible annual maximum, as discussed in Chapter 6 and as will be further explained later in this chapter.

If the client owns a disability income insurance policy and is nearing retirement, reallocation of the disability income insurance premium to purchase a long-term care insurance policy is an option to fund the long-term care insurance premium.

A reverse mortgage may be an option, with the client using the income from the reverse mortgage to pay the long-term care insurance premiums. However, the challenging housing market has sharply reduced home equity in many markets (**cf. Chapter 3, p. 60**).

If a client owns a life insurance policy that either is not performing up to expectations or is no longer needed due to a change in the client's life stage, the premium savings of a term life insurance policy, or the policy cash value of a permanent life insurance policy, can be used to fund a long-term care insurance policy.

Redirecting life insurance policy dividends that are purchasing paid-up additions in a whole life insurance policy is another possible funding method for the long-term care insurance premium.

---

16. Assumption: The funding of the premium of a tax-qualified long-term care insurance contract.

In the face of falling home and stock values, rising inflation, and depleted savings, a life settlement can be a financial alternative to fund the long-term care insurance policy. Life insurance values are generally guaranteed and somewhat uncorrelated with the economy, unlike real estate, stocks, and bonds, so there is predictable fluctuation.

A life settlement can be thought of somewhat like a reverse mortgage. It is an alternative way for clients to tap into an existing asset to generate liquidity to cover immediate needs. There are also important differences:

♦ A reverse mortgage is a loan that must be paid back, with interest and fees, once the secured property is no longer the primary residence—a prohibitive requirement for someone seeking to move into a continuum of care setting or care facility.

♦ A life settlement is the sale of a life insurance policy to a third party while the policy owner is still alive for a lump-sum payment; because it is not a loan, the funds are unrestricted and require no repayment. Potential ordinary income and capital gains tax implications of a life settlement should be considered prior to the transaction. The taxation of a life settlement may vary on a state-by-state basis. Taxes may also vary due to a client's tax bracket. Therefore, advice from and review of the settlement by a professional tax advisor is recommended.

The Pension Protection Act of 2006 (PPA) permits insurance contracts, endowment contracts, annuity contracts, and qualified long-term care insurance contracts that are exchanged for qualified long-term care insurance contracts to be treated as tax-free exchanges. Clients may have older annuities in their portfolios, and even though they are designed to provide retirement income, many people decease owning unused annuities.[17]

If the client currently owns a tax-deferred annuity and is at the age that he or she can annuitize, one option is to use the payments to pay a limited, ten-premium payment policy. After ten years, the long-term care insurance policy is paid up with no further premium payments due.

A funding strategy that is growing in popularity is using a single-premium immediate annuity to pay the annual premiums on a traditional long-term care insurance policy. This can save both taxes and premium dollars over the life of the long-term care insurance policy.

An advisor may find that his or her clients do not wish to withdraw from their individual retirement accounts (IRA) starting at the mandatory age 70½. Instead of fully funding the IRA, clients could consider diverting money starting in their early 60s or younger to fund the premium on the long-term care insurance policy.

---

17. Lincoln Financial Advisors (2011).

A client may choose to draw a distribution of his or her qualified retirement plan, such as a 401(k), 403(b), or other qualified plan arrangement, at 59½ and purchase an annuity with a long-term care insurance rider. An advisor will need to evaluate if this is a viable option; because the withdrawal is from a pre-tax retirement vehicle, there will now be a tax consequence.

Early retirees are able to withdraw specific amounts of money in substantially equal period payments (SEPP).[18] This is also known as the 72(t) rule, after the IRS code section to which it refers. A SEPP plan must be in place for at least five years or until the owner turns 59½, whichever is longer. For example, if a SEPP plan is started at age 58, it will have to continue until age 63, even though the owner will have already reached the early retirement age of 59½. A SEPP plan allows the withdrawal of money without receiving the 10 percent penalty, as long as the owner adheres to specific rules set out by the IRS. With proper structuring, the distributions can be applied toward premiums for a long-term care insurance policy.

If a client has reached age 70½ and is withdrawing the required minimum distributions (RMD), those distributions can be used to pay the premium. If the client has a substantial IRA and does not need most or all of it to meet daily living expenses during retirement, upon the client's death, the remaining balance will pass to his or her heirs. Depending on the size of the IRA owner's estate, the IRA may be subject to both income and estate taxes. The combined effect of these taxes on the IRA may reduce the amount distributed to the client's heirs by as much as 60 percent or more. Using distributions from an IRA to purchase long-term care insurance can dramatically increase the wealth a client passes on to his or her heirs.[19] Additionally, because of how a RMD withdrawal is determined upon one's death, it may be more suitable for the account owner to utilize this option for paying for long-term care insurance premiums versus paying out of other sources of income. The RMD will be determined by who, if anyone, is named as a beneficiary of the account from which the RMD is withdrawn. If the deceased account owner's spouse is the beneficiary, then the account will be treated as the beneficiary's own, and RMDs will be required, or not required, based on his or her age. If someone else is a beneficiary, RMDs will have to start immediately, based on the beneficiary's age. If no personal beneficiary is named, RMDs will be based on the account owner's age at death if the owner has already started taking RMDs, or the entire fund will need to be paid out within five years if the owner has not started taking withdrawals yet.

Of course, a client may choose to use the cash from his or her savings account, a maturing certificate of deposit (CD), and Social Security benefit payments to pay for the long-term care insurance policy.

---

18. I.R.C. § 72(t).
19. Pacific Life Insurance Company (Jan. 2011).

Building the anticipated long-term care insurance premium into the client's retirement is a possible solution. If the client, and the client's spouse if applicable, wants $10,000 a month on which to live in retirement, the advisor can build a planning model to include $11,000 a month of income or less, depending on long-term care plan design, health status, and age of the client. The $1,000 differential represents the premium for long-term care insurance policies.

The standard assumption is that policyholders pay their own premium, but the arrangement can be modified. One alternative is to ask clients' adult children to pay for their parents' policies when the parents want to preserve their estate but lack the liquidity to pay for long-term care insurance premiums. Another alternative is to have the parents and children jointly fund the policy. These options serve the best interest for both parents and children because they protect the estate of the parents, provide care, and preserve the estate for the children, who have a vested interest.

Just as children can fund the premium for parents' policies, wealthier parents are able to fund their adult children's policies. This is especially attractive when their children are in the life stage of educating the grandchildren while simultaneously trying to save for retirement. One example is for the parents to fund the first five years to secure the coverage, and then the children take over the premium payments after five years.

## Policy Premium Payment Options

There are two main premium payment options: the continuous payment of premium over the lifetime of the policy or an accelerated premium payment option, also known as a limited premium payment option.

### Lifetime Payments

The lifetime premium payment option is automatically assigned if the policyholder does not choose an option. Under the lifetime payment option, a policyholder pays the premium on the policy until the benefits are initiated with a claim. Premium payment modes are offered on a monthly, quarterly, semi-annual, or annual basis. Premiums are usually the lowest cost under this payment option. Paying on an annual basis can save a client up to 8 percent each year.[20]

### Accelerated Payment Options

Most insurance companies now offer policyholders the ability to pay their premiums in full over a defined period of time. Accelerated payment options, also called limited pay options, are typically available as a single premium or as twenty-pay, ten-pay, or paid-up-at-65 premiums. They may have limited appeal to policyholders who are personally paying their premium, for the following reasons:

---

20. American Association for Long-Term Care Insurance, The 2011 Sourcebook for Long-Term Care Insurance Information (2011).

- No discount is given for paying over a shorter period of time.
- All payments are lost if the owner dies during the payment period.
- On some policies, the premium could be increased during the payment period.
- If personally paying the premium, there is no additional tax benefit because deductibility is capped by age.

However, limited pay premiums are appealing to those who are owners of a C Corporation, have just sold a business, or have substantial resources and want to pay for the policy in a shorter period of time, while at the same time guaranteeing no premium increases by paying the premium early. Some insurance companies reserve the right to increase premiums on their accelerated payment policies. The substantial advantages to business owners will be explained in Chapter 9.

Some states require accelerated payment policies to offer a non-forfeiture benefit, which means the policyholder will still have benefits equal to the amount of premium paid if the policyholder is unable to complete the premium obligation for the limited pay period for any reason. However, some states do not allow this option at all and do not mandate a non-forfeiture benefit.

## Demographic Long-Term Care Planning

The U.S. is facing concerns that pose long-lasting implications for both baby boomers and the providers of senior residential settings and long-term care:

- The economy, in recent years, has experienced the worst decline since the Great Depression, and this generation may not see home values or commodity prices (fuel, groceries, etc.) return to where they were previously.
- The population over age 65 has begun to explode with the aging of the baby boomers, and as they age, life expectancies will continue to increase.

For an advisor, when first evaluating who in the client base may be most willing to discuss the subject of long-term care planning, and the best approach to design and funding, it is wise to begin by focusing on those with substantial income for the following reasons:

- with substantial income comes substantial responsibilities
- with substantial responsibilities come substantial consequences if the client cannot meet those substantial responsibilities
- consider those who have acted responsibly by already purchasing:
  - disability income
  - life insurance to fund buy-sell agreements
  - annuities to guarantee income

Determining insurability is the key to the entire process. Generally, the younger generation is healthier. As a result, age is to be considered as well as overall health. Some clients can pass underwriting requirements well into their 70s and occasionally mid-80s. But as one ages, insurability becomes more challenging and premiums become more expensive. Ideally, applicants should be between 45 and 65 years of age. An accelerated premium payment option may be attractive to the younger client who has the financial ability to pay the premium amount. It allows the client to finish paying the premium in ten years or to align premium payments to be completed in the client's working years. As well, it addresses the concern of rate increases.

According to American Association for Long-Term Care Insurance research, three-fourths (78 percent) of long-term care insurance policies are purchased by couples where either both or just one spouse purchases coverage. The average age for individual purchasers is 57, with some 76.3 percent of purchases made between ages 45 and 64, according to the Association's research. [21]

Planning for long-term care is particularly vital for women. Women are generally aware of the risk, as this chart illustrates:

### FIGURE 8-8

### Sixty Percent of Women Affected by the Economic Downturn in Their Ability to Plan for Their Future Care

Considering the current economic situation in the United States, what impact has the economy had on your ability to plan for your future long-term care?

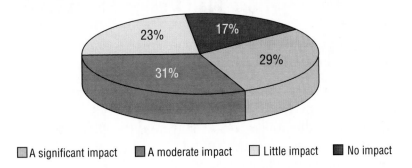

☐ A significant impact  ☐ A moderate impact  ☐ Little impact  ■ No impact

Source: Paul Petillo, *Retiring with a Plan* (2009), http://retiringwithaplan.blogspot.com/.

♦ Women face more risk of needing long-term care.
♦ Women represent a greater proportion of older Americans, accounting for almost 58 percent of the population age 65 and older.
♦ Women who reach age 65 have a life expectancy of another 20 years versus men who have a life expectancy of another 17 years.
♦ Women are twice as likely to be living alone. Between ages 65 and 74, 28 percent of women live alone compared to 15 percent of men. After age 75, 49 percent of women live alone compared to 22 percent of men.

---

21. *Id.*

+ The percentage of women living in poverty is highest among divorced or separated women (37 percent) followed by widowed women (28 percent), never married women (22 percent), and married women (10 percent).
+ Women are far more likely to go into a nursing home. After age 65, 40 out of every 1,000 women are in nursing homes, versus 24 men. After age 85, that figure is 265.2 for women versus 80.0 for men.
+ Women over age 65 include 980,000 nursing home residents versus 337,000 men.
+ Women are more likely to suffer from Alzheimer's disease, by far the leading health condition that requires long-term care. One in six women are at risk for developing Alzheimer's disease in their lifetime, while the risk for men is one in ten.
+ Women are more likely to suffer a stroke than men, another leading cause of needing long-term care. In 2004, 373,000 females and 327,000 males suffered a new or recurrent stroke.[22]

These statistics illustrate the importance of developing a strategy to protect this particular demographic with long-term care planning. The discussion of long-term care planning needs to focus not only on needing care, but also on the real hardship of initially providing care.

## Long-Term Care Insurance Plan Design Strategies

When designing the optimal long-term care insurance plan, there are many factors to consider and evaluate. The major factors include the following:

+ amount of the aggregate benefit pool or benefit payment period—the specific number of years or lifetime benefits
+ self-funding deductibility period, known as the elimination period in long-term care insurance policies
+ premium for various plan designs
+ investment opportunity lost on long-term care insurance premiums paid and the self-funded care cost (the elimination period and/or the exhaustion of benefits)
+ the cost of waiting
+ estimated tax savings

### Types of Policies

The long-term care insurance products in the market today are traditional "pool-of-money" products or life insurance and annuity-based products (linked products).

22. *Id.*

## Underwriting

Of the long-term care insurance products in the market today, traditional pool-of-money products have the strictest underwriting guidelines. These compose the vast majority of products sold. Life and annuity-based products tend to be more lenient.[23]

It is common for an insurance company to issue a traditional policy to an applicant with some medical conditions and charge a higher premium. Annuity products are the most lenient because applicants are paying higher premiums for these products and offsetting the insurance company's risk.[24]

A comprehensive long-term care insurance policy should include coverage for all levels of care—custodial, intermediate, and skilled—as well as all types of care settings—home care (to include, or offer as an option, informal care by a loved one), adult day care, assisted living facilities, skilled nursing facilities, and hospice care.

A pool-of-money policy provides a total dollar amount that can be used for various long-term care services. These policies pay a daily, weekly, or monthly dollar limit for one or more covered services. Policyholders can combine benefits in ways that best meet their needs. This provides more control over how the benefit dollars are spent. A policyholder may choose to combine the benefit for home care with the benefit for community-based care instead of using the nursing home benefit, for example.

An alternative to the more traditional approach of a pool-of-money policy is a lifetime maximum policy, similar to purchasing a face amount, as life insurance is structured. Upon certification of eligibility to receive benefits, the policyholder is reimbursed up to a specified percentage of his or her actual eligible long-term care expenses, up to the policy's lifetime maximum.

## Individual Policies

An individual long-term care insurance policy insures one policyholder only. Those who should consider these types of policies include

- ◆ individuals with no spouse,
- ◆ individuals whose spouse will not qualify for long-term care insurance, and
- ◆ individuals with a spouse where each wants his or her own policy and pool of money. Shared benefits are an option in policies and will be reviewed throughout the chapter.

## Joint Policies

A joint policy is a single policy that has either one policyholder with additional insured lives or two policyholders who are each insured. In both designs, the insured individuals can receive benefits in a number of ways:

---

23. Nicole Gurley, GurleyLTCI.com (2011).
24. *Id.*

- Each person can have his or her own pool of money to draw from, but benefits can be shared.
- Both insured individuals can share one pool of money.
- In some designs, up to three or more family members can be added as insured individuals by the policyholder.

The insured individuals may be a husband and wife, two partners, or two or more related adults.

Couples who think there is a good chance they both may need to use their benefits would be the best candidates for an individual policy. In the last two design considerations mentioned in the previous bullet points, the pooled benefit has a total benefit that applies to all the individuals insured in the policy. If one of the covered individuals collects benefits, that amount is subtracted from the total policy benefit.

Advantages to a joint policy design include the following:

- Many insurance companies offer substantial discounts when a couple purchases a joint policy.
- A joint policy can also provide tax benefits if one is self-employed or the insured individuals are in a business partnership.

However, there are also disadvantages to a joint policy design:

- If there is only one pool of funds, there may not be enough benefits for all insured family members in case more than one insured individual needs to utilize the benefits.

## Linked Policies

Many companies now offer products that are not standalone, pool-of-money long-term care insurance, but rather a life insurance or annuity contract with either a long-term care insurance rider or an accelerated death benefit provision (**cf. Chapter 4, p. 83**).

The life insurance linked product provides two types of protection: life insurance, which is guaranteed to pay at some future date, and long-term care coverage. Long-term care benefits are funded from the death benefit. There are currently two benefit payment options to draw against the death benefit:

- a monthly percentage of the death benefit, generally 2–4 percent
- a monthly benefit payment determined by dividing the death benefit by a number of years provided in the contract (generally two, three, or four years)

Most policies offer a rider that allows the policyholder to extend the benefit period, thereby increasing the pool of funds. For example, a two-year payout can be increased to four years, or a three-year benefit can be extended to six years. Most insurance companies also allow a return of premium within a period of time, usually 15 years, with no prepayment penalty.

A life insurance contract with an accelerated death benefit provision does not have a long-term care insurance rider, but rather accelerates the death benefit to pay for chronic illness care. A linked product accelerated death benefit differs from the traditional accelerated benefit feature in a standalone life insurance contract, which allows payment only when the death of the insured is anticipated or skilled nursing-home care is required.

One insurance company offers a rider, for an additional premium, that will continue paying benefits for chronic illness care if the death benefit is exhausted.

Another type of linked policy is a conversion policy, which gives the policyholder the right to convert another product to long-term care insurance. Two examples of conversion are

- a life insurance policy with an option, valid up to a certain age, to purchase long-term care insurance, usually without proof of insurability; and
- a disability income insurance policy with the option to convert it to a long-term care policy.

Combining a life insurance policy, owned by an irrevocable life insurance trust (ILIT), with a long-term care insurance rider will provide a client a way to pay for his or her long-term care needs with funds that have been removed from the client's estate. This allows for a more tax-efficient transfer of wealth. The indemnity method of a long-term care insurance rider will need to be used because the trust must verify that the insured qualifies for the long-term care benefit. The long-term care benefit is paid to the trust, because the trust owns the policy, so the insurance benefit is actually adding funds to the trust. The insured, or grantor, must never have had the money in hand or file a claim against the trust for such money as a direct distribution. A reimbursement method of a long-term care insurance rider cannot work in a trust because the receipts for care expenses are submitted to the insurance company by the trust, which owns the insurance policy. The insurance company then reimburses the insured, or the care provider on behalf of the insured. This chain of events provides a direct monetary benefit from the trust to the insured and therefore rescinds the integrity of the trust. Indemnity and reimbursement methods of benefit payments will be explained later in the chapter.

Through a linked annuity with long-term care insurance, the policyholder commits a lump sum to an annuity. The annuity issuer generally will match the amount with a long-term care benefit. Because the policyholder's money is used first, the insurance company is able to issue the policy using only five or six insurability questions. The questions generally include stroke, dementia, Parkinson's disease, multiple sclerosis, and insulin-dependent diabetes. If the applicant has already been diagnosed with any of these conditions, he or she is generally declined.

Through an impaired-risk single-premium immediate annuity (SPIA), a few insurance companies offer people who already need long-term care, or will shortly need it, a product that provides a lifelong income stream at a reduced upfront cost. Known as an impaired risk or medically underwritten SPIA, this product is underwritten on the basis of the annuitant's health rather than life expectancy. The more grave the illness, the less the upfront payment to purchase a given lifetime monthly benefit.

Of course, as with all SPIAs, the benefit ends at the death of the annuitant. Some companies, however, offer a "principal back" option—a refund of some of the principal when the annuity holder deceases. The beneficiary will receive a reduced amount of the principal in monthly payments.

Table 8-2 illustrates what a powerful tool this can be. As the table demonstrates, it is possible to buy lifetime care through a medically underwritten SPIA for almost half the cost of a traditional, age-based SPIA annuity. The disadvantage of this strategy is that repayment on an annuity ceases when the annuitant deceases. If the annuitant deceases sooner than the insurance company expects, the insurance company retains the portion of the premium that has not been repaid.

**TABLE 8-2**
**Traditional vs. Medically Impaired SPIA**

|  | Traditional SPIA | Medically Impaired SPIA |
| --- | --- | --- |
| Gender and Age | Male, 80 | Male, 80 |
| Health | Moderate Alzheimer's | Moderate Alzheimer's |
| Desired Monthly Income | $3,000 | $3,000 |
| Income Duration | Lifetime | Lifetime |
| Return of Principal | Available | Available |
| Premium Required | $255,890 (85 months) | $118,000 (39 months) |
| Difference |  | $137,890 |

Source: CLTC Course Handbook (Release 8.0, Jan. 2009)

Research studies show the typical demographic for linked products are individuals

♦ between the ages of 50 and 80 with a minimum liquid net worth ranging anywhere from $300,000 to $10 million or more, depending on the research study,[25] or

♦ who tend to think with their heads, not hearts; they are willing to pay for long-term care but have been shown how they can both leverage their money and maintain liquidity.

---

25. MILLIMAN RESEARCH REPORT, ANNUITY/LONG-TERM CARE COMBINATION PRODUCTS (2009); American Association for Long-Term Care Insurance (2011).

Generally, the product combines a universal life chassis with a full long-term care insurance policy linked to the death benefit. The long-term care insurance contract derives 100 percent of its funding from the death benefit. As an acceleration of the death benefit, the long-term care benefit payout will reduce both the death benefit and cash surrender values. The product's benefits are generally presented by an advisor as follows:

- A lump sum, commonly $100,000 but can be more or less, is used to pay for the death benefit. The funds to pay the premium do not need to come from the broader pool of assets under management but rather those that are in easily accessible and thus low-return assets such as CDs, money market accounts, and savings accounts.
- The client is shown how he or she obtains instant leverage through at least doubling the funds used to purchase the product and quickly realizes it would be close to impossible to get such a return on investment in existing accounts.
- The client is then informed that the funds remain liquid for a period of time, usually 15 years or greater, and that there is no surrender penalty.
- The product allows the insured to increase the pool of funds for long-term care coverage in the form of a rider.
- Asset-based benefits can multiply the amount of money in a policy, allowing $100,000 to result in perhaps $300,000 worth of benefits and a death benefit.

The advantages of linked products include the following:

- A payout from the policy, one way or the other, is assured.
- Most insurance companies guarantee a minimal death benefit.
- The policy qualifies for favorable tax status under IRC Section 1035. For example, the policyholder can roll over a cash surrender value to fund the policy.
- The policy's cash value grows at a guaranteed rate that is tax-deferred, and any funds withdrawn from the account and used to pay for long-term care are also tax-free. The premium paid plus any future earnings on the cash value of the policy can all be used for long-term care completely tax-free.
- Provides for loved ones in the event of premature death.
- Enables policyholders to re-accumulate lost assets by re-engaging in the upside potential of equity market participation, with reduced volatility risk.
- Allows portfolio diversification.
- Helps protect retirement assets from erosion caused by long-term care costs.
- Provides an alternative for those clients who do not think they will need long-term care.
- Provides an alternative for those clients who may not qualify for a traditional long-term care insurance policy.

♦ Provides an alternative for those clients who may wish to supplement an existing long-term care insurance policy.

The disadvantages of linked products include

♦ In states with a high cost of long-term care, the client has to buy a substantial death benefit.

♦ A client can purchase a greater death benefit with a standalone life insurance policy.

The following is an example of a $120,000 single-premium life insurance policy with long-term care benefits for a 55-year-old male, non-smoker, with a 30-day elimination period for home health care and a 60-day elimination period for other long-term care expenses:

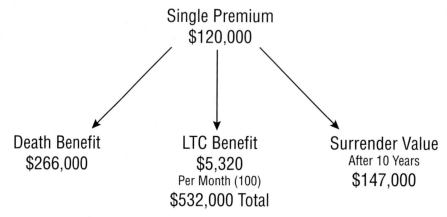

Single Premium
$120,000

Death Benefit
$266,000

LTC Benefit
$5,320
Per Month (100)
$532,000 Total

Surrender Value
After 10 Years
$147,000

Use of linked products: "Decease" OR "Live" OR "Quit"

## Benefit Amount Considerations

It is wise to always regard the highest form of long-term care in the client's geographical area as the minimum amount to be protected in the long-term care plan. Take into consideration where the client plans to retire geographically, as well. Most likely, the most expensive care will be that provided in nursing homes but could be 24-hour home care.

As part of the suitability solution, the client's income has already been calculated. It is recommended to include the annual income from investments that would normally be rolled over and then subtract the client's probable annual expenses, including any nonessentials that he or she would like to afford. The difference is the amount available for coinsurance. Coinsurance is the discretionary income available to reduce the cost of long-term care insurance, or the amount of money the client is willing to pay out of pocket toward the cost of care. From the highest cost of care, subtract the coinsurance. Divide the amount by 365. The result is the daily benefit. Further detail of how to calculate the daily benefit is provided below.

Depending on the financial situation, covering the entire maximum cost of long-term care with insurance does not, for some clients, provide the best value. If they opt to fully transfer the risk, they may pay higher premiums, while being unable to use the disposable income and income subject to reinvestment, from which coinsurance could be drawn. Most clients' concern is not that an illness will threaten the continued growth of their principal, but rather that it may force an invasion of principal.

Coinsurance is an important component of funding long-term care, because it keeps premiums at a manageable level. Premiums generally come from investments that would normally be reinvested.

Nursing home care is generally considered to be the costliest form of long-term care, but 24-hour home care may be more expensive. Conceivably, 24-hour home care can be impractical, for the following reasons:

- It is difficult to find and coordinate formal caregivers for three shifts and be confident that they will show up consistently.
- Few people are comfortable with strangers continuously coming in and out of their home.
- If the family decides on such care, it is likely that a full-time worker in the home, not employed by a home health care agency, would provide the services at a lower cost than a skilled nursing facility.

Calculating the coinsurance and daily benefit requires the following steps:

- Determine the maximum likely cost of long-term care, which is probably that of nursing home care, in the client's geographical area.
- Calculate the annual net income expected at retirement, including income from non-pension investments that will normally be reinvested.
- Determine what expenses, other than those for which long-term care insurance will pay, are likely to be. This should be relatively straightforward if the clients have been working with the advisor.
- Many clients have continuing commitments after retiring. Ask clients if they are:
  - Helping children in financial trouble because of divorce, poor judgment in handling money, or other reasons.
  - Providing for a handicapped child after the parents' deaths.
  - Assisting grandchildren with education costs.
  - Committed to making donations to charities or religious organizations.
- Subtract the total expenses from the net income.
- The net of the previous step divided by 365 is the daily amount available for coinsurance.
- The highest cost of care previously determined, less the amount available for coinsurance, equals the recommended long-term care insurance daily benefit.

## Benefit Periods and Pooling

The sum of the daily benefit amount chosen, multiplied by the benefit period that has been broken down to a daily basis (for example, a five-year benefit period equals 1,825 days) will be the benefit pooling amount, or pool of money, referred to earlier in the chapter.

> **$200 daily benefit amount x 1,825 days = $365,000 benefit pool of money**

The benefit period represents the period of time the insurance policy will pay benefits. There are various statistics on how long care is needed. The most prevalent length of time tends to be just less than three years. The possibility of having a long-term care insurance claim that lasts longer than three or four years is relatively low based on today's statistics:[26]

More than three years: 13.1 percent
More than four years: 7.6 percent
More than five years: 4.5 percent

However, if an individual's claim exceeds the expected number of years of the individual's policy, he or she can expect to need care for anywhere from two to six years. According to a study by Milliman, Inc., a 55-year-old who exhausts a three-year benefit period can expect to need care for another 3.7 years if a male, or 5.3 years if a female. An 82-year-old who exhausts a three-year benefit period can expect to need long-term care for another 1.9 years if a male, or 2.9 years if a female.[27]

It is necessary to consider family history and the financial consequences of an incorrect determination.

If premium cost is a material issue:

♦ A three- or four-year benefit based on reimbursement of incurred claims makes sense because the benefit period is stretched.

♦ After taking advantage of all available discounts, if the cost of the long-term care insurance protection is still an issue, selecting a shorter term policy can be a prudent option. When it comes to the cost of long-term care, some insurance coverage is indeed far better than none at all.

If premium cost is not a significant issue:

♦ Consider a longer benefit period such as five or six years.

If there is a history of longevity or chronic illness in the family:

♦ Lifetime is to be considered, but again it is important to keep in mind the average claim period. Alzheimer's disease likely requires at least a five-

26. THE AMERICAN ASSOCIATION FOR LONG-TERM CARE INSURANCE, HOW LONG DO LONG-TERM CARE INSURANCE CLAIMS LAST—A GUIDE FOR CONSUMERS (May 2010).

27. MILLIMAN, INC., AALTCI STUDY: A SPECIAL REPORT ON LONG-TERM CARE INSURANCE PROTECTION (2010).

or six-year benefit. Based on reimbursement, if the situation calls for an indemnity or cash payout, lifetime is the safest choice.

♦ If recommending lifetime benefits to a younger client, be aware that the client could face multiple rate increases by the insurance company, as this is the most costly benefit period actuarially to insurance companies. Also, insurance companies are closely monitoring their lifetime benefit policyholder block of business, and can request rate increases based on that criterion alone.[28]

Tax considerations:

♦ If the client has substantial tax-deferred (qualified) or low-cost-basis assets, a lifetime benefit allows the advisor to design a plan that executes properly. If a lifetime benefit period is not chosen and benefits are depleted, the client may be forced to liquidate the funds and pay substantial taxes.

If the client chooses an indemnity or cash payout, keep in mind that these options may limit the ability to stretch the benefit period. Stretching the benefit period takes place when the client does not use all of the allotted daily benefit, so it remains in the pool of money, allowing the benefit period to be stretched beyond the stated benefit period in the policy.

Additionally, skilled care facilities and home care are not mutually exclusive in that home care can progress to assisted living and then on to the skilled care facility. Such a combination can easily add up to five or six, or more, years. Many people who have the income and a healthy spouse usually have the stamina to survive one to two years of long-term care at home. However, it is the long-term care situation that continues past two years that is highly problematic, not only for assets but also the well-being and health of loved ones. Even if there is only a small chance that long-term care will last for more than five years, one should strongly consider the longest benefit period affordable.

## Short Duration/High Benefit Amount Planning

Selecting a shorter benefit period with a larger daily or monthly benefit amount provides greater flexibility to meet higher than expected expenses, while not sacrificing the overall size of the benefit pool.

**TABLE 8-3**
**Long-Term Care Plan Design Comparison**

| Benefit Design | Benefit Amount | Benefit Period | Total Pool of Money |
|---|---|---|---|
| Short and Fat | $6,000/month | 36 months | $216,000 |
| Long and Thin | $3,000/month | 72 months | $216,000 |

Source: Choices for Long-Term Care Insurance.

---

28. National Association of Insurance and Financial Advisors (NAIFA) (2008).

## Benefit Payment Methods

There are three methods insurance companies employ in paying long-term care insurance claims: reimbursement, indemnity, or cash benefits.

### Reimbursement

Under the reimbursement method, policyholders do not necessarily receive the entire daily benefit; the policyholder or care provider is reimbursed for the money spent on care, up to the daily maximum benefit. A policyholder may assign a care provider to receive the benefit payment.

The advantages of the reimbursement method:

♦ It presents the opportunity to stretch the benefit period because it is possible the policyholder will not use the maximum daily benefit at the beginning of the illness. Since most insurance companies use a pool of money approach, what is not used each day stays in the pool of money, thereby extending the benefit period.

♦ Reimbursement benefit payouts are the least expensive option; the premium will cost less than indemnity or cash benefit policies.

The disadvantages of the reimbursement method:

♦ Most insurance companies only allow the policy to reimburse actual payments for formal care defined as services provided by licensed professionals, yet some policies offer informal care to be purchased as an optional rider or offer it with a specified monthly maximum.

### Indemnity

This method allows the policyholder to receive the maximum daily benefit, regardless of actual expenses, as long as the policyholder shows he or she received at least one qualified service. The insurance company will send the policyholder a payment once a month for the maximum daily, weekly, or monthly benefit in the policy. Included in allowable expenses are items that are not specifically stated in the policy, such as personal need items, toileting supplies, medications, doctor visits, transportation, to name a few. Any remaining amount, after paying monthly expenses, is deposited into a personal account to pay future costs when the policy benefits are exhausted. Under the indemnity plan, an insured is more likely to receive the full benefit in the policy before the insured recovers or deceases. At the time of claim, most policies will require a "plan of care" from the attending physician, and then ongoing, periodic proof that a policyholder is still eligible for benefits.

Not all insurance companies offer the indemnity method. For those insurance companies that do offer this benefit payment method, it may be offered as part of the base policy provisions or as a separate rider that is purchased with additional premium. Additionally, some insurance companies include the indemnity method for nursing home care but not home care, and some include it for all types of care settings.

The advantages of the indemnity method:

♦ Ability to pay informal caregivers such as family members or friends.
♦ Fewer administrative requirements (no reimbursement paperwork).
♦ A valuable option if a policyholder plans to reside outside the United States.
♦ If a client qualifies for long-term care insurance but the client's spouse does not, the indemnity method may provide some options in planning. A plan design to consider:
  ○ A $300 daily benefit that pays on an indemnity basis is purchased,
  ○ The spouse does not have coverage.
  ○ If the insured spouse needs long-term care services, the insured will receive the entire $300 daily benefit, even if he or she receives only one service per day that costs less than $300. The balance of the money can be used for the spouse's care.
  ○ It needs to be noted that the spouse will only receive such coverage if the insured spouse's benefits are triggered due to a long-term care need.

The disadvantages of the indemnity method:

♦ It is more difficult to stretch the benefit period if the policyholder is receiving the entire daily benefit.
♦ Indemnity benefit payout is more expensive than the reimbursement method, averaging an additional 15 percent to 25 percent in premium. It is not as expensive as a full cash method, though.

## Cash

The cash benefit method provides the entire daily benefit without the need to show proof of care. A policyholder simply needs to submit a plan of care. However, the care plan is not actually required to be executed. The cost of this method can increase the premium as much as 50 percent over the cost of a reimbursement method.

According to a Milliman, Inc. study on cash versus reimbursement methods of benefit payments, the premium for a cash long-term care insurance policy is arguably more stable and less risky than for a conventional reimbursement method. Cash based long-term care insurance policies are insulated from the inevitable changes in the long-term care delivery system and from regulatory actions, which are likely given the legislative climate. Regulators continue to investigate insurance company claim paying practices. Of particular concern is the practice of not reimbursing for long-term care services because of the manner or setting in which services were provided. Cash method policies provide what consumers want, but are priced accordingly for it.[29]

The advantages of the cash method:

♦ This method works best if the advisor and client are looking for maximum flexibility, because the benefit payment can be used for any purpose. Examples of use of this method include:
  ○ If a client lives in a rural area, professional, formal care may be difficult to find.
  ○ A client may prefer a holistic approach to his or her care, to include yoga, alternative healing, and medical supplements.
  ○ For those who may have been turned down for disability income insurance due to adverse health history, a cash benefit method policy may offer an alternative, as there are less stringent underwriting criteria.
  ○ To supplement a disability income insurance policy in the event the client has an income protection need beyond a disability income insurance company's issue and participation limitation.

The disadvantages of the cash method:

♦ There is not an opportunity to stretch the benefit period because the policyholder is receiving the entire daily benefit each day or month.
♦ This is the most expensive method.
♦ Not many insurance companies offer this option.

## Benefit Payout Frequency

The benefit payout is the maximum amount that an insurance policy will pay out on a daily or monthly basis. The benefit payout allows a policyholder to carry over unused benefits to help offset for days when the actual cost of care may exceed the daily or monthly benefit.

### Daily Benefits

Generally, long-term care insurance policies contain provisions stating that the maximum daily benefit can only be for a day of care and whatever is not used remains in the pool of money. This can be a concern if the daily cost of care differs substantially during the week or month and a reimbursement method has been chosen.

### Weekly Benefits

The weekly benefit payout is generally available as a rider for additional premium, but some insurance companies build it into the base policy. The balance of the unused benefit amount can be transferred to cover care that exceeds the daily benefit on a weekly basis.

---

29. MILLIMAN, INC., CASH MODEL LTCI PRODUCTS—MORE STABLE AND LESS RISKY THAN REIMBURSEMENT (2008).

### Monthly Benefits

This benefit payout method is the most flexible form of payout. A policyholder is able to add up all the qualified care expenses received for a month and submit a claim. The policyholder will receive full payment regardless of whether he or she exceeded the maximum daily benefit as long as the aggregate claims are less than or equal to the total monthly benefit. Most insurance companies that offer this option do so as a rider for additional premium. However, there are some insurance companies that build this method into the base policy.

## Elimination Period

The elimination period is also referred to as the deductibility or waiting period. It is the period of time after being diagnosed with a loss of activities of daily living (ADL) or a cognitive impairment. During this period, expenses are paid out of pocket before the insurance company begins claim payments. Actuarially, it is a waiting period that the insurance company uses to gauge the number of days they will be liable for a period of services. One can purchase a zero-day elimination period, where benefits begin immediately, or a 30-day, 60-day, 90-day, or longer elimination period, but a 90-day elimination period is most common. This is predictably a result of the erroneous information that Medicare will pay for long-term care services for the first 100 days of care. During this period the policyholder is most likely responsible for payment for his or her care.

There are many different ways that insurance companies define and calculate the elimination period. Many policies define a day during the elimination period as a day of needing care. But more insurance companies are defining it as a calendar day, with no care required every day. Some policies have two pools of money, one for home care and one for facility care, which may have two mutually exclusive elimination periods.

Some policies require a policyholder to meet only one lifetime elimination period, whereas other policies require an elimination period to be met for each claim incident. Some policies waive the elimination period for home care but require it to be met for facility care. Of those waived days used for home care, although waived for elimination period purposes, some insurance companies will allow such days to count toward the facility elimination period.

Some insurance companies require that the accumulation of days to meet the elimination period be met in a certain calendar period, six months for example. If unmet, the insured must start the elimination period over.

Some insurance companies recognize that home care may only be received a few days a week, and that meeting a 90-day elimination period could actually take six months or longer, if the policy has a service day definition. Such companies credit a certain minimum number of home care days, three or more days a week for example, with a full seven days of elimination period credit, even though there were fewer actual days. Other companies' policies require that the elimination period be consecutive days of care. If one does not receive care at least seven days a week, the person will not qualify for benefit payments.

With some policies, and under some circumstances, a 90-day elimination period could result in an actual waiting period of six or more months before claims are paid.

With all the various elimination period definitions, it is important to thoroughly understand the differences, review the insurance contract, and make sure the elimination period meets the client's long-term care planning objectives.

## Inflation Protection Options

There is no doubt that the cost of care will continue to escalate. Deciding how the insurance coverage purchased today will still meet needs in 20 to 30 years is an important consideration. There are a variety of strategies for ensuring the benefits keep up with the rising cost of care, and keep pace with inflation. A benefit amount that is adequate to current long-term care costs will have much less buying power in future dollars without some form of inflation protection.

Looking back over the previous century, the core inflation rate for all goods and services has been close to 3 percent, whereas the inflation rate for long-term care services has been closer to 5 percent. The reason for the higher inflation rate for long-term care services is that these services have a high medical component; medical costs and services have been increasing exponentially in comparison to the core inflation rate.

### FIGURE 8-9

### 2011 Milliman Medical Index

Healthcare costs for American families double in less than nine years

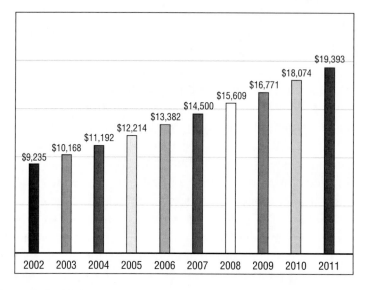

Source: 2011 Milliman Medical Index.

There are four general inflation protection methods available in a long-term care insurance policy: simple, compound, consumer price index (CPI), and guaranteed purchase option.

## Simple Inflation

With simple inflation growth, the daily benefit increases a set percentage, typically 5 percent per year, without compounding. For example, if a $200 daily benefit is purchased, on the first anniversary, $10 is added to the benefit, and another $10 is added each year thereafter.

This type of inflation is less expensive than compound inflation because it presents significantly less risk to the insurance company over time. Considering two-thirds of long-term care insurance claims begin after age 80,[30] simple inflation protection is likely to be the best option for 65- to 75-year-olds because compound inflation does not show a significant benefit increase before 12 to 14 years.

**FIGURE 8-10**

**Effect of Inflation on Daily Rates for Nursing Home Care**

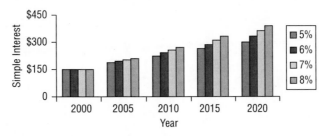

Source: National Association of Insurance Commissioners (2009).

## Compound Inflation

Compound inflation is the most expensive inflation option available in a long-term care insurance policy, yet it provides the greatest growth to the long-term care benefits. It is most commonly offered with a 3 or 5 percent growth rate. Some insurance companies offer this option with a limitation to the growth, along with an option to grow for the lifetime of the policy.

Using 5 percent as the example, if a client purchases a $200 daily benefit with 5 percent inflation growth, beginning in year two of the contract, the client's daily benefit will be $210. In year three, the 5 percent growth will be based on the $210, and the benefit will be $220.50.

This option is chosen by 47 percent of purchasers, according to the American Association of Long-Term Care.[31] In considering age appropriateness for inflation growth benefits, if affordable to the client, general benchmarks to use are: for

---

30. AMERICAN ASSOCIATION FOR LONG-TERM CARE INSURANCE, THE 2011 SOURCEBOOK FOR LONG-TERM CARE INSURANCE INFORMATION (2011).

31. American Association for Long-Term Care Insurance (2009).

clients ages 50 to 64, a 3 percent compound inflation growth is sufficient, and for clients under age 50, a 5 percent compound inflation growth is sufficient.[32]

The advantage of compound inflation growth:

◆ It provides those under age 65 with a significantly larger benefit due to the compounding of the inflation, compared to simple inflation growth.

◆ If there is longevity in a client's family history, compound inflation will likely provide a superior benefit.

The disadvantage of compound inflation growth:

◆ Compound inflation option is very expensive: it has the potential to almost double the cost of the premium.

**FIGURE 8-11**

**The Effect of Inflation on Nursing Home Costs**

(assumption: daily cost=$270, inflation rate=5% compounded)

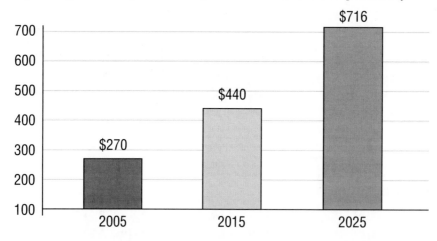

## Consumer Price Index (CPI)

The CPI inflation option fluctuates according to the consumer price index. Every year, on the policyholder's policy anniversary, the benefit and the total pool of money will automatically be adjusted on a compounded basis, according to the CPI. The CPI tracks the price of goods and services, which include such items as housing, food, and transportation. The CPI is often used to provide cost-of-living wage adjustments to millions of American workers. As a result, the CPI has a strong association with housing and labor costs, which are two key drivers of long-term care costs. In fact, Social Security benefits and many U.S. pension plans are linked to the CPI. It is the most widely used measure of inflation. However, it fails to fully reflect the higher cost of health care inflation.

---

32. NAIFA (2008).

## Guaranteed Purchase Option

Also known as the guaranteed increase option, there are many variations to this option that can keep the premium more affordable. In the most basic plan design, the policyholder reserves the right to purchase the inflation benefit in the future by having the ability to purchase additional benefits while receiving benefits. The policyholder is able to purchase additional benefits at periodic intervals without reapplying for insurance or providing evidence of insurability. It is typical that the policy offers a 15 percent increase every three years. The additional premium for any increase under this option is based on the policyholder's attained age as of the option date, original underwriting risk classification, and the premium rates in effect on the option date. If the policyholder exercises this option, the benefit and premium are added to the original policy benefit amount.

This inflation option may be a good planning approach if there are short-term cash flow concerns. Over time, as one's income increases, the future premium increases are more affordable than a level premium policy, while still allowing the ability to keep pace with inflation. It is less expensive than securing long-term care insurance with the automatic inflation options. However, it is important that the policyholder does not disregard election of the increase options, because most policies will rescind the option if the insured fails to elect a certain number of consecutive options. If increases are elected, the cost of the additional coverage will be more over the life of the policy than if the policyholder had elected level-premium, automatic inflation protection options.

If a client is between the ages of 65 and 75, instead of an inflation growth option, the advisor may want to consider having the client purchase a higher benefit amount. This plan design is slightly less desirable for a client at this age compared to a client who is over age 75, because the younger client is not as close to the average claim age.

**FIGURE 8-12**

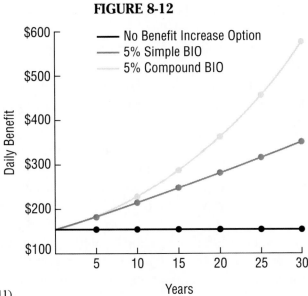

## *Types of Care in Policies*

Although HIPAA specifically defines the minimum policy standards for tax-qualified long-term care insurance, it permits several different forms of coverage. In general, tax-qualified policies adopt one of three possible forms:

◆ Facility care only (home health care may be included by rider)
◆ Home health care only
◆ Comprehensive care

### Facility Care Only

Some policies cover only long-term care provided in licensed facilities, such as nursing homes and assisted living facilities. Policy applicants should understand that home health care, although it represents a significant share of all long-term care, is not covered by this type of policy. Some insurance companies offer an optional rider for an additional premium cost that covers home health care expenses. Such insurance products are sometimes called unbundled long-term care policies.

Because a 60 percent premium savings for this type of plan is not uncommon, purchasers of facility-care-only policies tend to be older due to the plan's affordability.

### Home Health Care Only

Recognizing that most long-term care is provided in the home, some insurers offer policies that cover only home health care services. Such limited coverage is ideal for people who already have access to facility-only care, or who plan to apply for Medicaid assistance if and when they require institutionalization.

The home health care provision typically covers

◆ adult day care centers;
◆ licensed home health aides who assist the care recipient with activities of daily living;
◆ homemaker services like cooking, cleaning, transportation, and telephoning; and
◆ respite care for caregivers—temporary (typically 14–20 days) institutional or home care provided to a recipient while the home-based caregiver takes vacation time.

Home health care coverage is not typically designed to provide 24-hour care, which can potentially be far more expensive than facility care. However, when combined with an informal primary caregiver—a family member or friend—the home health care benefit may be the only thing that keeps a policyholder out of a nursing home.

Caution needs to be taken when selling a home-care-only policy to people who assure you they will never use facility care. Nine percent of recent policies purchased were for home care only, and very few insurance companies offer them, because it is difficult to guarantee that any particular person will never use facility care.[33] If a policyholder eventually needs to enter a facility, a lack of insurance may force the client onto Medicaid, in stark opposition to the client's original objectives.

## Comprehensive Care

The most common policies are those that cover a full range of care services, whether provided in the home, in a nursing or assisted living facility, or even through some forms of community-based care. If services delivered outside of a nursing home are included and not optional, the policy is known as a comprehensive benefit plan.

Most of these types of policies stipulate different elimination periods, benefit periods, and benefit amounts for each of the four principal types of care: home care, assisted living, adult day care centers, and nursing home care. Home care and adult day care center benefits may be offered as a percentage of facility care, ranging from 50 to 100 percent of the daily facility care benefit.

## *Other Important Policy Features*

### Time Limit on Denial of Coverage for Pre-Existing Conditions

Insurance companies may have a legitimate right to avoid insuring applicants with pre-existing medical conditions. People with known medical issues may be rejected in underwriting. If an insurance company elects to issue a policy to someone with a known pre-existing medical condition, most states limit the time period during which the policy may deny coverage for that condition. The time limit is generally two years after the policy's effective date.

### Pre-Existing Conditions and Policy Replacement

HIPAA prohibits insurers from imposing any restrictions on replacement policies because of pre-existing conditions.

### 30-Day Free Look

Policyholders must be offered a 30-day free-look period, beginning on the date the policy is delivered, during which time it may be returned for a full refund of all premiums and other fees paid. The policyholder may also make certain changes to the policy during this specified time.

### Coverage of Alzheimer's Disease

Once a policy has become effective, Alzheimer's disease may not be excluded as a covered condition or trigger. While policies must cover Alzheimer's and other "organic cognitive disabilities" (disabilities that result from changes to the structure of the brain), they are not required to cover non-organic mental disorders such as schizophrenia. Some states, however, require long-term care policies to

---

33. GORDON, *supra* note 1, CERTIFICATION IN LONG-TERM CARE COURSE HANDBOOK (2009).

cover all mental conditions, regardless of their origin. Some insurance companies offer this coverage independently of state requirements.

## Non-forfeiture

No other form of health insurance includes non-forfeiture benefits as part of its policy design. The request to include non-forfeiture options in long-term care policies comes from two groups:

1.  Consumer organizations that believe people should receive a refund if they do not claim benefits or if they cancel their policies. This belief is driven, primarily, by the expectation that insurance companies will raise premiums because the insurance companies have priced policies artificially low to attract business or because they have failed to understand the risks. The consumer groups are backed by many insurance regulators.
2.  Many consumers who do not believe in or fully understand the concept of insurance as risk-management, a practice that still makes sense even if benefits are not drawn.

One of the four following non-forfeiture options must be offered to policyholders:

1.  Return of premium

A policyholder with this option is refunded some or the entire premium upon the death of the insured. Under the typical return of premium arrangement, a relatively small return is payable for cancellations occurring after the fifth policy year. However, there is usually no refund for cancellations occurring prior to then. The refund increases until, after as little as 15 policy years, it can equal 100 percent of premiums paid. The premium returned is reduced by any claims.

2.  Full non-forfeiture

This option provides the same benefits as the return of premium, but the premium return is unaffected by claims.

3.  Shortened benefit period

Also known as a premium bank account, this is the most common form of non-forfeiture in tax-qualified policies, as it is the recommended option in recent revisions to the NAIC LTC Model Act. The shortened benefit period method entitles policyholders to a paid-up benefit equal to the greater of all premiums paid or 30 days of benefits when the policy has been in force for three years or more. In California, the benefit is the greater of premium paid or 90 days of benefits, and the policy has to be in force for at least ten years, not three.

4.  Reduced paid up

When this option is exercised, all provisions of the cancelled policy remain effective, with one exception: the daily benefit is reduced. The level to which it is reduced is dependent upon the length of time the policy has been in force. This benefit is allowed in a tax-qualified policy but is rare because most companies are using the NAIC's recommended form of non-forfeiture, the shortened benefit period.

## Waiver of Premium

Waiver of premium is a standard provision in almost all long-term care insurance policies. However, its application is not widely standardized. In general, this provision waives the payment of premium while benefits are being paid to the policyholder. Premiums are waived after a certain number of days from the date benefits began. This is usually 60 or 90 days.

Some waivers do not take effect until the first day of the month following the month in which the waiver period was met. Many policies only waive premiums for facility care claims, and premium paid is required for other types of care settings. Some of these policies offer riders to provide a blanket waiver of premium. A few policies will waive premiums after a claim for nursing care facilities, even if the policyholder recovered and is no longer receiving benefits.

## Joint Waiver of Premium

Some long-term care insurance policies include or provide the option to add a joint waiver of premium benefit. The insurance company waives the premium payments each month that the insured individual, spouse, or partner is receiving care, as defined by the policy. The waivers begin after the elimination period of the policy has been satisfied.

The joint waiver of premium benefit can relieve the financial obligation associated with long-term care expenses. For example, this feature can provide additional peace of mind in that a spouse may be able to take more time off from work, knowing the premium payments will be waived when the other spouse is in need of care.

Joint policies covering two insured individuals will usually waive premiums for both insured individuals.

## Bed Reservation

This benefit is in most long-term care policies. The benefit continues to pay the daily benefit to reserve, or maintain, the policyholder's residential space in a nursing home facility for any absence. A stricter definition in a long-term care insurance policy states that the daily benefit will continue to be paid when the insured must be hospitalized temporarily. Some policies offer coverage for a short period of time, such as two weeks, or limit the number of payment periods, whereas superior policies offer a benefit that will pay up to 60 days per year.

If the nursing home or assisted living facility has a waiting list, as many do, the resident may find that he or she no longer has a bed or room there upon return to the facility, so this becomes a very important feature.

## Respite Care

Respite care is generally defined as temporary institutional or home care provided to a recipient while the home-based caregiver takes vacation time, or a period of rest and relaxation. These riders typically provide 14 to 30 days of benefits. Some insurance policies pay respite care only in the home, but the ideal respite care benefit pays for facility care as well to cover the 24-hour care that will be needed if the caregiver is absent for several days.

Generally the respite care benefit differs from the daily benefit, in that

♦ Respite care will pay to bring someone in during the elimination period. However, the care provided does not satisfy the elimination period.

♦ Some insurance companies will pay for respite care even though it exceeds the maximum.

### Alternative Plan of Care

The claim departments of early long-term care insurance companies used to experiment with benefit utilization by offering alternatives to nursing home confinement to those filing claims. This feature allows the family and the insurance company's claim department to negotiate the level of care needed and coverage available.

This process is intended to be mutually beneficial to both the insurance company and the policyholder. If completed properly, it can save insurance companies thousands of dollars per claim and provide the policyholder with more comfortable care. It relies on compromise: by authorizing benefit payments for sources of services that are not usually covered, insurance companies try to save claim dollars, while at the same time helping policyholders obtain care and services that better meet their needs.

Today, most long-term care policies include a provision that permits either the insurance company or the insured individual to propose an alternative plan of care when the final result is at least as favorable to the insured as the policy would normally permit. This option is also valuable because it provides a way for a policy to pay for new services that are not specifically covered by policy language. The insurance company generally does not have the right to demand implementation of an alternative plan of care.

### Home Modification

Every insurance company offers the policyholder the ability to receive a lump sum of a specified amount in the policy, to be deducted from the pool of money, to renovate their home to be care-accessible. Some examples of modification include ramps for a wheelchair and a handicap-accessible bathroom and kitchen.

### Care Coordination

This feature allows the insurance company to pay for a third party to establish and manage the policyholder's care. The coordinator, usually a nurse or a social worker, will provide the following services:

♦ Help choose where the care is best delivered (home, assisted living, adult day care centers, nursing home, or even hospice)

- Help negotiate prices and coordinate schedules
- Provide constant monitoring of the policyholder's status and report it to family members who might not live nearby

Some insurance companies consider this benefit very important because they allow benefits payable under this provision to not deplete the overall benefit maximum in their policies. Some provide unlimited benefits for insurance company-employed care coordinators, a specific benefit for a private care coordinator of the policyholder's own choosing, or both.

Several insurance companies offer policyholders a variety of incentives to elect the care coordination option, including

- waiving the elimination period for any home or community-based care recommended by the care coordinator;
- providing benefit levels for home care of up to 100 percent of the nursing home benefit, versus 80 percent if the policyholder does not use a care coordinator; and
- basing benefits on a weekly, rather than a daily, amount, thus allowing flexibility in scheduling care.

### Caregiver Training

Many insurance companies will pay a modest amount, usually between three and five times the maximum daily benefit, to train the informal caregiver to lift, move, feed, bathe, give medicines, for example.

## Price Discounts

There are a wide variety of discounts available to married adults and unmarried adults who are living together. These discounts generally range from 15 to 40 percent each year when more than one individual purchases a policy simultaneously. A partial "couples discount" may even be offered if only one partner purchases a policy.

Multiple policy discounts for unmarried situations vary from one insurance company to another. Some offer discounts to domestic partners or individuals in committed relationships.

Some insurance companies will extend their multiple policy discounts to same-generation family members such as siblings. Some insurance companies offer multi-generational family discounts that allow several generations of a family to buy a single pool of benefits to be used by anyone in the family who needs the long-term care benefits.

Some insurance companies are now offering multi-line-of-coverage discounts, where if a policyholder also has other lines of coverage with the insurance company, the company will offer the policyholder a discount on the long-term care insurance policy. Examples of other lines of coverage may include life insurance, annuities, disability income, homeowners, or automobile insurance.

## Other Optional Benefits to Consider

The following optional benefits are available in some long-term care insurance policies for an additional cost:

### Survivor Waiver of Premium

Also known as survivor benefit, this benefit is similar to survivorship life insurance for couples, and is only available in individual long-term care insurance policies when both individuals purchase policies. Typically, if one spouse deceases after the policies have been in effect for a certain number of years, usually ten years, the policy becomes paid up for the survivor, and no additional premiums are due. The deceased does not have to be receiving long-term care insurance benefits at the time of death. This is generally offered as an optional benefit in a policy, but there are insurance companies that offer it as a policy feature with the ability to purchase an enhanced benefit as an optional rider.

This option should be considered for couples when there is a greater than seven-year disparity between their ages; include it on the older spouse's policy.[34]

### Shared Care

This optional rider allows couples to share each other's benefits. If one spouse needs long-term care and uses all of the benefits in the pool of money in his or her own policy, he or she then can access the other spouse's pool of money policy benefits. Some insurance companies offer policies where two people share one pool of benefits. This may be used to maximize the eligible tax deductibility when there is a difference in ages between the spouses.

The "shared care" option is highly attractive to couples because it provides the ability to purchase a more affordable, shorter-duration policy while offering access to a much larger combined pool of money.

### International Benefits

For clients who spend time outside the U.S., or plan to retire outside the U.S., this optional benefit should be seriously considered. Some policies have international benefits included, whereas others do not. Of those policies that include this option, it is important to evaluate the details of the benefit if this benefit is applicable to a client's lifestyle.

### Restoration of Benefits

This benefit restores the full benefit period after some level of benefits has already been paid. To qualify, the policyholder must have fully recuperated and may not have suffered a relapse for a minimum period, usually six months. If the policyholder requires long-term care within six months of recovering from a prior period of care, some policies will restore full benefits if the cause is different from the first illness or

---

34. NAIFA (2008).

injury. But most will not restore benefits for any reason until the policyholder has, for at least six months, regained the ADL or cognitive capacity he or she was lacking.

This provision will most likely be used by a younger person who stands a better chance of recovering from a chronic illness. In considering this benefit for an older client, generally, after extended periods of care of perhaps more than a year, older long-term care patients typically do not recover from their illness or injury.

### Home Support Services

Family members may live in a different city than their parents or relatives. Home support services help bridge the gap by providing dependable care, enabling the policyholder to remain safe at home. Some of the services provided may include

- bill payment;
- companionship;
- escort to appointments, events, and religious services;
- light housekeeping and laundry;
- maintaining calendars and appointments;
- meal preparation;
- medication reminders; and
- shopping and errands.

### Short-Term Recovery Care

In addition to including a long-term care insurance plan in a client's portfolio for long-term, catastrophic medical conditions, the insurance market offers protection for short-term recovery care. Medicare will protect such care for only a specified time period and includes stipulations. Short-term recovery care insurance can be used in conjunction with a long-term care insurance policy to lower premiums, by extending the elimination period of the long-term care insurance policy. It is quite affordable, with monthly premiums averaging less than $100. This type of policy also allows for less coinsurance (self-insurance) to be allocated from the client's financial plan. By combining the two products, the advisor designs a fully comprehensive yet affordable package that covers both a client's short- and long-term care needs.

## Maximizing Tax-Qualified Status

As discussed in Chapter 7, only tax-qualified long-term care insurance premiums are considered a deductible medical insurance expense.[35] Eligible long-term care insurance premiums are the lesser of the age-based premium and the actual premiums paid.

---

35. I.R.C. § 213 (d)(1)(D).

## Gifting

Federal gift tax law allows one to pay the eligible long-term care insurance premiums for another person without having to treat the premium as a taxable gift. Anyone may pay anyone else's medical care expenses without the payment being treated as a gift, as long as the person pays it directly to the insurance company. If an individual pays the premium on behalf of another person, only the eligible premium will be exempted from gift tax treatment. The balance of the premium will be treated as a gift. No gift tax will be owed if the total gifts the benefactor makes to an individual during the year do not exceed the annual gift tax exclusion. There will be no tax deductibility for federal income tax purposes, though the taxpayer may be able to obtain some tax deductibility or a tax credit on state income taxes, depending on the state.

Premiums of tax-qualified long-term care insurance policies represent qualifying medical expenses for the purposes of the annual gift tax exclusion, if they are paid directly to the insurance company, service provider, or institution that provides the care.[36]

Individuals may pay the premium for their spouses and eligible dependents without those premiums being treated as a gift. In general, taxpayers who itemize their deductions may also deduct such premiums on their federal income tax return to the extent that all the eligible premiums that are paid, plus all other unreimbursed medical expenses, exceed 7.5 percent of adjusted gross income (AGI).

Long-term care insurance policy premiums paid for a parent are deductible as qualifying medical expenses for income tax purposes if the parent is a dependent of the child by IRS definition.

## Internal Revenue Code (IRC) Section 1035 Exchange

As reviewed in Chapter 5, as a result of the Pension Protection Act of 2006 (PPA), beginning in 2010, federal regulations began permitting IRC Section 1035 exchanges from both life insurance and annuities to a long-term care insurance policy, with no taxable gain in the policy cash values. This is accomplished without the individual being taxed on any unrealized gain at the time of transfer.

Product exchanges can provide funds in the right circumstances. A non-qualified deferred annuity, immediate annuity, or life insurance policy can be exchanged tax-free for a standalone, traditional tax-qualified long-term care insurance policy. Any non-qualified deferred annuity may be used, subject to the limitations set by the transferring insurance company.

Any capital gains transferred as part of the IRC Section 1035 exchange to pay long-term care insurance premiums will be tax-free. The exchange may be either a full or partial exchange. If it is a partial exchange, gain and basis are transferred pro-rata, as a proportionate allocation. By exchanging an annuity to pay the

---

36. *Id.* §§ 2503(e)(2)(B), 7702(B).

long-term care insurance premiums, the client may avoid taxes on the capital gain portion of the amount exchanged, which would otherwise be taxable when withdrawn from the annuity.

In addition to using the IRC Section 1035 exchange for traditional long-term care insurance policy, a 1035 exchange to a linked product that has a guaranteed minimum income benefit that doubles or triples if the client needs long-term care services may serve as a vital planning instrument.

Be aware that the release of IRC Section 1035 and other sourced funds from a financial or legal organization that has control over said funds may be delayed. Coordinating the availability of funds with the requirement of a premium payment from the long-term care insurance company may prove difficult. In cases where the applicant was declined coverage by the insurance company, returning funds to an annuity, trust, or other legal agreement may not be possible and/or may result in a loss of tax advantages.

## Health Savings Account (HSA)

As reviewed in Chapter 6, contributions to an HSA are made on a pre-tax basis, while withdrawals for qualified medical expenses are made tax-free. Any growth inside an HSA is tax-free if withdrawals are for qualified medical expenses or tax-deferred if withdrawals are for other purposes. This instrument is advantageous in long-term care planning, as it allows for payment of qualified medical expenses over and above expenses covered by an insurance product.

Qualified long-term care insurance premiums are a tax-qualified medical expense.[37] As a result, an individual may withdraw funds tax-free from the individual's HSA to pay qualified long-term care insurance premiums. Qualified long-term care insurance premiums are eligible premiums; therefore only eligible premiums are tax-free.

### Transfer of Individual Retirement Account (IRA) Money to HSA

Individuals may make a one-time tax-free transfer of money from their traditional or Roth IRA to their HSA in the amount of the maximum deductible contribution they can make to their HSA for the year of the transfer.

IRA money transferred in a direct trustee-to-trustee transfer to an HSA will not be treated as income, nor will it be subject to the 10 percent federal penalty tax applicable to premature distributions from IRAs and qualified plans.[38] The transfer must be a direct trustee-to-trustee transfer. A rollover, in which the IRA owner withdraws money from their IRA and deposits it to their HSA, will not receive the favorable tax treatment this law provides. Transfers of amounts to an HSA from an ongoing Simplified Employee Pension (SEP IRA) or SIMPLE IRA do not qualify for the tax treatment under these IRC sections.

---

37. IRS Notice 2004-50, Q & A 41.
38. I.R.C § 408(d).

### *Return of Premium*

Qualified long-term care insurance policies cannot provide for a cash surrender value or other money that can be borrowed, paid, assigned, or pledged as collateral for a loan.[39] Premium refunds, policy dividends, or similar amounts must be applied to reduce premiums or increase future benefits.[40] There are two exceptions to this general rule:

1. Premium refunds paid on the individual insured's death are generally not taxable income to the policyholder's estate or beneficiary.[41]
2. Premium refunds paid on a complete surrender or cancellation of a long-term care insurance policy must be included in the taxpayer's gross income to the extent that the taxpayer was allowed a deduction or exclusion for the premium payments.[42]

In addition, it is now possible to cancel a policy, although not recommended, and receive a full refund, if one chooses such an option.

## Conclusions

Long-term care insurance continues to evolve to meet the changing needs and desires of the baby boomer generation, making it easier to develop a tailored plan.

Long-term care insurance policy provisions, features, and optional benefits are not standardized between insurance companies; therefore, it is important to carefully analyze the contracts in detail. The premium is driven by the policy features and optional benefits.

Long-term care planning can be complicated; therefore, it requires the same commitment that financial and estate planning advisors pledge to financial and estate planning.

It is the responsibility of advisors to protect clients and help them prepare for unforeseen challenges. Though it may be difficult for clients to discuss, many will need long-term care as they age. It is important to educate clients, especially baby boomers, on the benefits of long-term care insurance. Even though they may think it only will happen to someone else, they may be the "someone else" who experiences the unthinkable hardship.

Understanding the impact and delivery of long-term care allows the right questions to be asked, which leads to the discussion regarding a client's belief that he or she will live a long life. This belief manifests itself every time a client asks for reassurance that his or her principal will remain intact after retiring. Establishing

---

39. *Id.* § 7702B(b)(1)(D).
40. *Id.* § 7702B(b)(1)(E).
41. *Id.* § 7702B(b)(2)(C).
42. *Id.*

this baseline leads to a discussion of the effects long-term care has on the family and the client's retirement plan. This, in turn, leads to the establishment of a plan for providing care by having the client consider who will provide care and where it will be delivered. This allows the advisor to discuss the impact of needing care on the client's retirement plan and ultimately how to pay for the plan. This engagement should focus on how the client's plan allocates income and assets for retirement, rather than invading principal for long-term care. Affluent people live on income, not assets. Long-term care insurance is a product that protects income. The discussion of long-term care planning should be in the context of protecting one's family against the consequences a long-term care event causes. Protecting assets, providing choices, and not being a burden come with having a plan in place.

Long-term care insurance is a financial tool that, when used properly, can protect a family from the devastating financial and emotional impact long-term care can cause. Advisors who seize this opportunity will build stronger relationships with clients and deliver greater value to them at the same time.

# Long-Term Care and the Employer

**9**

EMPLOYEE AND EXECUTIVE BENEFIT programs are an integral part of America's workplace and have existed in this country since colonial times. In the early 20th century, these programs began to evolve from simple pension plans to include more comprehensive benefits, such as medical coverage and life insurance. The federal government recognized the important role these plans play in providing financial security to working Americans, and over time, the nation's tax policy has strengthened the incentive for employers to provide such programs. This voluntarily employer-based system has served Americans well for decades, and continues to provide workers and their families with protection against life's financial risks. In fact, 41 percent of workers consider workplace benefits to be the foundation of their personal safety net.[1] These benefit plans include health care, retirement savings, and financial protection products—inclusive of long-term care insurance. Perhaps least-recognized and -understood are the financial protection products, as described below, that help working families manage life's uncertainties.[2]

The life insurance industry is the leading provider of products and services for employer-sponsored benefit packages, including products that protect against the risk of premature death, extended

---

1. METLIFE, STUDY OF THE AMERICAN DREAM (2008).

2. This chapter draws in part from HARLEY GORDON, CERTIFICATION IN LONG-TERM CARE COURSE HANDBOOK, Sections A, C, D (Releases 8.0, 9.0, Corporation for Long-Term Care Certification 2009, 2011).

disability, long-term care, or the non-medical expenses often associated with serious medical conditions. For most American workers, the insurance coverage they receive at the workplace is the only insurance they have for such events, making the benefits provided through the employer and insurance company a partnership that is a vital component to the financial security of families across the nation. Fifty-one percent of all employees report obtaining the majority of their financial protection products, such as life, disability income, and long-term care insurance, as well as retirement savings plans, through the workplace.[3] The workplace is an efficient and a cost-effective way to provide American workers and their families with the tools they need to attain financial security.

Employers conduct extensive research before choosing a provider of insurance that meets the needs of their employees, negotiating favorable pricing that makes the coverage affordable. Employers also provide a range of educational information that helps guide their employees through the process of selecting appropriate benefits for their families' needs. In many instances, employees would not have access to these products without the convenient and efficient venue provided by their employers.

Employers can help to make these insurance products affordable by offering various subsidy levels for their employees. Some employers pay 100 percent of the cost of employee benefits; others share the costs with their employees; still others offer employees discounted rates on benefits programs that employees pay for themselves. Long-term care insurance is becoming an increasingly more popular employee benefit. As well, of the employee benefit programs offered in the workplace, long-term care insurance is becoming an important component of employee and executive benefit planning. An increasing number of employers, including the federal government and many state governments, offer long-term care insurance as part of their employee benefit packages. Many employers offer plans that allow employees to purchase long-term care insurance for the employee and the employee's spouse and parents. Generally, the employee pays the premium for the dependent coverage. The result is a system in which workers and their families have access to affordable coverage through their employers. In fact, 90 percent of Americans believe that it is important for employers to continue to offer benefits even if the employee must pay most or all of the cost.[4] With the volatility of the economy, working Americans are able to find the financial protection they need through these vitally important, employer-sponsored plans.

Federal legislation was introduced in the 111th Congress that would have permitted employees to pay for long-term care insurance premiums with pre-tax dollars in employer-sponsored cafeteria plans and flexible spending accounts (FSAs). Although this legislation was voted down, if similar legislation is passed in

---

3. METLIFE, *supra* note 1.
4. METLIFE, STUDY OF EMPLOYEE BENEFITS TRENDS (2009).

the future, hopefully it will encourage more employers and employees to consider long-term care insurance in their employee benefit programs.

Employees and their families who purchase long-term care insurance through the workplace receive substantial benefits. In 2007, insurance companies paid $7.2 billion in long-term care insurance claim benefits, helping families pay for long-term care needs and often making it possible for the insured to live at home with formal care.

Ninety-eight percent of the people who purchased group long-term care insurance in 2010 were between the ages of 18 to 64, while 86 percent of this same age group purchased individual policies through an employer multi-life insurance arrangement.[5] Although group insurance plans once implied 100 percent employer-paid coverage, this is no longer the case. Group insurance plans have transformed into shared contribution plans.

Research shows how strongly a benefit plan influences employees' decisions on where to work:

◆ Sixty percent of employees have stayed in a job because of the benefit program.

◆ Forty-nine percent of employees have taken a job because of the benefit program.[6]

Many employees make career decisions based on the relative strength of the employee benefit package. Adding long-term care insurance to an employee benefit program can help an employer gain an edge in a tight labor market.

## Employer's and Caregiver's Burden

As the American workforce ages, U.S. employers increasingly face an emerging business challenge that is the result of the elder care and caregiving resource dilemma. Today's workforce, often referred to as the "sandwich generation," is challenged with caring for both their children and their parents. As a result, employees face more elder care and caregiving issues than ever before in this country's history. Coping with this challenge places an enormous demand on employees, wearing them emotionally, physically, and financially, which in turn creates enormous challenges for employers. Ultimately, these commitments significantly impact the work-life balance of employees, therefore affecting the productivity and success of our country's businesses. It is estimated that 62 percent of employed caregivers report their caregiving responsibilities have negatively affected their work.[7] For the aging workforce, elder care is replacing child care as the number one concern.

5. AMERICAN ASSOCIATION FOR LONG-TERM CARE INSURANCE, THE 2011 SOURCEBOOK FOR LONG-TERM CARE INSURANCE INFORMATION (2011).

6. METLIFE, 9TH ANNUAL STUDY OF EMPLOYEE BENEFIT TRENDS (2011).

7. AGIS Network, *Caregiving & Long Term Care Executive Overview* (Oct. 7, 2010), http://www.labormanagementcoalition.org/pdf/AGIS-Executive-Summary.pdf.

Additionally, there are increased employer-sponsored health care costs due to the stress caregiving places on employees. The MetLife Mature Market Institute in conjunction with the National Alliance of Caregiving released a study with these key findings:[8]

- Eight percent higher medical costs for working caregivers
- Eleven percent higher medical costs for blue-collar working caregivers
- Eighteen percent higher medical costs for male working caregivers
- Caregiver health problems are estimated to cost U.S. companies about $13.4 billion per year
- Younger caregivers, those ages 18 to 39, demonstrate significantly higher rates of cholesterol, hypertension, chronic obstructive pulmonary disease, depression, kidney disease, and heart disease than non-caregivers of the same ages

The National Alliance for Caregiving reported in a recent study that 44.4 million Americans, 21 percent of the U.S. population age 18 and over, provides long-term care informally to someone over age 50. Most caregivers (89 percent) are helping relatives. Nearly 80 percent of care recipients are over age 50; the other 20 percent are ages 18 to 49. The value of this informal care is estimated at $257 billion per year.[9]

Caregivers surveyed stated the following as their most predominant concerns:

- The most frequently reported unmet needs are finding time for themselves (35 percent), managing emotional and physical stress (29 percent), and balancing work and family responsibilities (29 percent).
- About three in ten caregivers say they need help keeping the person they care for safe (30 percent) and finding easy activities to do with the person they care for (27 percent).
- One in five caregivers say they need help talking with doctors and other health care professionals (22 percent) or making end-of-life decisions (20 percent).

Reports show that employees who are caregivers display lower work performance, decreased physical well-being, and diminished levels of satisfaction at work and at home. The workers may be present at their place of employment but coping with impairments themselves, such as depression, chronic stress, and fatigue, that cause them to work less efficiently and less safely. Millions of Americans fall into the category of presenteeism—they are physically at work but mentally and emotionally affected by elder care distractions that impair productivity.[10] Actual costs of employee stress related to legal and financial matters can be found in increased absenteeism and presenteeism, increased mistakes, increased accidents and injuries, and decreased work productivity. The real difficulty for

---

8. The Mature Market Institute and National Alliance of Caregiving (Feb. 2010).

9. National Family Caregivers Association and the National Alliance for Caregiving (2004).

10. U.S. EQUAL EMPLOYMENT OPPORTUNITY COMMISSION, EMPLOYER BEST PRACTICES FOR WORKERS WITH CAREGIVING RESPONSIBILITIES (Jan. 19, 2011).

employers is that when an employee has one or more of these major stressful legal and financial problems, it becomes the employer's problem, too.

With 46 being the average age of a caregiver, the responsibility of caregiving impacts retirement and educational savings plans. Caregiving, additionally, places career limits on one's key wage earning years. Employees who have faced caregiving issues with loved ones become increasingly concerned about their own long-term care needs, as sharply rising care costs risk a secure retirement.

When offering long-term care insurance, it is important that the insurance plan design includes caregiver services. These services can help reduce the burden of employees caring for elder family members and provide helpful resources to reduce stress, which can then help employees remain more productive. In addition to a caregiver services provision in the policy, a cost-of-living-adjustment provision will help benefit amounts keep pace with inflation.

Children rarely want to provide care but almost always will provide care. It is the right thing to do, and they are concerned about their parents' safety. Suggesting that the advisor knows the adult children will care for their parents provides an opportunity for the advisor to express the essence of long-term care insurance. Long-term care insurance allows children to provide care better and longer by bringing in formal caregivers to handle the work that children and spouses find the most time-consuming, embarrassing, and stressful. It then allows the children to maintain their relationship as children supervising care, not providing care. It serves no lesser a purpose for a spouse, sibling, or friend. If one wonders why children will purchase long-term care insurance for their parents, it is because, one way or another, children will end up paying for their parents' care—emotionally, physically, or financially.

A noteworthy survey has indicated that 62 percent of employees would like their employers to offer long-term care insurance.[11] These employees have several motives to buy long-term care insurance through the workplace for themselves, their spouses, and their parents:

- ◆ They have personally experienced, or learned from the experience of acquaintances, the impact of chronic illness on families.
- ◆ They may have to reduce work hours or even leave their jobs to take care of a parent who is without long-term care insurance.
- ◆ Group insurance may offer discounted pricing for the employees and their spouses.
- ◆ Group insurance may offer guaranteed issue underwriting for employees under a certain age. Many insurance companies offer employees a one-time opportunity to buy long-term care insurance with limited or no health questions, even when employees pay 100 percent of the premium.[12]
- ◆ If individual long-term care insurance policies are offered, as with a multi-life product, an insurance company may underwrite individual purchasers under age 64 by asking a series of short questions in a phone interview. For

---

11. PRUDENTIAL FINANCIAL, 2003 LTC INSURANCE EMPLOYEE BENEFIT STUDY (2003).
12. Phyllis Shelton, LTCI Worksite Toolbox (2011).

older purchasers, the insurance company generally requires an attending physician's statement (APS).

♦ Extended family members such as parents, siblings, and adult children are eligible to apply for coverage with medical underwriting. Simplified underwriting is sometimes available to spouses of employees, as well.[13]

♦ The employer may contribute to the cost of the policy.

Employers should look to long-term care insurance advisors as educators, to explain to employees the facts regarding funding sources and out-of-pocket costs for the various levels of care throughout the country. When educating, there are a lot of parallels that can be drawn between long-term care insurance and other types of insurance, as well as financial, investment, and estate planning. Employers can integrate long-term care insurance education within their financial education campaign, as it plays a significant role in wealth accumulation and preservation.

### FIGURE 9-1

### Knowledge of Insurance Products

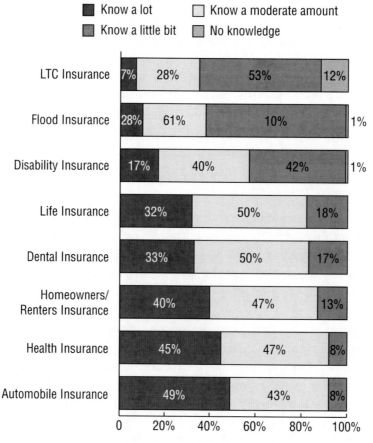

Source: Prudential, Long-Term Care Insurance: A Piece of the Retirement & Estate Planning Puzzle (2011).

13. *Id.*

In addition, because evidence shows a link between family caregiving and health care costs, corporate wellness programs and employee assistance programs should be linked to corporate long-term care planning. For example, where stress can clearly be an issue for caregivers trying to manage work and family, wellness programs that offer a variety of stress-management seminars and stress-reduction programs, such as onsite yoga and exercise classes and relaxation techniques, can be helpful. Online decision support systems, which help caregivers know which services are the best for themselves and their relatives, fit in with other health care decision support systems.

Working caregivers need to be encouraged to stop or reduce negative behaviors as well as to take full advantage of the preventive opportunities employers offer. Smoking cessation programs are a prime example, because there is a clear link between elder caregiving and smoking, especially among white-collar workers. Incentives can help drive utilization in wellness programs.

Other elder care education programs include caregiver fairs, line supervisor training, lunchtime seminars, flex-time and shared work, and dependent care accounts. About 1 percent of employers offer the services of a geriatric care manager to conduct an in-home assessment, develop a care plan, and spend a small number of free professional hours (usually one to three hours) to put into place the services the older person needs. Ways to redesign traditional employee benefits and human resource offerings to become compatible with the realities of long-term care include the following:[14]

- ♦ Paid time off (PTO) programs: A PTO program can replace traditionally distinct programs (i.e., vacation, sick, and personal days) with a single block of time that gives employees more control over their time. Additionally, PTO programs encourage responsible time management and give employees the flexibility to take time off when they need it, not because they need to "use it or lose it."
- ♦ Telecommuting arrangements: Helping employees successfully manage between work and home can help address productivity, loyalty, and retention. Giving employees the flexibility to choose where they work can allow them to be fully engaged in their work without the pressure to leave the office at a certain time to fulfill their personal responsibilities.
- ♦ Flexible schedules: In many industries, the traditional "nine-to-five schedule" is not necessary to keep the business running and customers satisfied. In these cases, allowing employees to work a schedule that is convenient for them, as long as the work is done on time, is a great way to help employees balance work and life.

The integration of available resources, the modernizing of employee benefit and human resource programs, and the education provided by an employer-sponsored

14. University of Pittsburgh Institute on Aging, MetLife Mature Market Institute, The MetLife Study of Working Caregivers and Employer Health Care Costs National Alliance for Caregiving (Feb. 2010).

long-term care insurance plan are more relevant than ever; they are valuable to both the employer and the employee.

## Employee and Executive Benefit Planning Issues

As health care and other core benefit costs continue to rise, developing benefit strategies that provide value to both the organization and the employee, in particular the executive, has become especially challenging. In addition, the aging of the U.S. workforce is causing many companies, especially large, highly diversified employers, to change the way they conduct business and deliver benefit offerings to their employees.

Employers' concerns regarding long-term care include

- loss of key employees;
- employees' preoccupation with their caregiving duties;
- lost productivity;
- lost revenue; and
- reduced value of the business.[15]

Solutions for the employer include:

- providing individual or group long-term care insurance on a voluntary basis;
- providing caregiver services as an employee benefit or provide access to long-term care insurance beyond the employee to family members who may potentially be dependent on the employee to be the family member's caregiver;
- providing executive carve-out plans; and
- utilizing limited premium payment options.[16]

### Employer-Sponsored Long-Term Care Insurance Plans

The profile of group long-term care insurance purchasers is different from the profile of individual product purchasers in that

- the average age of a group insurance purchaser is 43;
- the monthly benefit purchased is less than $4,000;
- the benefit period purchased is three years or less;
- ninety-three percent choose a 90-day elimination period; and

---

15. National Association of Insurance and Financial Advisors (NAIFA) (2008).
16. *Id.*

♦ eighty-eight percent of new long-term care insurance sales were funded using employer funds, implementing guaranteed-issue policies, with an option for the employee to personally purchase additional coverage.[17]

Some group long-term care insurance plans are guaranteed-issue or modified guaranteed-issue. The former term means there is no underwriting and all applicants are accepted. The latter term means that there is limited underwriting.

Employer long-term care insurance plans are generally divided into three markets: true group, multi-life, and group trust. Association plans are known as affinity plans.

## True Group Long-Term Care Insurance Plans (GLTCI)

True group long-term care insurance plans are offered as an employee benefit, typically to persons employed at least 30 hours per week. Eligible employees' family members—parents, grandparents, siblings, and adult children who are age 18 and older, as well as aunts and uncles—are also eligible to apply for coverage. In some plans, relatives of a group member may apply even if the group member does not.

Additionally, group long-term care insurance plans offer advantages to family members:

♦ Some insurance companies allow employees' family members to be billed directly to their homes or through bank account withdrawal. This advantage is available on individual long-term care insurance policies, as well.

♦ If the employee is paying the premium for a parent's tax-qualified long-term care insurance policy, the employee may deduct it as a medical expense as long as the parent is a dependent.

Following is a summary of the true group long-term care insurance marketplace:

### True Group Long-Term Care Insurance (GLTCI) Market Update

♦ GLTCI market grew by 20+ percent in new premiums in 2010
♦ New GLTCI premiums were $150+ million in 2010
♦ GLTCI industry averaged approximately $700 in per employee annual premium
♦ Cumulative market growth rate for past 13 years is 892 percent
♦ Employee family members' needing care contributes to growth
♦ Growth driven by benefits community diversification
  ○ Voluntary benefits proliferation
  ○ Competition drives differentiation
♦ The top four insurance companies accounted for 90 percent of new premiums

Source: Genworth True Group Market Update (June 1, 2011); LTCI Partners (Apr. 8, 2011).

---

17. UNUM, BUYERS STUDY: BENEFITS STRATEGIES FOR A NEW ERA (2011).

## Executive Long-Term Care Insurance Plans

Executive long-term care insurance plans are emerging as an appealing method for attracting, rewarding, and retaining "key" executives, for any size business. An executive long-term care insurance plan protects the assets of the key employees and executives who control business relationships and spending authority of the corporation.

Some employers may consider paying key employees' long-term care insurance premiums instead of offering them annual bonuses. While bonuses are taxed at an exorbitant rate, long-term care insurance allows for favorable tax treatment. Included in the advantages are less costly premiums due to the premium discounts of purchasing with a multi-life arrangement.

More than ever, executives are viewing corporate-sponsored long-term care insurance plans as an attractive and economically favorable method to pre-fund this risk, and at the same time protect retirement assets and income from rapid depletion. A corporate-sponsored executive long-term care insurance plan protecting a key employee and the key employee's spouse potentially creates a lifetime multimillion dollar, tax-free wealth preservation value.

Strategies for these plans, such as the use of limited premium payment options, will be addressed later in the chapter.

## Multi-Life (Individual Insurance) Plans

Individual insurance policies issued with discounts and more relaxed underwriting are referred to as "multi-life" plans.

Many advisors work in the multi-life market, helping to design executive "carve-out" solutions for a group of executives or other key employees. Multi-life long-term care insurance continues to be a fast growing segment of the long-term care insurance market, accounting for 14 percent of total individual long-term care insurance sales in the first half of 2008 according to LIMRA International data, an increase of 21 percent from the first half of 2007.[18]

This type of long-term care insurance policy allows business owners to purchase coverage for themselves and their families, as well as their key employees and their families, offering favorable tax treatment.

Multi-life insurance policies also present a significant opportunity for advisors to serve their more affluent clients. By introducing clients to this type of long-term care insurance planning, advisors can also reinforce their position as trusted advisors who are truly knowledgeable about the long-term care insurance industry, and committed to finding the best solutions for clients.

## Group Trust Plans

Similar to multiple employer trusts (METs) that are utilized to provide group medical insurance coverage to small employer groups, a group trust plan establishes a trust as the master policyholder.

---

18. LIMRA International, Inc. (2009).

Once it is established, it accepts for group coverage employer groups that are too small to be eligible for their own policies. Like METs, these plans are usually established for the benefit of specific industry groups, such as medical care providers or law firms.

More often, group trust long-term care insurance plans are used by insurance companies to sell, in particular states, individual long-term care insurance plans that are not or cannot be approved in those states. A master trust is set up in a state that has lenient insurance laws, and certificates of coverage are issued from the master trust.

Because most states do not have the same discretion over group trusts as they do over individual plans, such a group trust avoids the state's insurance regulation for individual long-term care insurance, and the certificate may be sold within that state.

### Affinity Group Plans

Associations frequently contract with a long-term care insurance company to provide long-term care insurance to their members. Often, such plans are supported by individual policies that are usually issued with family discounts. While these are not traditional group plans covering employees of a single employer or members of a labor union, associations meet the definition of a group for insurance purposes—they offer premium discounts to their members and underwriting concessions, such as simplified underwriting.

### Workplace Insurance Policy Continuation Options

All states allow group long-term care insurance policies to convert their certificates of coverage to individual long-term insurance care policies, without having to provide evidence of insurability, in the event the group policy is cancelled by the insurance company, employer, or group policyholder. In many cases, the conversion period is 60 days from the date of policy cancellation. Some states require insurance companies to charge a premium for the individual conversion policy, based on the insured individual's group application age, rather than the individual's attained age. For example, if a group certificate holder was 50 years old when he or she enrolled in a group long-term care insurance plan and the plan is cancelled when the insured individual is 55 years old, the insured's premium rate for an individual policy obtained by exercising the conversion privilege will be the rate of a 50-year-old with the same gender.

In addition, long-term care insurance purchased through the workplace is portable; employees can retain coverage if they change employers or retire.

To summarize, the various types of employer "group setting" plan design considerations include:

- ◆ providing access to large numbers of people;
- ◆ minimum participation requirement of 6 to 15 percent in order to implement the plan (generally, six lives, not six employees, need to enroll in the plan, for example);

- a simpler application;
- a 5 to 10 percent discount off individual premium rates;
- reduced underwriting requirements compared to individual application requirements;
- employees could potentially collect upward of 45 percent in total premium discounts by purchasing long-term care insurance through their employer; and
- many group insurance policies offer only basic coverage, with few options. This tends to keep the price affordable for the general employee population, but also creates an opportunity for selling individual policies that can be better customized to the employer's objectives.

More affordable group long-term care insurance plan design considerations include

- guaranteed purchase option instead of 5 percent compound inflation protection if there are short-term cash flow concerns;
- fifty percent instead of 100 percent home health care benefits;
- shorter benefit periods, such as, a two- or three-year benefit period; and
- longer elimination period, such as a 90- or 180-day elimination period.

In order to properly educate employers and employees and achieve maximum participation, group long-term care insurance should be enrolled during a time of year when other benefits are not being enrolled simultaneously. This reduces distractions and allows for greater focus.

In working with employer groups, employees are not the only ones who need to understand that long-term care insurance coverage is an important and valuable benefit. Employers may be concerned that a third party will only try to sell products, not educate the employees, raising more questions than answers. If this objection occurs, the advisor can respond to management's concern by pointing out the impact of lost productivity and presenteeism and how long-term care insurance can provide a solution to these issues.

Group long-term care insurance typically is offered as a voluntary benefit for which the employee pays some or all of the premium. Some employers may choose to purchase a base plan, allowing the employees to purchase additional units of coverage or enhance the plan design. At the very least, long-term care insurance should be offered as a voluntary benefit.

For those employers that have already implemented a long-term care insurance program, offering advice on in-force policies may be a valuable benefit for employers and their employees. A program analysis can help them validate the program, analyze the current coverage offering to make sure it is meeting their objectives, and decide whether to make adjustments to it, supplement it, or, if necessary, replace it with a more current plan.

# Planning Strategies

There are many valid reasons for an employer to secure long-term care insurance for its employees. The employer has the flexibility to discriminate in terms of to whom coverage will be offered and for whom coverage will be paid for by the employer. For example, an employer can offer employer-paid long-term care insurance to management and offer voluntary coverage to the rest of the employee population. In addition, there is flexibility in terms of who pays the premium.

As discussed in Chapter 6, currently, the federal tax code provides employers and employees with favorable tax treatment of premiums and benefits for qualified long-term care insurance policies. Corporate tax deductions are available to employer-paid qualified long-term care insurance policies in the form of premium deductions as a usual business expense.

Employees are not taxed on premiums paid by their employer for long-term care insurance policies owned by the employee, the employee's spouse, and the employee's eligible dependents,[19] even if the premiums exceed the age-based eligible premium limitation.[20] The benefits paid to reimburse long-term care expenses are not taxable to the employee.

Executive long-term care insurance can be an attractive benefit for both the company offering it and the insured. An employer can carve out selected key employees for long-term care insurance. In designing an executive carve-out long-term care insurance plan, there is flexibility in defining the class of employees to be included. Similar to all benefit plans, it should be formalized in the corporate minutes and approved at a corporate board or management meeting. The plan may be based on years of service and income criteria, to recruit, retain, and reward employees. To review a sample corporate resolution, please see Appendix 3.

Linked policies in small to medium business situations work well to protect key employees or protect buy-sell agreements. Traditional life insurance only pays when a death occurs, whereas a linked policy provides both a death benefit and a living benefit in the event the executive can no longer participate in the business.

## *Maximizing Tax Leverage within the Business Entity*

There are several ways a corporation can maximize the tax leverage on qualified long-term care insurance plans while providing key employees and executives significant benefits.

For a profitable corporation with retained earnings, fiscal year-end planning with long-term care insurance offers a solution. Retained earnings are created when a C corporation decides not to spend or distribute earnings at the end of its fiscal year. In order for the C corporation to retain earnings, it must pay corporate

---

19. I.R.C. § 152.
20. *Id.* § 106(a).

income taxes on the amount retained. Retained earnings create a double tax; it unfavorably affects the corporation and the owner of the corporation. The fiscal (tax) year for C corporations does not necessarily end on December 31st, as it does for "pass through" entities and individuals. At the beginning of the fourth quarter of the C corporation's fiscal year, profitable companies generally start looking for tax deductions. Long-term care insurance is an excellent way to offer an important benefit and reduce taxes; benefits are far more valued than new office furniture. The premium paid by the business is excluded from the employee's adjusted gross income even if the premium exceeds the age-based eligible premium amount. In the next section, the planning strategy is put into practice, using the accelerated premium payment option.

For an S corporation, limited liability company, sole proprietor, or partnership entity:

♦ If the sole proprietor's or partner's spouse is on the payroll and meets the criteria of a bona fide employee, the entire premium is deductible on the sole proprietor's Schedule C.[21]

♦ If that spouse's policy has a shared benefit rider, the rider is to be included in the deductible premium amount; the actual total premium is deductible.

Additional strategies for self-employed business owners and sole proprietors include the following:

♦ If a business owner's parent is on the payroll, purchasing a joint policy makes sense, because the employed parent can pick up the parent's spouse (the other parent) as an insured.

♦ Most insurance companies underwrite joint policies covering domestic partners, if they share living expenses. Premium paid on a policy that also covers a dependent is deductible on Schedule C. It appears that in a domestic partner relationship, the premium is deductible if the couple meets the following criteria:

  ○ The dependent received over half of his or her support from the taxpayer during the tax year.[22]

  ○ The dependent was a member of the taxpayer's household, which the taxpayer maintained by paying more than half the household expenses, and the dependent lived with the taxpayer during the entire tax year, in a relationship recognized by local law.[23]

For business owners and sole proprietors, consider also the favorable tax treatment of a ten-year premium payment policy for these business situations.

---

21. IRS Tech. Adv. Mem. 94-09-006 (Ltr. Rul. 94-09-006).
22. I.R.C. § 152(d)(1)(C).
23. *Id.* § 152(d)(2)(H).

## Accelerated Premium Payment Options

The use of accelerated premium options, such as a single payment, ten-year payments, or to-age-65 payments, provides a higher tax deduction for the corporation and enables the long-term care insurance premium to be fully "paid up" by the time the owner retires or sells the owner's portion of the business.

Implementing an executive long-term care insurance plan allows the corporation to offer customized benefits to a select group of highly compensated employees, while capitalizing on favorable tax treatment for the corporation and the policyholders. Additionally, accelerated payment options provide an abbreviated period of premium expenditures that can mirror the duration of an executive's employment. For example, the policy can be used as a retention tool for key employees. If they stay with the corporation for ten years, they will receive a paid-up long-term care insurance policy as a reward for their loyalty. The employer can then purchase a ten-premium payment policy for the executive and the executive's spouse and, in doing so, provide benefits and asset protection beyond retirement.

The accelerated pay options represent a creative approach to employer-sponsored executive long-term care insurance plans. A long-term care insurance plan is usually an especially meaningful benefit for executives, as they are typically older and have accumulated significant assets.

Long-term care insurance plans help executives finance their long-term care expenses, secure retirement assets, and preserve their estates for future generations, while providing tax benefits and an efficient revenue distribution for the corporation. It is an effective compensation and retention instrument.

---

*Frontloading the premium may create a challenge from the IRS on the following points:*

Reasonableness: Employees can deduct tax-qualified policy premiums to the extent that these are "ordinary and necessary expenses for reasonable compensation paid to employees."[24]

Deferred compensation versus welfare benefits: Another issue is whether limited-pay policies actually provide employees deferred compensation rather than deferred welfare benefits.[25]

*The benefit design must be justified to the IRS, as reviewed in Chapter 6.*

---

24. *Id.* § 162.

25. *Id.* § 404(b); *see also* Wellons v. Comm'r, 31 F.3d 569 (7th Cir. 1994).

## Fiscal Year-End Planning for Profitable Companies with a Retained Earnings Issue

Because the deductibility of premium is not limited to the age-based eligible premium limitations for non-owner employees or any employee of a C corporation, the objective will be to maximize the amount of premium being paid for by the corporation on the employees' behalf.

This can be accomplished by having the corporation determine participation criteria (which employees it would like in this group of insured individuals), and then secure long-term care insurance policies for this group. It is usually desirable to design a comprehensive benefit consisting of the highest daily or monthly indemnity benefit available, lifetime or the longest benefit duration available, 5 percent compound inflation, and full non-forfeiture or return of premium riders. Other optional benefits should also be considered. Including the employees' spouses in the plan is also a good idea because the spouses' premiums are also deductible. Without insurance, long-term care expenses incurred by either the employee or spouse will be paid from a common pool of personal assets. Lastly, yet importantly, accelerated-pay premium options will further increase the premiums for the long-term care insurance.

The following is a worksheet illustrating the tax leverage and benefit value of an executive long-term care insurance plan, providing the plan design, as described above, to five executives of a C corporation:

### C Corporation Executive LTC Plan

| Corporate Tax Bracket | Premium Payment Option | Estimated Rate of Inflation | Number of Covered Employees |
|:---:|:---:|:---:|:---:|
| 40% | 5 | 4% | 5 |

### Corporate Deduction & Tax Savings

| Year | Annual Premium for Covered Group | Corporate Tax Deduction on LTCi * | Net Cost of LTCi After Tax |
|:---:|:---:|:---:|:---:|
| 1 | $195,522 | ($78,209) | $117,313 |
| 2 | $195,522 | ($78,209) | $117,313 |
| 3 | $195,522 | ($78,209) | $117,313 |
| 4 | $195,522 | ($78,209) | $117,313 |
| 5 | $195,522 | ($78,209) | $117,313 |
| **TOTALS** | **$977,611** | **($391,044)** | **$586,567** |

| Net Present Value of Future Premium Payments at Estimated Rate of Inflation | $522,258 |
|:---|:---:|

| Value of Long Term Care Benefits (5% Compound) at end of premium payment period | $3,327,448 |
|:---|:---:|

Looking past the five-year accelerated premium term, the value of the long-term care insurance benefits after 20 years will grow to over $6.9 million, with no additional premiums required.

## Conclusions

Many employers are now beginning to understand that long-term care insurance functions as a firewall around an employee's retirement plan.[26]

Common disabilities requiring long-term care services for the workforce under age 65 are accidents, cancer, and strokes.[27] Forty-three percent of those needing long-term care are under age 65.[28] A long-term care event can occur at any time. Employers and employees alike need to be educated that ownership of a long-term care insurance policy protects them not only as they age, but also in their working years. In addition, long-term care insurance reduces the amount an employee needs to save for retirement and protects the employee's earnings.

The CLASS Plan has prompted discussions about the importance of long-term care planning and has raised awareness among many people who had overlooked this important matter. The best advice to any employer or individual concerned about the cost and availability of long-term care services is to consider purchasing private long-term care insurance now.

By incorporating long-term care insurance into one's financial planning, one can secure protection at current age rates, take advantage of current health status, and avoid paying higher premiums due to waiting or being rated or declined for coverage in the future.

Reasons for employers to include long-term care insurance in their employee benefit programs include the following:

- Key employee retention
- Limited premium payment options leverage tax savings
- Control of their business
- Business wealth preservation
- Tax savings, which may be the key selling point

Long-term care insurance resonates with many advisors because of their own long-term care experiences with loved ones. Some have said this career path is their social calling.

26. Mike Skiens, Business Insurance (Mar. 18, 2007).

27. Kaiser Commission on Medicaid and the Uninsured, Georgetown University Health Policy Institute (Nov. 2005).

28. National Care Planning Council (2011).

# *Life Table for the United States Social Security Area 1900–2100*

**ACTUARIAL STUDY NO. 120**
**by Felicitie C. Bell and Michael L. Miller**

To use the table: Calendar Year column represents the year on which life expectancy is based. Depending on male or female, current age determines life expectancy. For example: In 2011, a 60-year-old male has an additional life expectancy of 20.4 years, for a total life expectancy of 80.4 years.

## Period Life Expectancies at Selected Ages, by Sex and Calendar Year

| Calendar Year | Male 0 | 30 | 60 | 65 | 70 | 100 |
|---|---|---|---|---|---|---|
| 1900 | 46.41 | 34.57 | 14.18 | 11.35 | 8.85 | 1.61 |
| 1901 | 47.87 | 34.33 | 14.09 | 11.33 | 8.85 | 1.63 |
| 1902 | 49.02 | 35.1 | 14.53 | 11.71 | 9.17 | 1.76 |
| 1903 | 49.2 | 34.76 | 14.21 | 11.43 | 8.92 | 1.66 |
| 1904 | 48.08 | 34 | 13.74 | 11.09 | 8.61 | 1.53 |
| 1905 | 48.73 | 34.52 | 14.04 | 11.35 | 8.85 | 1.54 |
| 1906 | 48.27 | 34.49 | 14.18 | 11.44 | 8.94 | 1.55 |
| 1907 | 48.29 | 33.79 | 13.69 | 11.01 | 8.58 | 1.5 |
| 1908 | 50.22 | 35.26 | 14.41 | 11.61 | 9.03 | 1.61 |
| 1909 | 51.12 | 35.53 | 14.43 | 11.6 | 9.08 | 1.6 |
| 1910 | 50.08 | 35.02 | 14.18 | 11.38 | 8.87 | 1.6 |
| 1911 | 51.8 | 35.26 | 14.31 | 11.47 | 8.94 | 1.64 |
| 1912 | 52.34 | 35.35 | 14.34 | 11.49 | 8.98 | 1.67 |
| 1913 | 51.72 | 35.33 | 14.43 | 11.55 | 9.03 | 1.71 |
| 1914 | 52.87 | 35.63 | 14.49 | 11.59 | 9.06 | 1.76 |
| 1915 | 53.51 | 35.63 | 14.38 | 11.44 | 8.88 | 1.68 |
| 1916 | 52.42 | 35.13 | 14.17 | 11.26 | 8.77 | 1.64 |
| 1917 | 52.18 | 34.85 | 14.11 | 11.22 | 8.75 | 1.67 |
| 1918 | 45.34 | 32.05 | 14.49 | 11.63 | 9.19 | 1.83 |
| 1919 | 54.19 | 36.59 | 15.3 | 12.27 | 9.65 | 1.81 |
| 1920 | 54.51 | 36.75 | 14.87 | 11.81 | 9.18 | 1.66 |
| 1921 | 57.25 | 38.06 | 15.3 | 12.24 | 9.53 | 1.75 |
| 1922 | 57.02 | 37.24 | 14.72 | 11.76 | 9.11 | 1.68 |
| 1923 | 56.32 | 36.81 | 14.42 | 11.54 | 8.87 | 1.57 |
| 1924 | 57.15 | 37.11 | 14.65 | 11.75 | 9.1 | 1.67 |
| 1925 | 57.23 | 36.97 | 14.55 | 11.65 | 9.03 | 1.58 |
| 1926 | 56.57 | 36.53 | 14.28 | 11.37 | 8.81 | 1.49 |
| 1927 | 57.94 | 37.09 | 14.69 | 11.75 | 9.2 | 1.58 |
| 1928 | 56.78 | 36.35 | 14.27 | 11.33 | 8.83 | 1.43 |
| 1929 | 56.99 | 36.37 | 14.34 | 11.42 | 8.94 | 1.44 |

| Calendar Year | Female 0 | 30 | 60 | 65 | 70 | 100 |
|---|---|---|---|---|---|---|
| 1900 | 48.96 | 35.8 | 14.96 | 12.01 | 9.36 | 1.61 |
| 1901 | 50.86 | 35.9 | 14.88 | 11.99 | 9.35 | 1.63 |
| 1902 | 52.08 | 36.97 | 15.59 | 12.61 | 9.91 | 1.76 |
| 1903 | 52.12 | 36.48 | 15.14 | 12.22 | 9.57 | 1.66 |
| 1904 | 51.1 | 36 | 14.77 | 11.87 | 9.22 | 1.53 |
| 1905 | 51.88 | 36.38 | 14.96 | 12.05 | 9.43 | 1.54 |
| 1906 | 51.96 | 36.77 | 15.18 | 12.22 | 9.56 | 1.55 |
| 1907 | 52.22 | 36.29 | 14.72 | 11.79 | 9.15 | 1.5 |
| 1908 | 53.59 | 37.3 | 15.32 | 12.32 | 9.63 | 1.61 |
| 1909 | 54.46 | 37.6 | 15.41 | 12.36 | 9.68 | 1.6 |
| 1910 | 53.58 | 37.23 | 15.16 | 12.1 | 9.43 | 1.6 |
| 1911 | 55.05 | 37.38 | 15.27 | 12.19 | 9.49 | 1.64 |
| 1912 | 55.87 | 37.65 | 15.35 | 12.26 | 9.56 | 1.67 |
| 1913 | 55.45 | 37.74 | 15.49 | 12.37 | 9.64 | 1.71 |
| 1914 | 56.33 | 37.85 | 15.56 | 12.44 | 9.71 | 1.76 |
| 1915 | 56.79 | 37.64 | 15.28 | 12.16 | 9.44 | 1.68 |
| 1916 | 55.98 | 37.38 | 15.15 | 12.03 | 9.35 | 1.64 |
| 1917 | 55.91 | 37.31 | 15.16 | 12.06 | 9.38 | 1.67 |
| 1918 | 49.08 | 35.08 | 15.53 | 12.48 | 9.84 | 1.83 |
| 1919 | 56.45 | 37.82 | 16.02 | 12.85 | 10.12 | 1.81 |
| 1920 | 56.27 | 37.46 | 15.48 | 12.34 | 9.6 | 1.66 |
| 1921 | 59.26 | 38.97 | 15.99 | 12.82 | 9.99 | 1.75 |
| 1922 | 59.33 | 38.5 | 15.56 | 12.45 | 9.64 | 1.68 |
| 1923 | 58.74 | 38.25 | 15.29 | 12.2 | 9.37 | 1.57 |
| 1924 | 59.91 | 38.83 | 15.75 | 12.65 | 9.75 | 1.67 |
| 1925 | 59.93 | 38.7 | 15.62 | 12.52 | 9.69 | 1.58 |
| 1926 | 59.33 | 38.31 | 15.33 | 12.23 | 9.46 | 1.49 |
| 1927 | 60.86 | 39.05 | 15.91 | 12.73 | 9.95 | 1.58 |
| 1928 | 59.82 | 38.34 | 15.44 | 12.29 | 9.55 | 1.43 |
| 1929 | 60.16 | 38.52 | 15.56 | 12.41 | 9.67 | 1.44 |

| Calendar Year | Male 0 | 30 | 60 | 65 | 70 | 100 |
|---|---|---|---|---|---|---|
| 1930 | 57.96 | 36.91 | 14.69 | 11.83 | 9.29 | 1.62 |
| 1931 | 58.57 | 37.09 | 14.86 | 11.98 | 9.36 | 1.64 |
| 1932 | 59.44 | 37.39 | 14.79 | 11.92 | 9.23 | 1.6 |
| 1933 | 59.58 | 37.5 | 14.85 | 12.02 | 9.33 | 1.66 |
| 1934 | 58.85 | 37.2 | 14.7 | 11.88 | 9.22 | 1.65 |
| 1935 | 59.42 | 37.31 | 14.8 | 11.93 | 9.32 | 1.64 |
| 1936 | 58.75 | 36.68 | 14.4 | 11.56 | 9 | 1.52 |
| 1937 | 59.36 | 37.04 | 14.63 | 11.77 | 9.22 | 1.59 |
| 1938 | 60.81 | 37.99 | 15.05 | 12.11 | 9.52 | 1.67 |
| 1939 | 61.44 | 38.07 | 14.99 | 12.04 | 9.43 | 1.61 |
| 1940 | 61.43 | 37.99 | 14.84 | 11.92 | 9.32 | 1.64 |
| 1941 | 61.9 | 38.31 | 15.11 | 12.17 | 9.56 | 1.69 |
| 1942 | 62.58 | 38.54 | 15.33 | 12.39 | 9.78 | 1.75 |
| 1943 | 62.25 | 38.34 | 15.05 | 12.11 | 9.46 | 1.62 |
| 1944 | 62.68 | 38.79 | 15.41 | 12.46 | 9.78 | 1.72 |
| 1945 | 62.87 | 38.86 | 15.56 | 12.63 | 9.95 | 1.73 |
| 1946 | 64.25 | 39.47 | 15.8 | 12.86 | 10.14 | 1.78 |
| 1947 | 64.57 | 39.28 | 15.54 | 12.64 | 9.95 | 1.72 |
| 1948 | 64.84 | 39.47 | 15.63 | 12.71 | 10.04 | 1.77 |
| 1949 | 65.26 | 39.76 | 15.74 | 12.82 | 10.16 | 1.88 |
| 1950 | 65.63 | 39.88 | 15.75 | 12.81 | 10.16 | 1.92 |
| 1951 | 65.66 | 39.91 | 15.79 | 12.83 | 10.21 | 1.98 |
| 1952 | 65.78 | 40.06 | 15.9 | 12.97 | 10.35 | 2.05 |
| 1953 | 65.98 | 40.13 | 15.86 | 12.93 | 10.31 | 2 |
| 1954 | 66.74 | 40.7 | 16.21 | 13.22 | 10.59 | 2.08 |
| 1955 | 66.72 | 40.64 | 16.09 | 13.08 | 10.44 | 1.96 |
| 1956 | 66.73 | 40.61 | 16.03 | 13.04 | 10.41 | 1.92 |
| 1957 | 66.47 | 40.35 | 15.82 | 12.88 | 10.32 | 1.9 |
| 1958 | 66.64 | 40.49 | 15.9 | 12.93 | 10.34 | 1.91 |
| 1959 | 66.8 | 40.63 | 16.03 | 13.06 | 10.44 | 1.96 |

| Calendar Year | Female 0 | 30 | 60 | 65 | 70 | 100 |
|---|---|---|---|---|---|---|
| 1930 | 61.31 | 39.23 | 16.04 | 12.91 | 10.11 | 1.62 |
| 1931 | 62.02 | 39.54 | 16.25 | 13.12 | 10.26 | 1.64 |
| 1932 | 62.59 | 39.64 | 16.1 | 12.95 | 10.03 | 1.6 |
| 1933 | 63.03 | 40.01 | 16.34 | 13.18 | 10.25 | 1.66 |
| 1934 | 62.68 | 39.97 | 16.27 | 13.13 | 10.19 | 1.65 |
| | | | | | | |
| 1935 | 63.32 | 40.14 | 16.41 | 13.21 | 10.31 | 1.64 |
| 1936 | 62.85 | 39.72 | 16.02 | 12.81 | 9.94 | 1.52 |
| 1937 | 63.58 | 40.2 | 16.38 | 13.14 | 10.24 | 1.59 |
| 1938 | 64.74 | 40.93 | 16.75 | 13.45 | 10.51 | 1.67 |
| 1939 | 65.41 | 41.03 | 16.71 | 13.4 | 10.41 | 1.61 |
| | | | | | | |
| 1940 | 65.74 | 41.28 | 16.78 | 13.42 | 10.42 | 1.64 |
| 1941 | 66.46 | 41.84 | 17.21 | 13.81 | 10.78 | 1.69 |
| 1942 | 67.36 | 42.25 | 17.46 | 14.05 | 10.99 | 1.75 |
| 1943 | 67.1 | 41.9 | 17.13 | 13.72 | 10.65 | 1.62 |
| 1944 | 67.82 | 42.49 | 17.55 | 14.1 | 10.98 | 1.72 |
| | | | | | | |
| 1945 | 68.44 | 42.88 | 17.85 | 14.38 | 11.23 | 1.73 |
| 1946 | 69.21 | 43.34 | 18.08 | 14.59 | 11.38 | 1.78 |
| 1947 | 69.68 | 43.4 | 18.02 | 14.52 | 11.31 | 1.72 |
| 1948 | 70.16 | 43.79 | 18.24 | 14.72 | 11.48 | 1.77 |
| 1949 | 70.66 | 44.15 | 18.47 | 14.93 | 11.69 | 1.88 |
| | | | | | | |
| 1950 | 71.13 | 44.41 | 18.6 | 15.06 | 11.79 | 1.92 |
| 1951 | 71.36 | 44.57 | 18.71 | 15.15 | 11.86 | 1.98 |
| 1952 | 71.62 | 44.84 | 18.9 | 15.31 | 12.01 | 2.05 |
| 1953 | 71.98 | 45.03 | 18.98 | 15.34 | 12.05 | 2 |
| 1954 | 72.74 | 45.64 | 19.42 | 15.75 | 12.41 | 2.08 |
| | | | | | | |
| 1955 | 72.81 | 45.67 | 19.34 | 15.64 | 12.3 | 1.96 |
| 1956 | 72.94 | 45.74 | 19.39 | 15.68 | 12.34 | 1.92 |
| 1957 | 72.73 | 45.59 | 19.28 | 15.6 | 12.27 | 1.9 |
| 1958 | 72.92 | 45.79 | 19.39 | 15.69 | 12.32 | 1.91 |
| 1959 | 73.24 | 46.05 | 19.6 | 15.88 | 12.49 | 1.96 |

| Calendar Year | Male 0 | 30 | 60 | 65 | 70 | 100 |
|---|---|---|---|---|---|---|
| 1960 | 66.66 | 40.45 | 15.86 | 12.91 | 10.3 | 1.95 |
| 1961 | 67.07 | 40.73 | 16.04 | 13.08 | 10.47 | 1.95 |
| 1962 | 66.89 | 40.55 | 15.89 | 12.93 | 10.34 | 1.88 |
| 1963 | 66.64 | 40.31 | 15.69 | 12.75 | 10.17 | 1.84 |
| 1964 | 66.84 | 40.51 | 15.91 | 13 | 10.39 | 1.94 |
| 1965 | 66.79 | 40.44 | 15.83 | 12.92 | 10.32 | 1.91 |
| 1966 | 66.69 | 40.33 | 15.79 | 12.86 | 10.27 | 1.93 |
| 1967 | 66.95 | 40.5 | 15.95 | 13.01 | 10.38 | 1.99 |
| 1968 | 66.61 | 40.2 | 15.73 | 12.8 | 10.19 | 1.84 |
| 1969 | 66.88 | 40.44 | 15.99 | 13.02 | 10.38 | 1.94 |
| 1970 | 67.15 | 40.59 | 16.11 | 13.13 | 10.51 | 2.06 |
| 1971 | 67.4 | 40.75 | 16.15 | 13.13 | 10.48 | 2.05 |
| 1972 | 67.42 | 40.72 | 16.1 | 13.09 | 10.43 | 2.04 |
| 1973 | 67.64 | 40.92 | 16.23 | 13.19 | 10.52 | 2.01 |
| 1974 | 68.27 | 41.39 | 16.56 | 13.48 | 10.79 | 2.13 |
| 1975 | 68.74 | 41.77 | 16.81 | 13.7 | 10.98 | 2.21 |
| 1976 | 69.08 | 41.97 | 16.87 | 13.75 | 11.01 | 2.1 |
| 1977 | 69.4 | 42.25 | 17.07 | 13.91 | 11.14 | 2.2 |
| 1978 | 69.57 | 42.39 | 17.12 | 13.95 | 11.17 | 2.21 |
| 1979 | 69.96 | 42.73 | 17.4 | 14.18 | 11.37 | 2.29 |
| 1980 | 69.94 | 42.67 | 17.31 | 14.04 | 11.23 | 2.2 |
| 1981 | 70.37 | 42.94 | 17.53 | 14.24 | 11.39 | 2.29 |
| 1982 | 70.83 | 43.29 | 17.75 | 14.45 | 11.58 | 2.4 |
| 1983 | 70.92 | 43.27 | 17.63 | 14.31 | 11.41 | 2.31 |
| 1984 | 71.08 | 43.39 | 17.73 | 14.41 | 11.49 | 2.28 |
| 1985 | 71.06 | 43.36 | 17.73 | 14.39 | 11.45 | 2.22 |
| 1986 | 71.12 | 43.48 | 17.87 | 14.52 | 11.55 | 2.29 |
| 1987 | 71.3 | 43.61 | 18 | 14.64 | 11.66 | 2.36 |
| 1988 | 71.3 | 43.62 | 18.01 | 14.64 | 11.61 | 2.07 |
| 1989 | 71.59 | 43.88 | 18.31 | 14.92 | 11.86 | 2.18 |

| Calendar Year | Female 0 | 30 | 60 | 65 | 70 | 100 |
|---|---|---|---|---|---|---|
| 1960 | 73.24 | 46.02 | 19.57 | 15.89 | 12.48 | 1.97 |
| 1961 | 73.63 | 46.32 | 19.8 | 16.11 | 12.67 | 1.98 |
| 1962 | 73.5 | 46.2 | 19.72 | 16.02 | 12.59 | 1.91 |
| 1963 | 73.42 | 46.11 | 19.67 | 15.99 | 12.55 | 1.89 |
| 1964 | 73.74 | 46.41 | 19.98 | 16.29 | 12.84 | 1.98 |
| 1965 | 73.84 | 46.47 | 20.05 | 16.34 | 12.89 | 1.98 |
| 1966 | 73.9 | 46.5 | 20.07 | 16.32 | 12.88 | 2 |
| 1967 | 74.29 | 46.78 | 20.34 | 16.58 | 13.13 | 2.09 |
| 1968 | 74.21 | 46.68 | 20.34 | 16.6 | 13.09 | 2.05 |
| 1969 | 74.59 | 47.03 | 20.66 | 16.9 | 13.35 | 2.16 |
| 1970 | 74.86 | 47.24 | 20.87 | 17.11 | 13.58 | 2.27 |
| 1971 | 75.06 | 47.34 | 20.91 | 17.14 | 13.59 | 2.26 |
| 1972 | 75.22 | 47.44 | 20.96 | 17.18 | 13.65 | 2.26 |
| 1973 | 75.47 | 47.64 | 21.13 | 17.35 | 13.78 | 2.25 |
| 1974 | 76.02 | 48.09 | 21.45 | 17.66 | 14.08 | 2.36 |
| 1975 | 76.55 | 48.56 | 21.83 | 18.02 | 14.42 | 2.45 |
| 1976 | 76.77 | 48.7 | 21.89 | 18.08 | 14.48 | 2.38 |
| 1977 | 77.16 | 49.02 | 22.15 | 18.33 | 14.75 | 2.46 |
| 1978 | 77.25 | 49.08 | 22.15 | 18.33 | 14.74 | 2.34 |
| 1979 | 77.71 | 49.47 | 22.45 | 18.6 | 15 | 2.56 |
| 1980 | 77.52 | 49.24 | 22.2 | 18.35 | 14.78 | 2.42 |
| 1981 | 77.85 | 49.49 | 22.43 | 18.58 | 15.01 | 2.5 |
| 1982 | 78.2 | 49.78 | 22.64 | 18.8 | 15.22 | 2.68 |
| 1983 | 78.12 | 49.65 | 22.47 | 18.63 | 15.06 | 2.53 |
| 1984 | 78.2 | 49.7 | 22.5 | 18.66 | 15.09 | 2.54 |
| 1985 | 78.22 | 49.68 | 22.47 | 18.62 | 15.04 | 2.46 |
| 1986 | 78.3 | 49.76 | 22.51 | 18.66 | 15.1 | 2.48 |
| 1987 | 78.39 | 49.84 | 22.59 | 18.73 | 15.15 | 2.5 |
| 1988 | 78.37 | 49.82 | 22.57 | 18.71 | 15.09 | 2.39 |
| 1989 | 78.63 | 50.08 | 22.8 | 18.92 | 15.28 | 2.45 |

| Calendar Year | Male 0 | 30 | 60 | 65 | 70 | 100 |
|---|---|---|---|---|---|---|
| 1990 | 71.82 | 44.09 | 18.47 | 15.06 | 11.99 | 2.18 |
| 1991 | 72.02 | 44.26 | 18.64 | 15.2 | 12.11 | 2.25 |
| 1992 | 72.26 | 44.39 | 18.76 | 15.28 | 12.18 | 2.21 |
| 1993 | 72.09 | 44.23 | 18.64 | 15.16 | 12.05 | 2.15 |
| 1994 | 72.31 | 44.41 | 18.83 | 15.34 | 12.22 | 2.12 |
| 1995 | 72.5 | 44.52 | 18.91 | 15.4 | 12.25 | 2.09 |
| 1996 | 72.97 | 44.88 | 19.01 | 15.49 | 12.33 | 2.08 |
| 1997 | 73.44 | 45.28 | 19.16 | 15.58 | 12.41 | 2.05 |
| 1998 | 73.71 | 45.49 | 19.29 | 15.68 | 12.47 | 2.06 |
| 1999 | 73.83 | 45.57 | 19.36 | 15.73 | 12.47 | 2.01 |
| 2000 | 74.03 | 45.77 | 19.55 | 15.91 | 12.61 | 1.98 |
| 2001 | 74.14 | 45.9 | 19.72 | 16.05 | 12.75 | 2 |
| 2002 | 74.35 | 46.02 | 19.7 | 16.02 | 12.71 | 1.95 |
| 2003 | 74.5 | 46.13 | 19.79 | 16.1 | 12.78 | 1.94 |
| 2004 | 74.64 | 46.25 | 19.87 | 16.16 | 12.83 | 1.92 |
| 2005 | 74.78 | 46.36 | 19.95 | 16.23 | 12.87 | 1.91 |
| 2006 | 74.91 | 46.46 | 20.03 | 16.29 | 12.92 | 1.9 |
| 2007 | 75.04 | 46.57 | 20.11 | 16.36 | 12.98 | 1.89 |
| 2008 | 75.16 | 46.67 | 20.18 | 16.42 | 13.03 | 1.89 |
| 2009 | 75.28 | 46.77 | 20.26 | 16.49 | 13.08 | 1.89 |
| 2010 | 75.4 | 46.87 | 20.33 | 16.55 | 13.13 | 1.89 |
| 2011 | 75.52 | 46.96 | 20.4 | 16.61 | 13.19 | 1.9 |
| 2012 | 75.63 | 47.06 | 20.48 | 16.68 | 13.24 | 1.91 |
| 2013 | 75.74 | 47.16 | 20.55 | 16.74 | 13.3 | 1.92 |
| 2014 | 75.85 | 47.25 | 20.62 | 16.8 | 13.35 | 1.93 |
| 2015 | 75.96 | 47.35 | 20.69 | 16.87 | 13.41 | 1.94 |
| 2016 | 76.07 | 47.44 | 20.76 | 16.93 | 13.46 | 1.95 |
| 2017 | 76.18 | 47.53 | 20.83 | 16.99 | 13.52 | 1.96 |
| 2018 | 76.29 | 47.63 | 20.9 | 17.05 | 13.57 | 1.97 |
| 2019 | 76.39 | 47.72 | 20.97 | 17.12 | 13.63 | 1.98 |

| Calendar Year | Female 0 | 30 | 60 | 65 | 70 | 100 |
|---|---|---|---|---|---|---|
| 1990 | 78.9 | 50.27 | 22.96 | 19.07 | 15.44 | 2.51 |
| 1991 | 79.04 | 50.38 | 23.07 | 19.17 | 15.53 | 2.55 |
| 1992 | 79.22 | 50.51 | 23.16 | 19.25 | 15.61 | 2.61 |
| 1993 | 78.95 | 50.25 | 22.92 | 19.01 | 15.37 | 2.47 |
| 1994 | 79.07 | 50.33 | 22.99 | 19.07 | 15.43 | 2.48 |
| 1995 | 79.08 | 50.3 | 22.97 | 19.05 | 15.4 | 2.44 |
| 1996 | 79.2 | 50.38 | 22.99 | 19.06 | 15.41 | 2.43 |
| 1997 | 79.35 | 50.5 | 23.05 | 19.11 | 15.44 | 2.39 |
| 1998 | 79.41 | 50.53 | 23.03 | 19.07 | 15.39 | 2.38 |
| 1999 | 79.32 | 50.44 | 22.94 | 18.95 | 15.27 | 2.29 |
| 2000 | 79.39 | 50.48 | 22.97 | 18.98 | 15.29 | 2.26 |
| 2001 | 79.45 | 50.53 | 23.06 | 19.06 | 15.35 | 2.29 |
| 2002 | 79.47 | 50.53 | 22.99 | 18.99 | 15.29 | 2.24 |
| 2003 | 79.52 | 50.56 | 23.01 | 19 | 15.3 | 2.22 |
| 2004 | 79.57 | 50.59 | 23.02 | 19.01 | 15.3 | 2.21 |
| 2005 | 79.62 | 50.61 | 23.03 | 19.01 | 15.3 | 2.19 |
| 2006 | 79.67 | 50.65 | 23.05 | 19.02 | 15.31 | 2.18 |
| 2007 | 79.73 | 50.69 | 23.08 | 19.05 | 15.33 | 2.18 |
| 2008 | 79.8 | 50.75 | 23.11 | 19.08 | 15.35 | 2.17 |
| 2009 | 79.87 | 50.81 | 23.16 | 19.12 | 15.38 | 2.18 |
| 2010 | 79.95 | 50.87 | 23.2 | 19.16 | 15.42 | 2.18 |
| 2011 | 80.03 | 50.94 | 23.26 | 19.2 | 15.46 | 2.19 |
| 2012 | 80.11 | 51.01 | 23.31 | 19.25 | 15.51 | 2.19 |
| 2013 | 80.19 | 51.08 | 23.37 | 19.31 | 15.55 | 2.2 |
| 2014 | 80.28 | 51.15 | 23.43 | 19.36 | 15.6 | 2.22 |
| 2015 | 80.37 | 51.23 | 23.49 | 19.42 | 15.65 | 2.23 |
| 2016 | 80.45 | 51.3 | 23.55 | 19.47 | 15.7 | 2.24 |
| 2017 | 80.54 | 51.38 | 23.62 | 19.53 | 15.76 | 2.25 |
| 2018 | 80.63 | 51.46 | 23.68 | 19.59 | 15.81 | 2.27 |
| 2019 | 80.71 | 51.53 | 23.74 | 19.65 | 15.86 | 2.28 |

| Calendar Year | Male 0 | 30 | 60 | 65 | 70 | 100 |
|---|---|---|---|---|---|---|
| 2020 | 76.5 | 47.81 | 21.04 | 17.18 | 13.68 | 2 |
| 2021 | 76.6 | 47.9 | 21.11 | 17.24 | 13.73 | 2.01 |
| 2022 | 76.71 | 47.99 | 21.17 | 17.3 | 13.79 | 2.02 |
| 2023 | 76.81 | 48.08 | 21.24 | 17.36 | 13.84 | 2.04 |
| 2024 | 76.91 | 48.17 | 21.31 | 17.42 | 13.9 | 2.05 |
| 2025 | 77.01 | 48.26 | 21.38 | 17.48 | 13.95 | 2.06 |
| 2026 | 77.11 | 48.35 | 21.45 | 17.54 | 14.01 | 2.08 |
| 2027 | 77.21 | 48.44 | 21.51 | 17.61 | 14.06 | 2.09 |
| 2028 | 77.31 | 48.52 | 21.58 | 17.67 | 14.11 | 2.11 |
| 2029 | 77.41 | 48.61 | 21.64 | 17.73 | 14.17 | 2.12 |
| 2030 | 77.51 | 48.7 | 21.71 | 17.78 | 14.22 | 2.13 |
| 2031 | 77.61 | 48.78 | 21.78 | 17.84 | 14.27 | 2.15 |
| 2032 | 77.71 | 48.87 | 21.84 | 17.9 | 14.33 | 2.16 |
| 2033 | 77.8 | 48.95 | 21.91 | 17.96 | 14.38 | 2.18 |
| 2034 | 77.9 | 49.04 | 21.97 | 18.02 | 14.43 | 2.19 |
| 2035 | 77.99 | 49.12 | 22.03 | 18.08 | 14.48 | 2.21 |
| 2036 | 78.09 | 49.21 | 22.1 | 18.14 | 14.53 | 2.22 |
| 2037 | 78.18 | 49.29 | 22.16 | 18.19 | 14.59 | 2.23 |
| 2038 | 78.28 | 49.37 | 22.23 | 18.25 | 14.64 | 2.25 |
| 2039 | 78.37 | 49.45 | 22.29 | 18.31 | 14.69 | 2.26 |
| 2040 | 78.46 | 49.54 | 22.35 | 18.37 | 14.74 | 2.28 |
| 2041 | 78.55 | 49.62 | 22.41 | 18.42 | 14.79 | 2.29 |
| 2042 | 78.64 | 49.7 | 22.48 | 18.48 | 14.84 | 2.31 |
| 2043 | 78.73 | 49.78 | 22.54 | 18.54 | 14.89 | 2.32 |
| 2044 | 78.82 | 49.86 | 22.6 | 18.59 | 14.94 | 2.34 |
| 2045 | 78.91 | 49.94 | 22.66 | 18.65 | 14.99 | 2.35 |
| 2046 | 79 | 50.02 | 22.72 | 18.7 | 15.04 | 2.36 |
| 2047 | 79.09 | 50.09 | 22.78 | 18.76 | 15.09 | 2.38 |
| 2048 | 79.17 | 50.17 | 22.84 | 18.81 | 15.14 | 2.39 |
| 2049 | 79.26 | 50.25 | 22.9 | 18.87 | 15.19 | 2.41 |

| Calendar Year | Female 0 | 30 | 60 | 65 | 70 | 100 |
|---|---|---|---|---|---|---|
| 2020 | 80.8 | 51.61 | 23.81 | 19.71 | 15.92 | 2.3 |
| 2021 | 80.89 | 51.69 | 23.87 | 19.77 | 15.97 | 2.31 |
| 2022 | 80.98 | 51.77 | 23.94 | 19.83 | 16.03 | 2.32 |
| 2023 | 81.06 | 51.84 | 24 | 19.89 | 16.08 | 2.34 |
| 2024 | 81.15 | 51.92 | 24.07 | 19.95 | 16.13 | 2.36 |
| 2025 | 81.24 | 52 | 24.13 | 20.01 | 16.19 | 2.37 |
| 2026 | 81.32 | 52.08 | 24.2 | 20.07 | 16.24 | 2.39 |
| 2027 | 81.41 | 52.15 | 24.26 | 20.13 | 16.3 | 2.4 |
| 2028 | 81.49 | 52.23 | 24.32 | 20.18 | 16.35 | 2.42 |
| 2029 | 81.57 | 52.3 | 24.39 | 20.24 | 16.4 | 2.43 |
| 2030 | 81.66 | 52.38 | 24.45 | 20.3 | 16.46 | 2.45 |
| 2031 | 81.74 | 52.46 | 24.51 | 20.36 | 16.51 | 2.47 |
| 2032 | 81.83 | 52.53 | 24.58 | 20.42 | 16.57 | 2.48 |
| 2033 | 81.91 | 52.6 | 24.64 | 20.48 | 16.62 | 2.5 |
| 2034 | 81.99 | 52.68 | 24.7 | 20.53 | 16.67 | 2.51 |
| 2035 | 82.07 | 52.75 | 24.76 | 20.59 | 16.72 | 2.53 |
| 2036 | 82.15 | 52.82 | 24.82 | 20.65 | 16.78 | 2.55 |
| 2037 | 82.23 | 52.9 | 24.88 | 20.71 | 16.83 | 2.56 |
| 2038 | 82.31 | 52.97 | 24.95 | 20.76 | 16.88 | 2.58 |
| 2039 | 82.39 | 53.04 | 25.01 | 20.82 | 16.93 | 2.59 |
| 2040 | 82.47 | 53.11 | 25.07 | 20.87 | 16.98 | 2.61 |
| 2041 | 82.54 | 53.18 | 25.13 | 20.93 | 17.03 | 2.63 |
| 2042 | 82.62 | 53.25 | 25.18 | 20.98 | 17.08 | 2.64 |
| 2043 | 82.7 | 53.32 | 25.24 | 21.04 | 17.13 | 2.66 |
| 2044 | 82.78 | 53.39 | 25.3 | 21.09 | 17.18 | 2.67 |
| 2045 | 82.85 | 53.46 | 25.36 | 21.15 | 17.23 | 2.69 |
| 2046 | 82.93 | 53.53 | 25.42 | 21.2 | 17.28 | 2.71 |
| 2047 | 83 | 53.6 | 25.48 | 21.26 | 17.33 | 2.72 |
| 2048 | 83.08 | 53.67 | 25.53 | 21.31 | 17.38 | 2.74 |
| 2049 | 83.15 | 53.73 | 25.59 | 21.36 | 17.43 | 2.75 |

| Calendar Year | Male 0 | 30 | 60 | 65 | 70 | 100 |
|---|---|---|---|---|---|---|
| 2050 | 79.35 | 50.33 | 22.96 | 18.92 | 15.24 | 2.42 |
| 2051 | 79.43 | 50.4 | 23.02 | 18.98 | 15.29 | 2.44 |
| 2052 | 79.52 | 50.48 | 23.08 | 19.03 | 15.33 | 2.45 |
| 2053 | 79.6 | 50.55 | 23.14 | 19.08 | 15.38 | 2.47 |
| 2054 | 79.69 | 50.63 | 23.2 | 19.14 | 15.43 | 2.48 |
| 2055 | 79.77 | 50.71 | 23.25 | 19.19 | 15.48 | 2.49 |
| 2056 | 79.86 | 50.78 | 23.31 | 19.24 | 15.53 | 2.51 |
| 2057 | 79.94 | 50.85 | 23.37 | 19.29 | 15.57 | 2.52 |
| 2058 | 80.02 | 50.93 | 23.43 | 19.35 | 15.62 | 2.54 |
| 2059 | 80.1 | 51 | 23.48 | 19.4 | 15.67 | 2.55 |
| 2060 | 80.18 | 51.07 | 23.54 | 19.45 | 15.71 | 2.57 |
| 2061 | 80.26 | 51.15 | 23.6 | 19.5 | 15.76 | 2.58 |
| 2062 | 80.34 | 51.22 | 23.65 | 19.55 | 15.81 | 2.6 |
| 2063 | 80.42 | 51.29 | 23.71 | 19.61 | 15.85 | 2.61 |
| 2064 | 80.5 | 51.36 | 23.77 | 19.66 | 15.9 | 2.62 |
| 2065 | 80.58 | 51.43 | 23.82 | 19.71 | 15.95 | 2.64 |
| 2066 | 80.66 | 51.5 | 23.88 | 19.76 | 15.99 | 2.65 |
| 2067 | 80.74 | 51.57 | 23.93 | 19.81 | 16.04 | 2.67 |
| 2068 | 80.81 | 51.64 | 23.99 | 19.86 | 16.08 | 2.68 |
| 2069 | 80.89 | 51.71 | 24.04 | 19.91 | 16.13 | 2.7 |
| 2070 | 80.97 | 51.78 | 24.1 | 19.96 | 16.17 | 2.71 |
| 2071 | 81.05 | 51.85 | 24.15 | 20.01 | 16.22 | 2.73 |
| 2072 | 81.12 | 51.92 | 24.2 | 20.06 | 16.26 | 2.74 |
| 2073 | 81.2 | 51.98 | 24.26 | 20.11 | 16.31 | 2.76 |
| 2074 | 81.27 | 52.05 | 24.31 | 20.16 | 16.35 | 2.77 |
| 2075 | 81.34 | 52.12 | 24.36 | 20.21 | 16.39 | 2.78 |
| 2076 | 81.42 | 52.19 | 24.42 | 20.25 | 16.44 | 2.8 |
| 2077 | 81.49 | 52.25 | 24.47 | 20.3 | 16.48 | 2.81 |
| 2078 | 81.56 | 52.32 | 24.52 | 20.35 | 16.53 | 2.83 |
| 2079 | 81.64 | 52.38 | 24.57 | 20.4 | 16.57 | 2.84 |

| Calendar Year | Female 0 | 30 | 60 | 65 | 70 | 100 |
|---|---|---|---|---|---|---|
| 2050 | 83.22 | 53.8 | 25.65 | 21.42 | 17.48 | 2.77 |
| 2051 | 83.3 | 53.87 | 25.7 | 21.47 | 17.53 | 2.79 |
| 2052 | 83.37 | 53.93 | 25.76 | 21.52 | 17.58 | 2.8 |
| 2053 | 83.44 | 54 | 25.82 | 21.57 | 17.62 | 2.82 |
| 2054 | 83.51 | 54.07 | 25.87 | 21.62 | 17.67 | 2.83 |
| 2055 | 83.58 | 54.13 | 25.93 | 21.68 | 17.72 | 2.85 |
| 2056 | 83.66 | 54.2 | 25.98 | 21.73 | 17.77 | 2.87 |
| 2057 | 83.73 | 54.26 | 26.04 | 21.78 | 17.81 | 2.88 |
| 2058 | 83.8 | 54.32 | 26.09 | 21.83 | 17.86 | 2.9 |
| 2059 | 83.86 | 54.39 | 26.15 | 21.88 | 17.91 | 2.91 |
| 2060 | 83.93 | 54.45 | 26.2 | 21.93 | 17.95 | 2.93 |
| 2061 | 84 | 54.51 | 26.25 | 21.98 | 18 | 2.95 |
| 2062 | 84.07 | 54.58 | 26.31 | 22.03 | 18.05 | 2.96 |
| 2063 | 84.14 | 54.64 | 26.36 | 22.08 | 18.09 | 2.98 |
| 2064 | 84.21 | 54.7 | 26.41 | 22.13 | 18.14 | 3 |
| 2065 | 84.27 | 54.76 | 26.47 | 22.18 | 18.18 | 3.01 |
| 2066 | 84.34 | 54.83 | 26.52 | 22.23 | 18.23 | 3.03 |
| 2067 | 84.41 | 54.89 | 26.57 | 22.28 | 18.27 | 3.04 |
| 2068 | 84.47 | 54.95 | 26.62 | 22.33 | 18.32 | 3.06 |
| 2069 | 84.54 | 55.01 | 26.67 | 22.37 | 18.36 | 3.08 |
| 2070 | 84.6 | 55.07 | 26.73 | 22.42 | 18.41 | 3.09 |
| 2071 | 84.67 | 55.13 | 26.78 | 22.47 | 18.45 | 3.11 |
| 2072 | 84.73 | 55.19 | 26.83 | 22.52 | 18.5 | 3.12 |
| 2073 | 84.79 | 55.25 | 26.88 | 22.56 | 18.54 | 3.14 |
| 2074 | 84.86 | 55.31 | 26.93 | 22.61 | 18.58 | 3.16 |
| 2075 | 84.92 | 55.37 | 26.98 | 22.66 | 18.63 | 3.17 |
| 2076 | 84.98 | 55.42 | 27.03 | 22.71 | 18.67 | 3.19 |
| 2077 | 85.05 | 55.48 | 27.08 | 22.75 | 18.71 | 3.2 |
| 2078 | 85.11 | 55.54 | 27.13 | 22.8 | 18.76 | 3.22 |
| 2079 | 85.17 | 55.6 | 27.18 | 22.84 | 18.8 | 3.23 |

| Calendar Year | Male 0 | 30 | 60 | 65 | 70 | 100 |
|---|---|---|---|---|---|---|
| 2080 | 81.71 | 52.45 | 24.62 | 20.45 | 16.61 | 2.86 |
| 2081 | 81.78 | 52.51 | 24.68 | 20.49 | 16.66 | 2.87 |
| 2082 | 81.85 | 52.58 | 24.73 | 20.54 | 16.7 | 2.89 |
| 2083 | 81.92 | 52.64 | 24.78 | 20.59 | 16.74 | 2.9 |
| 2084 | 81.99 | 52.71 | 24.83 | 20.64 | 16.78 | 2.92 |
| 2085 | 82.07 | 52.77 | 24.88 | 20.68 | 16.83 | 2.93 |
| 2086 | 82.13 | 52.84 | 24.93 | 20.73 | 16.87 | 2.94 |
| 2087 | 82.2 | 52.9 | 24.98 | 20.78 | 16.91 | 2.96 |
| 2088 | 82.27 | 52.96 | 25.03 | 20.82 | 16.95 | 2.97 |
| 2089 | 82.34 | 53.02 | 25.08 | 20.87 | 17 | 2.99 |
| 2090 | 82.41 | 53.09 | 25.13 | 20.91 | 17.04 | 3 |
| 2091 | 82.48 | 53.15 | 25.18 | 20.96 | 17.08 | 3.02 |
| 2092 | 82.55 | 53.21 | 25.23 | 21.01 | 17.12 | 3.03 |
| 2093 | 82.61 | 53.27 | 25.28 | 21.05 | 17.16 | 3.05 |
| 2094 | 82.68 | 53.33 | 25.33 | 21.1 | 17.2 | 3.06 |
| 2095 | 82.75 | 53.39 | 25.38 | 21.14 | 17.24 | 3.07 |
| 2096 | 82.81 | 53.45 | 25.43 | 21.19 | 17.28 | 3.09 |
| 2097 | 82.88 | 53.51 | 25.47 | 21.23 | 17.32 | 3.1 |
| 2098 | 82.94 | 53.57 | 25.52 | 21.27 | 17.37 | 3.12 |
| 2099 | 83.01 | 53.63 | 25.57 | 21.32 | 17.41 | 3.13 |
| 2100 | 83.07 | 53.69 | 25.62 | 21.36 | 17.45 | 3.15 |

| Calendar Year | Female 0 | 30 | 60 | 65 | 70 | 100 |
|---|---|---|---|---|---|---|
| 2080 | 85.23 | 55.65 | 27.23 | 22.89 | 18.84 | 3.25 |
| 2081 | 85.29 | 55.71 | 27.28 | 22.94 | 18.88 | 3.27 |
| 2082 | 85.35 | 55.77 | 27.32 | 22.98 | 18.93 | 3.28 |
| 2083 | 85.42 | 55.82 | 27.37 | 23.03 | 18.97 | 3.3 |
| 2084 | 85.48 | 55.88 | 27.42 | 23.07 | 19.01 | 3.31 |
| 2085 | 85.54 | 55.94 | 27.47 | 23.12 | 19.05 | 3.33 |
| 2086 | 85.6 | 55.99 | 27.52 | 23.16 | 19.09 | 3.35 |
| 2087 | 85.65 | 56.05 | 27.56 | 23.21 | 19.13 | 3.36 |
| 2088 | 85.71 | 56.1 | 27.61 | 23.25 | 19.18 | 3.38 |
| 2089 | 85.77 | 56.16 | 27.66 | 23.29 | 19.22 | 3.39 |
| 2090 | 85.83 | 56.21 | 27.7 | 23.34 | 19.26 | 3.41 |
| 2091 | 85.89 | 56.27 | 27.75 | 23.38 | 19.3 | 3.42 |
| 2092 | 85.95 | 56.32 | 27.8 | 23.43 | 19.34 | 3.44 |
| 2093 | 86 | 56.37 | 27.84 | 23.47 | 19.38 | 3.46 |
| 2094 | 86.06 | 56.43 | 27.89 | 23.51 | 19.42 | 3.47 |
| 2095 | 86.12 | 56.48 | 27.94 | 23.56 | 19.46 | 3.49 |
| 2096 | 86.17 | 56.53 | 27.98 | 23.6 | 19.5 | 3.5 |
| 2097 | 86.23 | 56.59 | 28.03 | 23.64 | 19.54 | 3.52 |
| 2098 | 86.29 | 56.64 | 28.07 | 23.68 | 19.58 | 3.53 |
| 2099 | 86.34 | 56.69 | 28.12 | 23.73 | 19.62 | 3.55 |
| 2100 | 86.4 | 56.74 | 28.16 | 23.77 | 19.66 | 3.57 |

# Resources

**American Association for Long-Term Care Insurance (AALTCI)** is the national professional organization exclusively dedicated to promoting the importance of planning for long-term care needs. Founded in 1998, the Association is the nation's leading independent organization serving those who offer long-term care insurance and other planning solutions. AALTCI's members constitute the nation's most knowledgeable and committed professionals along with leading long-term care providers. www.aaltci.org.

**The American College** is a nonprofit private educational institution located in Bryn Mawr, Pennsylvania. It offers several professional certifications and two types of master's degrees. Annually, The American College educates approximately 40,000 students, mainly through distance education. The institution was founded as The American College of Life Underwriters in 1927 by Dr. Solomon S. Huebner of the Wharton School at the University of Pennsylvania.

Huebner was a professional involved in the development of economic theory. His theory of human life value is used in the field of insurance. It was his vision for a college-level professional education program for insurance agents that led to the creation of The American College. Today the college offers professional training to all types of financial practitioners. When the institution began, its programs focused exclusively on providing education to life insurance professionals. The Chartered Life Underwriter (CLU) designation was the first credential offered by the college. www.theamericancollege.edu.

- Life Underwriter Training Council Fellow (LUTCF)—A program teaching product knowledge and sales skills for persons interested in pursuing a career in insurance and financial services
- Financial Services Specialist (FSS)—A training program to strengthen sales skills and technical knowledge for professionals in the insurance, securities, and banking industries
- Certified Financial Planner Educational Curriculum (CFP)—A program that prepares students for the certified financial planner certification examination
- Chartered Life Underwriter (CLU)—A program of advanced life insurance and estate planning
- Chartered Financial Consultant (ChFC)—A program of advanced comprehensive financial planning
- Chartered Advisor for Senior Living (CASL)—A program providing training in the special needs, issues, and decisions facing senior citizens
- Registered Health Underwriter (RHU)—A program for financial advisors assisting clients with health care needs, including medical, disability income, and long-term care insurance
- Registered Employee Benefits Consultant (REBC)—Specialty courses for financial advisors working in United States employee benefits services
- Chartered Leadership Fellow (CLF)—A program providing fundamentals of leadership and organizational structures, and management of financial services organizations
- Chartered Advisor in Philanthropy (CAP)—A program training professionals dealing with wealthy individuals involved in philanthropy
- Master of Science in Management (MSM)—A master's degree program that focuses on leadership and financial services organizations
- Master of Science in Financial Services (MSFS)—A master's degree program that focuses on financial planning topics, including business succession planning, pensions, charitable giving, and asset management

**America's Health Insurance Plans (AHIP)** is the national trade association representing the health insurance industry. AHIP's members provide health and supplemental benefits to more than 200 million Americans through employer-sponsored coverage, the individual insurance market, and public programs such as Medicare and Medicaid. AHIP advocates for public policies that expand access to affordable health care coverage to all Americans through a competitive marketplace that fosters choice, quality, and innovation. www .ahip.org.

**AssistGuide Information Services (AGIS)** was founded on its own caregiving experience, so it knows how important such questions are. In fact, its business depends on the ongoing trust and confidence of caregivers. It takes care to ensure that helping caregivers and their families live healthier, happier lives remains its guiding principle. Toward that goal, AGIS strives to provide caregivers with free access to the broadest possible range of worthwhile elder care information by combining its own content with material from many other unbiased sources.

**Center for Long-Term Care Reform, Inc.** President Stephen Moses and Executive Director David Rosenfeld founded the Center for Long-Term Care Financing in April 1998 to educate others about the problems that plague America's long-term care financing system and to advocate for public policy that targets our scarce public resources to the neediest, while encouraging everyone else to plan ahead for the risk of expensive long-term care. The Center's efforts continue to expand upon Moses's and Rosenfeld's prior work at LTC, Incorporated and upon Moses's seminal research as a senior analyst for the Health Care Financing Administration and for the Inspector General of the U.S. Department of Health and Human Services. Through frequent speeches to national audiences, hard-hitting reports, and its popular "LTC Bullets" online newsletter, the Center for LTC Financing quickly became the preeminent advocate for a rational and financially viable long-term care financing system. In February 2000, the Center became a 501(c)(3) charitable non-profit organization. The Center for Long-Term Care Financing was succeeded by the Center for Long-Term Care Reform, Inc. in May 2005. Although the operating structure has changed to "for profit," or perhaps more accurately "no profit," Moses's mission for the Center for Long-Term Care Reform remains the same: to ensure quality long-term care for all Americans. www.centerltc.com.

**The Center for Long Term Care Research and Policy** is dedicated to improving the quality of long-term care for all Americans. Using a multidisciplinary approach, the Center engages in research, education, and public policy development designed to address health care disparities, health care needs, and caregiving across the lifespan and to promote fair and equitable financing of long-term care in the United States. http://www.nymc.edu/shsp/CLTC/index.html.

**The Centers for Medicare & Medicaid Services (CMS),** previously known as the Health Care Financing Administration (HCFA), is a federal agency within the United States Department of Health and Human Services (DHHS) that administers the Medicare program and works in partnership with state governments to administer Medicaid, the State Children's Health Insurance Program (SCHIP), and health insurance portability standards. In addition to these programs, CMS has other responsibilities, including the administrative simplification standards from the Health Insurance Portability and Accountability Act of 1996 (HIPAA), quality standards in long-term care facilities (more commonly referred to as nursing homes) through its survey and certification process, and clinical laboratory quality standards under the Clinical Laboratory Improvement Amendments. www .cms.gov.

**Center for Technology and Aging** is a non-profit organization that was founded in 2009 with a grant from The SCAN Foundation (www.thescanfoundation.org) and is affiliated with the Public Health Institute (www.phi.org). Its purpose is to advance the diffusion of technologies that help older adults lead healthier lives and maintain independence. The Center identifies promising strategies to promote the diffusion and adoption of technologies and provides grant funding to test selected strategies. In collaboration with grantees and key stakeholders, the Center will disseminate best practices and lessons learned from grant-making initiatives. The Center serves as a state and national resource for those engaged in the promotion and implementation of successful technology diffusion strategies. www.techandaging.org.

**Certified Financial Planner Board of Standards, Inc.** The mission of Certified Financial Planner Board of Standards, Inc. is to benefit the public by granting the CFP® certification and upholding it as the recognized standard of excellence for competent and ethical personal financial planning. www.cfp-board.org.

**Corporation for Long-Term Care Certification (CLTC).** "CLTC" stands for "Certified in Long-Term Care," a designation granted by the Corporation for Long-Term Care Certification. CLTC graduates have completed a rigorous multidisciplinary course that focuses on the profession of long-term care. The program is recognized by state regulators, through the granting of continuing education credits, as having provided essential information necessary to the appropriate sale of long-term care insurance. www.ltc-cltc.com.

**ElderCare Matters** is designed to provide families with access to experts in all areas of elder care, plus useful information and answers about a wide range of elder care matters provided by the members of the ElderCare Matters Alliance. Members of their national ElderCare Matters Alliance are some of America's top elder care experts, with long and successful careers working with seniors and their families. www.eldercarematters.com.

**Financial Planning Association® (FPA®)** is a leadership and advocacy organization connecting those who provide, support, and benefit from professional financial planning. FPA is the Heart of Financial Planning™ and represents a promise of financial well-being, hoping to create a world where everyone thrives and prospers. Based in Denver, Colorado, FPA has 95 chapters throughout the United States representing tens of thousands of members involved in all facets of providing financial planning services. Working in alliance with academic leaders, legislative and regulatory bodies, financial services firms, and consumer-interest organizations, FPA is the premier resource for the public to find a financial planner who will deliver advice using an ethical, objective, client-centered process. www .fpanet.org.

**LTC Consultants** is a third-party training and consulting company for long-term care insurance founded by Phyllis Shelton in 1991. In addition to marketing a complete line of long-term care insurance marketing materials, LTC Consultants provides consulting and sales training to insurance companies, independent and captive agents and brokers, banks, and long-term care providers. LTC Consultants believes that planning for long-term care is not just a good idea but is essential for every American, and it is committed to agent and consumer education so that families may retain independence and choice when care is needed. Training programs being presented across the nation offer ongoing support and income-producing results. www.ltcconsultants.com.

**The MetLife Mature Market Institute** is MetLife's center of expertise in aging, longevity, and the generations, and is a recognized thought leader by business, the media, opinion leaders, and the public. The Institute's groundbreaking research, insights, strategic partnerships, and consumer education expand the knowledge and choices for those in, approaching, or working with the 40+ market. www.maturemarketinstitute.com.

**National Alliance for Caregiving** is dedicated to being the foremost national resource on family caregiving to improve the quality of life for families and care recipients. Established in 1996, the Alliance is a non-profit coalition of more than 40 national organizations focusing on family caregiving. It is the leading provider of caregiving research across health issues, life issues, and lifespans. From research to policy analysis to promoting national best practices, the Alliance works to increase public awareness of this vital health care asset—the American family caregiver. www.caregiving.org.

**National Association of Health Underwriters (NAHU)** represents more than 100,000 licensed health insurance agents, brokers, consultants, and benefit professionals through more than 200 chapters across America. NAHU members service the health insurance needs of large and small employers as well as people seeking individual health insurance coverage. They are not only involved in traditional health insurance products, but also coverage such as dental, long-term care, disability, Medicare Advantage and Medicare Supplements, and a variety of consumer-driven products. Members agree to abide by NAHU's Code of Ethics, which requires them to always make health care coverage recommendations with the customer's best interests in mind. www.nahu.org.

**National Association of Insurance and Financial Advisors (NAIFA)** comprises more than 600 state and local associations representing the interests of approximately 200,000 agents and their associates nationwide. NAIFA members focus their practices on one or more of the following: life insurance and annuities, health insurance and employee benefits, multi-line products, and financial advising and investments. The Association's mission is to advocate for a positive legislative and regulatory environment, enhance business and professional skills, and promote the ethical conduct of its members. www.naifa.org.

**National LTC Network** is an alliance of leading distributors of long-term care insurance. Network members work with multiple insurers and are dedicated to marketing long-term care insurance with knowledge, ethics, and excellence. Founded in November 1994, the alliance include some of the largest and most-respected distributors in the nation. www.nltcn.com.

**Society of Financial Service Professionals (FSP).** For more than 80 years, the Society of Financial Service Professionals has been helping individuals, families, and businesses achieve financial security. With their strong commitment to delivering only those financial products and planning services that are in their clients' best interests, the Society's approximately 15,000 members nationwide are uniquely qualified to assist the public in reaching their future financial goals—today, tomorrow, and into the next millennium. Society members can provide consumers expert assistance with estate, retirement, and financial planning; employee benefits; business and compensation planning; and life, health, disability, and long-term care insurance. Society members have earned recognized professional credentials in the financial services industry or are working toward attaining a professional credential. www.financialpro.org.

**U.S. Department of Veterans Affairs** provides patient care and federal benefits to veterans and their dependents. www.va.gov.

## Additional Websites

www.caregiving.com

Center for Health Care Strategies, Inc. www.chcs.org

www.elderlawanswers.com

Medicare. www.medicare.gov/nursing/alternatives/other.asp

National Clearinghouse for Long-Term Care Information. www.longtermcare .gov

National Care Planning Council. www.longtermcarelink.net

www.seniorresource.com

www.seniorresourceguide.com

# Corporate Resolution to Establish Long-Term Care Insurance Plan

---

# Sample Document

---

## Corporate Resolution to Establish Long-Term Care Insurance Plan

There was a discussion led by **NAME** concerning the establishment of a Long-Term Care Insurance plan, and after additional discussion and upon motion duly made, seconded and unanimously approved, the following resolution was adopted:

WHEREAS, it is the desire of **CORPORATION**, to establish an employee Long-Term Care plan, which provides the employee with coverage in the event of a loss of two or more Activities of Daily Living or a Cognitive Impairment, will advance the best interest of the corporation through the improvement of its relationships with its employees, and

WHEREAS, it is desirable to make said Long-Term Care Insurance available to specified classes of employees for reason of the valuable services performed by said employees, and

WHEREAS, the corporation believes that this assistance can be best provided by the adoption of a Long-Term Care plan insured by long-term care insurance policies.

THEREFORE, be it resolved that an employee will be a covered employee only if he or she meets all of the following requirements as of the Entry Date:

1. ***EXAMPLE*** Is an officer of the corporation
2. ***EXAMPLE*** Has accumulated 20 years of service

RESOLVED, that any Officer of this corporation is authorized and directed to take such steps as may be necessary to establish an insured Long-Term Care plan, under the provisions of Section 105 and 106 of the Internal Revenue Code of 1954 as amended, for the benefit of the aforementioned employees, and be it further RESOLVED, that in order to put the plan into effect, and Officer be and hereby is authorized to take steps necessary to institute such plan and pay insurance premiums due on a Long-Term Care policy issued to a covered employee to provide the benefits pursuant to the said Plan.

---

President

Attest:

---

Secretary
Recorded in the books of the company this _____ day of _____, 20___

*Inflation Chart*

## The Effect of Inflation Riders on Daily Benefits

| Policy Year | Daily | | Annually | |
|---|---|---|---|---|
| | 5% Simple Inflation | 5% Compound Inflation | 5% Simple Inflation | 5% Compound Inflation |
| 1 | $200 | $200 | $73,000 | $73,000 |
| 2 | $210 | $210 | $76,650 | $76,650 |
| 3 | $220 | $221 | $80,300 | $80,483 |
| 4 | $230 | $232 | $83,950 | $84,507 |
| 5 | $240 | $243 | $87,600 | $88,732 |
| 6 | $250 | $255 | $91,250 | $93,169 |
| 7 | $260 | $268 | $94,900 | $97,827 |
| 8 | $270 | $281 | $98,550 | $102,718 |
| 9 | $280 | $296 | $102,200 | $107,854 |
| 10 | $290 | $310 | $105,850 | $113,247 |
| 15 | $340 | $396 | $124,100 | $144,535 |
| 20 | $390 | $505 | $142,350 | $184,467 |
| 25 | $440 | $645 | $160,600 | $235,432 |

Notes: Benefit amounts rounded to the nearest dollar. Sample illustrates to 25 years although an actual policy provision may run for the lifetime of the policy.

Sources: Corporation for Long-Term Care 2009 (format); Author 2011 (figures).

# Index